CHICKEN SOUP
FOR THE
CHRISTIAN
SOUL 2

Stories of Faith, Hope and Healing

Jack Canfield
Mark Victor Hansen
LeAnn Thieman

Health Communications, Inc.
Deerfield Beach, Florida

www.bcibooks.com
www.chickensoup.com

To all Christians,
Christ's hands and feet
and voice on Earth

We would like to acknowledge the following publishers and individuals for permission to reprint the following material. (Note: The stories that were written by Jack Canfield, Mark Victor Hansen or LeAnn Thieman are not included in this listing.)

Magnolias. Reprinted by permission of Edna Ellison. ©2002 Edna Ellison.

A Reason to Celebrate. Reprinted with permission of Janet Lynn Mitchell. ©2002 Janet Lynn Mitchell.

A Special Prayer. Reprinted with permission of Michael Jordan Segal. ©2003 Michael Jordan Segal.

(Continued on page 369)

Library of Congress Cataloging-in-Publication Data

Chicken soup for the Christian soul 2 : stories of faith, hope, and healing / [compiled by] Jack Canfield, Mark Victor Hansen, LeAnn Thieman.
    p. cm
    ISBN 0-7573-0320-X
    1. Christian life—Anecdotes. I. Title: Chicken soup for the Christian soul 2. II. Canfield, Jack, 1944- III. Hansen, Mark Victor. IV. Thieman, LeAnn.

BV4517.C49 2006
242—dc22

2005052805

©2005 Jack Canfield, Mark Victor Hansen
ISBN 0-7573-0320-X

Publisher: Health Communications, Inc.
    3201 S.W. 15th Street
    Deerfield Beach, FL 33442–8190

Cover design by Kevin Stawieray
Inside formatting by Lawna Patterson Oldfield

Contents

3. ANSWERED PRAYERS

4. GOD'S HEALING POWER

8. DIVINE GUIDANCE

9. A MATTER OF PERSPECTIVE

10. MAKING A DIFFERENCE

Acknowledgments

The path to *Chicken Soup for the Christian Soul 2* has been made all the more beautiful by the people who have been there with us along the way. Our heartfelt gratitude to:

Our families, who have been Chicken Soup for our Souls!

Inga, Travis, Riley, Christopher, Oran, Kyle and Patty, Elisabeth and Melanie for once again sharing and lovingly supporting us in creating yet another book.

Mark, Angela, Brian, Dante, Lia Christie, Dave and Mitch, LeAnn's devoted, loving family, her greatest gifts from God.

Our publisher, Peter Vegso, for his vision and commitment to bringing *Chicken Soup for the Soul* to the world.

Patty Aubery and Russ Kamalski for being there on every step of the journey with endless creativity.

Barbara Lomonaco, for helping us select wonderful stories.

D'ette Corona, for being coauthor liaison extraordinaire. Your knowledge, patience and dedication brought this book to fruition.

Patty Hansen, for her thorough and competent handling of the legal and licensing aspects of the *Chicken Soup for the Soul* books. You are magnificent at the challenge!

Veronica Romero, Teresa Esparza, Robin Yerian, Jesse Ianniello, Lauren Edelstein, Laurie Hartman, Jody Emme, Debbie Lefever, Michelle Adams, Dee Dee Romanello, Shanna Vieyra, Lisa Williams, Gina Romanello, Brittany Shaw, Dena Jacobson, Tanya Jones, Mary McKay and David Coleman, who support Jack's and Mark's businesses with skill and love.

Bret Witter, Elisabeth Rinaldi, Allison Janse and Kathy Grant, the editorial department at Health Communications, Inc., for their devotion to excellence.

Terry Burke, Lori Golden, Kelly Maragni, Sean Geary, Patricia McConnell, Ariana Daner, Kim Weiss, Paola Fernandez-Rana and Julie De La Cruz, the sales, marketing and PR departments at Health Communications, Inc., for doing such an incredible job supporting our books.

Tom Sand, Claude Choquette and Luc Jutras, who manage year after year to get our books translated into thirty-six languages around the world.

The art department at Health Communications, Inc., for their talent, creativity and unrelenting patience in producing book covers and inside designs that capture the essence of Chicken Soup: Larissa Hise Henoch, Lawna Patterson Oldfield, Andrea Perrine Brower, Anthony Clausi and Dawn Von Strolley Grove.

All the Chicken Soup for the Soul coauthors, who make it so much of a joy to be part of this Chicken Soup family.

Our glorious panel of readers who helped us make the final selections and made invaluable suggestions on how to improve the book:

Annie Barnett, Jean Bell, Bobbie Bonk, Pat Cavallin, Teri Detwiler, Dierdre Dizon, Robin Dorf, Jan Duello, Richard and Deborah Duello, Bob and Leita Duello, Kerri Flanagan, Jackie Fleming, Karen Kilby, Renee King, Karen Kishpaugh, Terry LePine, Mary Panosh, Carol Rehme, Sallie Rodman, Christie L. Rogers, Kay Rosenthal, John and Sharon Raffensperger, Diane L. "Smitty" Smith, Wendy Staton, Mary Strait, Terry Tuck, Jeanie Winstrom.

And, most of all, everyone who submitted their heartfelt stories, poems, quotes and cartoons for possible inclusion in this book. While we were not able to use everything you sent in, we know it came from your hearts.

Because of the size of this project, we may have left out the names of some people who contributed along the way. If so, we are sorry; please know we appreciate you very much.

A special thanks to Amy Williams, LeAnn's marketing assistant. Thanks for keeping my speaking business booming while I pursue my writing ministry, too.

To Mark, LeAnn's husband. Without your unwavering support, my love, I could not answer His call. Together we serve Him. And to Berniece, LeAnn's mom. You taught me all I know, Mama. All I am today is because of you. And to God. Thanks for showing me the way and teaching me Your paths.

Introduction

"The public is crying for another Christian Soul book!" What a wonderful testament it is for our world and its future to hear the professional book-buyers proclaim that. And what an honor it was to comply.

The truth is, in many ways this book wrote itself. Every week Chicken Soup Enterprises receives hundreds of true stories from people all over the world. As they benevolently share their trials and tribulations, their hearts and souls, many recount how their faith in Christ guided their experiences. We read literally thousands of these inspirational true stories to select the wonderful ones you will find in the pages of *Chicken Soup for the Christian Soul 2*.

Yet, how can we be surprised with this phenomenon? Since Adam and Eve, from the Old Testament to the New, people have shared their lessons and wisdom through storytelling. We are grateful for these thousands more who now join the biblical writers in sharing their stories, telling the world about God in their lives. We invite you to journey with them as they give evidence of their faith, charity, hope, love and forgiveness.

Read the stories one at a time, alone or in a group. Savor the scripture verse or quotation. Embrace the message. Deepen your faith as Christ guides your walk with Him.

Take His hand as He leads you on your journey.

Share with Us

We would like to invite you to send us stories you would like to see published in future editions of *Chicken Soup for the Soul*.

We would also love to hear your reactions to the stories in this book. Please let us know what your favorite stories are and how they affected you.

Chicken Soup for the Soul
P.O. Box 30880
Santa Barbara, CA 93130
fax: 805-563-2945

Please submit your stories on our Web site:

www.chickensoup.com

We hope you enjoy reading this book as much as we enjoyed compiling, editing and writing it.

1

ANGELS AMONG US

The Angels have wider spheres of action and nobler forms of duty than ourselves, but truth and right to them and to us are one and the same thing.

E. H. Chapin

Magnolias

The manner of giving shows the character of the giver, more than the gift itself.

John Casper Lavater

I spent the week before my daughter's June wedding running last-minute trips to the caterer, florist, tuxedo shop and the church about forty miles away. As happy as I was that Patsy was marrying a good Christian young man, I felt laden with responsibilities as I watched my budget dwindle . . . so many details, so many bills and so little time. My son Jack was away at college, but he said he would be there to walk his younger sister down the aisle, taking the place of his dad, who had died a few years before. He teased Patsy, saying he'd wanted to give her away since she was about three years old!

To save money, I gathered blossoms from several friends who had large magnolia trees. Their luscious, creamy-white blooms and slick green leaves would make beautiful arrangements against the rich dark wood inside the church.

After the rehearsal dinner the night before the wedding, we banked the podium area and choir loft with magnolias.

As we left just before midnight, I felt tired but satisfied this would be the best wedding any bride had ever had! The music, the ceremony, the reception—and especially the flowers—would be remembered for years.

The big day arrived—the busiest day of my life—and while her bridesmaids helped Patsy to dress, her fiancé, Tim, walked with me to the sanctuary to do a final check. When we opened the door and felt a rush of hot air, I almost fainted; and then I saw them—all the beautiful white flowers were black. Funeral black. An electrical storm during the night had knocked out the air conditioning system, and on that hot summer day, the flowers had wilted and died.

I panicked, knowing I didn't have time to drive back to our hometown, gather more flowers and return in time for the wedding.

Tim turned to me. "Edna, can you get more flowers? I'll throw away these dead ones and put fresh flowers in these arrangements."

I mumbled, "Sure," as he bebopped down the hall to put on his cuff links.

Alone in the large sanctuary, I looked up at the dark wooden beams in the arched ceiling. "Lord," I prayed, "please help me. I don't know anyone in this town. Help me find someone willing to give me flowers—in a hurry!" I scurried out praying for four things: the blessing of white magnolias, courage to find them in an unfamiliar yard, safety from any dog that may bite my leg and a nice person who would not get out a shotgun when I asked to cut his tree to shreds.

As I left the church, I saw magnolia trees in the distance. I approached a house . . . no dog in sight. I knocked on the door and an older man answered. So far, so good . . . no shotgun. When I stated my plea the man beamed, "I'd be happy to!"

He climbed a stepladder and cut large boughs and

handed them down to me. Minutes later, as I lifted the last armload into my car trunk, I said, "Sir, you've made the mother of a bride happy today."

"No, ma'am," he said. "You don't understand what's happening here."

"What?" I asked.

"You see, my wife of sixty-seven years died on Monday. On Tuesday I received friends at the funeral home, and on Wednesday. . . . " He paused. I saw tears welling up in his eyes. "On Wednesday I buried her." He looked away. "On Thursday most of my out-of-town relatives went back home, and on Friday—yesterday—my children left."

I nodded.

"This morning," he continued, "I was sitting in my den crying out loud. I miss her so much. For the last sixteen years, as her health got worse, she needed me. But now nobody needs me. This morning I cried, 'Who needs an eighty-six-year-old wore-out man? Nobody!' I began to cry louder. 'Nobody needs me!' About that time, you knocked and said, 'Sir, I need you.'"

I stood with my mouth open.

He asked, "Are you an angel? The way the light shone around your head into my dark living room . . . "

I assured him I was no angel.

He smiled. "Do you know what I was thinking when I handed you those magnolias?"

"No."

"I decided I'm needed. My flowers are needed. Why, I might have a flower ministry! I could give them to every-one! Some caskets at the funeral home have no flowers. People need flowers at times like that, and I have lots of them. They're all over the backyard! I can give them to hospitals, churches—all sorts of places. You know what I'm going to do? I'm going to serve the Lord until the day He calls me home!"

I drove back to the church, filled with wonder. On Patsy's wedding day, if anyone had asked me to encourage someone who was hurting, I would have said, "Forget it! It's my only daughter's wedding, for goodness sake! There is no way I can minister to anyone today." But God found a way—through dead flowers.

Edna Ellison

A Reason to Celebrate

Behold I send an angel before you to keep you in the way and to bring you into the place I have prepared.

Exodus 23:20

Numbly, I left my husband, Marty, at the hospital where I had been visiting two of my children and headed for the grocery store. Since it was 11 P.M., I drove to the only store I knew was open twenty-four hours a day. I turned my car motor off and rested my head against the seat.

What a day, I thought to myself. With two of my young children in the hospital, and a third waiting at Grandma's, I was truly spread thin. Today I had actually passed the infant CPR exam required before I could take eight-week-old Joel home from the hospital. *Would I remember how to perform CPR in a moment of crisis?* A cold chill ran down my spine as I debated my answer.

Exhausted, I reached for my grocery list that resembled more of a scientific equation than the food for the week. For the past several days, I'd been learning the facts about juvenile diabetes and trying to accept Jenna's, my six-year-old daughter's, diagnosis. In addition to the CPR exam, I'd spent the day reviewing how to test Jenna's blood and give her insulin shots. Now I was buying the needed food to balance the insulin that would sustain Jenna's life.

"Let's go, Janet," I mumbled to myself while sliding out of the car. "Tomorrow is the big day! Both kids are coming home from the hospital." It didn't take long before my mumbling turned into a prayer.

God, I am soooo scared! What if I make a mistake and give Jenna too much insulin, or what if I measure her food wrong, or what if she does the unmentionable—and sneaks a treat? And God, what about Joel's apnea monitor? What if it goes off? What if he turns blue and I panic? What if? Oh, the consequences are certain to be great!

With a shiver, my own thoughts startled me. Quickly, I tried to redirect my mind away from the what ifs. I gave myself an emergency pep talk and recited what I knew to be true, "I can do all things through Christ who strengthens me. I can do all things. . . ."

Like a child doing an errand she wasn't up for, I grabbed my purse, locked the car and found my way inside the store. The layout of the store was different from what I was used to. Uncertain where to find what I needed, I decided to walk up and down each aisle.

Soon I was holding a box of cereal, reading the label, trying to figure out the carbohydrate count and sugar content. *Would three-fourths a cup of cereal fill Jenna up?* Not finding any "sugar free" cereal, I grabbed a box of Kellogg's Corn Flakes and continued shopping. Pausing, I turned back. *Do I still buy Froot Loops for Jason?* I hadn't even thought how Jenna's diagnosis might affect Jason, my typical four-year-old. *Is it okay if he has a box of Froot Loops while Jenna eats Kellogg's Corn Flakes?*

Eventually I walked down the canned fruit and juice aisle. *Yes, I need apple juice, but how much? Just how often will Jenna's sugar "go low" so she will need this lifesaving can of juice? Will a six-year-old actually know when her blood sugar is dropping? What if . . . ?* I began to ask myself again.

I held the can of apple juice and began to read the label. *Jenna will need fifteen carbohydrates of juice when her sugar drops. But this can has thirty-two.* Immediately I could see my hand begin to tremble. I tried to steady the can and reread the label when I felt tears leave my eyes and make their way down the sides of my face. Not knowing what to do, I grabbed a couple of six-packs of apple juice and placed them in my cart. Frustrated by feelings of total inadequacy, I crumpled up my grocery list, covered my face in my hands and cried.

"Honey, are you all right?" I heard a gentle voice ask. I had been so engrossed in my own thoughts that I hadn't even noticed the woman who was shopping alongside of me. Suddenly I felt her hand as she reached toward me and rested it upon my shoulder. "Are you all right? Honey, are you a little short of cash? Why don't you just let me . . . ?"

I slowly dropped my hands from my face and looked into the eyes of the silver-haired woman who waited for my answer. "Oh, no, thank you, ma'am," I said while wiping my tears, trying to gather my composure. "I have enough money."

"Well, honey, what is it then?" she persisted.

"It's just that I'm kind of overwhelmed. I'm here shopping for groceries so that I can bring my children home from the hospital tomorrow."

"Home from the hospital! What a celebration that shall be. Why, you should have a party!"

Within minutes this stranger had befriended me. She took my crumpled-up grocery list, smoothed it out and became my personal shopper. She stayed by my side until each item on my list was checked off. She even walked me to my car, helping me as I placed the groceries in my trunk. Then with a hug and a smile, she sent me on my way.

It was shortly after midnight, while lugging the groceries into my house, that I realized the lesson this woman had taught me. "My kids are coming home from the hospital!" I shouted with joy. "Joel is off life support and functioning on a monitor. Jenna and I can learn how to manage her diabetes and give her shots properly. And just as God met my needs in a grocery store, He will meet each and every need we have. What a reason to celebrate." I giggled to myself.

"I have a reason to celebrate!" I shouted to my empty house.

"Why, you should have a party!" the woman had exclaimed.

And a party there would be!

Janet Lynn Mitchell

A Special Prayer

Heal me, O Lord, and I shall be healed.

Jeremiah 17:14

My father is the most unselfish person I know—always thinking of others first before himself. Perhaps that is why he chose to be a rabbi, to serve God by helping other people.

Every Christmas, my father, Rabbi Jack Segal, volunteers at a hospital in Houston so Christian employees can spend Christmas with their loved ones. One particular Christmas he was working the telephone switchboard at the hospital, answering basic questions and transferring phone calls. One of the calls he received was from a woman, obviously upset.

"Sir, I understand my nephew was in a terrible car accident this morning. Please tell me how he is."

After the woman gave my father the boy's name, he checked the computer and said, according to protocol at that time, "Your nephew is listed in critical condition. I'm truly sorry. I hope he'll get better." As soon as my father said "critical," the woman immediately began to sob and she screamed, "Oh, my God! What should I do? What should I do?"

Hearing those words, my father softly stated, "Prayer might be helpful at this time."

The woman quickly replied, "Yes—oh, yes. But it's been ten years since I've been to a church and I've forgotten how to pray," then asked, "Sir, do you know how to pray? Could *you* say a prayer for me while I listen on the phone?"

My father quickly answered, "Of course," and began saying the ancient prayer for healing in Hebrew, the *Mee Shebayroch*. He concluded, "Amen."

"Thank you, thank you so much," the woman on the phone replied. "However," she went on, "I truly appreciate your prayer, but I have one major problem. I did not understand the prayer, since I do not speak Spanish."

My father inwardly chuckled and said, "Ma'am, that was not Spanish. I'm a rabbi, and that prayer was in Hebrew."

The woman sighed heavily in relief. "Hebrew? That's great. That's God's language. Now He won't need a translator!"

Michael Jordan Segal, M.S.W.

Alone

Do not fear, for I am with you; do not be dismayed, for I am your God.

Isaiah 41:10a

At El Toro Marine Corps Air Station in Southern California where my husband Joe was stationed, the clinic physician peered with a lighted instrument into my right eye. "Hmmm," he murmured to himself.

"What do you see?" I asked, anxious to learn the cause of my suddenly blurred vision.

"I'm . . . not . . . sure," he said, maneuvering his head for a different view.

"Is something wrong with my pregnancy?" I blurted out, near panic. *Please, God, this is our first baby. Don't let anything go wrong.*

"Mrs. Stargel," the young doctor's brow creased, "your vision has deteriorated. You need a specialist. I'm sending you to Camp Pendleton Naval Hospital." Then he added gently, "You'll need to go prepared to stay."

No, please, no. This can't be happening. Joe's getting discharged next week, and we're going home!

I was so homesick. It was my first year away from the rest of the family, and we hadn't told them about our baby due in four months. We wanted to surprise everyone, but now. . . . That afternoon, Joe and I drove down the Pacific Coast Highway toward San Diego and Camp Pendleton. Ordinarily, we enjoyed the spectacular scenery along Route 101—crashing waves on one side of the road, rolling hills on the other, wildflowers everywhere. But on this day, we saw none of the beauty—concern for my health and that of our baby nearly blocked out the sun.

I checked into the military hospital, a sprawling one-story structure painted battleship gray inside and out. The antiseptic smell assaulted my senses and threatened to reactivate my morning sickness. They assigned me to a ward with seven other women—eight beds lined up at attention, each with its own metal nightstand in which the washcloth and bedpan, even my toothbrush, had its precise location. Reluctantly, I changed from my fashionable maternity dress into gray-blue cotton pajamas bearing the stamp "U.S. Navy."

For the next eleven days doctors examined and X-rayed me head to toe, trying to locate the area of infection that caused inflammation of the choroid layer of my eye—inflammation that threatened blindness.

Meanwhile, they prescribed cortisone to be administered intravenously. My veins proved "uncooperative." Every day, the nurses probed with needles, again and again, while I cringed in pain.

Saturday night came. Joe had weekend duty at El Toro, fifty miles away. My closest neighbors in the ward had left. I hadn't even seen the IV team that day. Never had I felt so forlorn, so forsaken. As the outside darkness smothered the hospital, loneliness as thick as fog from the nearby ocean engulfed me.

Sometime after the ten o'clock "lights out," I heard the shuffling of padded feet and the rhythmic tinkle of metal hitting against a bottle. The sounds stopped by my bed. With lowered voices, working by flashlights so as not to waken the patients on the far end of the ward, the IV team started the vein search in my bruised arms. I bit my lip.

"I'm sorry, Mrs. Stargel," one of the nurses said. "I wish we didn't have to do this to you, especially at this time of night. Several emergencies kept us from getting to you sooner."

I turned away and clenched my teeth, waiting for the next puncture. Finally, sounding relieved for both of us, she said, "This one's going to work." As she taped the offending needle onto the back of my wrist, she added, "I'm afraid, though, you won't get much sleep tonight."

Handing me a flashlight, she motioned to the bottle of liquid swinging above my head. "Remember to check from time to time the number of drops per minute. We don't want the medication to enter the body too quickly—nor too slowly." With that bit of instruction, she retreated with the others.

I was alone again. With my free hand I hugged the sheet up under my chin, fighting an onrush of unspeakable sadness. Doubts piled on top of one another. *What if we can't go home next week? What if I lose my eyesight? And our baby! What are all these X-rays and chemicals doing to our baby?*

I wanted—needed—to pray, but was afraid to try. Would God remember me? After all, I had neglected Him this entire year. It was as if I had left God on the East Coast, too—rarely praying, let alone attending church services.

My arm throbbed. I reached for the flashlight, directed its beam on the bottle of medication, and counted the dripping clear liquid—one, two, three, four . . .

I switched off the light and stared up into the black void. Sinking into a pit of despair, my very soul cried out to God. *Lord, please help me. I know I don't deserve it, God, but please help me.*

Soon after I couldn't believe what I was hearing! From somewhere out in the shadowy hallway came the hauntingly beautiful sound of a young woman's voice, singing that lovely Rodgers and Hammerstein song, "You'll Never Walk Alone."

I dared not breathe—afraid the moment would vanish. *I must be dreaming. Who would be singing at this time of night?* But yes. She was singing all right. In a voice as clear, as soul lifting, as the music of a carillon's steepled bells echoing across a soft green meadow.

I listened, amazed, as the heaven-sent words of hope and comfort and courage winged their way into the ward—and into my aching heart. Instantly I was wrapped in a blanket of God's love. As I rested in that newfound refuge, tears I had fought back all evening spilled over, ran down the sides of my face and puddled in my ears. When the last note of the celestial song dissolved into memories, I lay there—awed—my fear replaced by perfect peace, my loneliness by the reassurance of a Holy Presence.

Finally, I took one more count of the IV drops, laid the flashlight beside my pillow and fell soundly asleep.

The identity of the singer remains a mystery. But I believe God sent an angel to sing for me that night to remind me of His promise, "Never will I leave you; never will I forsake you" (Hebrews 13:5b).

Five days after the angel sang, the hospital dismissed me and the Marine Corps dismissed Joe. We came home and later had a handsome, healthy son.

And I knew I'd "never walk alone" again.

Gloria Cassity Stargel

Pearls of Time

The older women likewise, that they be reverent, temperate, sound in faith, in love, in patience . . . that they admonish the young to love their husbands, to love their children.

Titus 2:3-4

I hadn't intended to isolate myself in my bedroom for three days, but the unexpected death of a dear friend had devastated me. I was a new Christian, unprepared for the questions and doubts that overwhelmed me.

The door opened and my husband, Jeff, came near.

"It's going to be okay," he said softly, stroking my hair.

I buried my head in his shoulder. I didn't understand this grief. Life seemed so perfect until this happened. One minute Jeff and I were rejoicing in the news of my pregnancy, the next, we were grieving over the loss of a friend. The future was an uncertain destiny, and how was I, a Christian and expectant mother, supposed to view life's sorrows and triumphs?

"I'm so confused," I confessed, lifting my tear-streaked face. "I wish God would just give me a simple answer. A vision of how to journey through life as a Christian woman."

Just then, the doorbell rang. Jeff kissed the top of my head, then left to answer it. When slow-moving footsteps returned to the doorway, I was surprised to find my elderly neighbor, Sarah, appraising me. I yearned for the wisdom her blue eyes held behind wire-rimmed glasses.

"I missed your visits to me these past days," she said, shuffling over to sit beside me. "I thought you might've been experiencing morning sickness, but then I learned your friend died."

I didn't say a word. Sarah was the godliest woman I had ever met. She rarely left her home unless it was an emergency. I suppose she figured this was an emergency.

"How do I look today?" she surprised me by asking.

"Beautiful," I answered, assessing her pale blue dress and pearl necklace. "I've never seen that necklace before. It's lovely."

"You have one too," she said, lifting a finger to point at my collarbone. "Only it's a spiritual one unseen by human eyes." She reached behind her neck and unlocked the necklace. Holding it between her fingers, she rubbed the pearls gently. "This necklace was handed down to me as a reminder of the heavenly necklaces women wear." Patting my knee, she continued, "God instilled in women an incredible sense of caring and compassion, Karen. We are the nurturers, the vessels of life. We take care of our husbands, our children, our houses, and sometimes we feel as though everyone's emotional well-being depends on us."

She paused, handing me a tissue, then smiled. "Long ago, when I was a child, an elderly woman told me that she believed there's a special blessing for women—a 'pearls of time' necklace that we're born with. During our lifetime, the pearls that adorn our necks represent momentous events in our lives."

Moved by her words, I instinctively touched my neck, as if I could sense adornment there.

"But," she emphasized, holding the necklace for me to see, "the most important part is the clasp that holds it together. That represents Jesus. Like a perfect circle—from beginning to end, He's with us. Holding us firmly in life's tragedies or triumphs. We only need to remember and trust in that." She sighed, slipping the necklace back on and waiting for me to speak.

Speechless, I absorbed her words, allowing them to soothe my soul. "I don't know what to say," I whispered.

"Don't say anything, then," she chuckled, standing up. "I'm just fulfilling the scripture in Titus 2:4 for older women to be holy, so that they can teach the younger ones. One day you will, too. Right now, you're a young, uncertain Christian woman, but you have a teachable spirit and a great desire to obey God. That's a winning combination."

We embraced, and I inhaled the familiar scent of lilac soap. "Thank you, Sarah. Thank you."

"You don't have to thank me, honey," she said, "but I do have to go. My son is waiting." She was almost out of the doorway when she stopped briefly and turned to me. Lifting her hand, she brought my attention to her neck. "Just remember, dear."

"I will," I promised, walking over to help her down the stairs.

As I watched the car disappear around a curve, I suddenly felt renewed. "Thank you, Jesus," I murmured, closing my eyes. "Thank you for answering my prayers." When I reopened them, my vision was clear.

Four years later, I clutched the hand of my three-year-old daughter Abigail as we stood beside Sarah's hospital bed. "You're going to get better," I told her, watching in despair as her face grew paler.

"I'm not worried, dear," she grinned, squeezing my hand. "I'm looking forward to seeing the Lord."

"But we'll miss you," I blurted, clutching her hand. "I love you! You've not only been my friend, but you've been a godly teacher to me. I'll miss our talks, our laughter, our—"

"Shhh," she smiled, meeting my eyes. "You'll do just fine without me." She pointed to a small box lying on the bedside table. "Take that. Open it tonight with Abigail. It'll help both of you. Now, promise me."

"I promise," I said, slipping the box into my purse.

We said our tearful good-byes, each being a little more lighthearted for Abigail's sake, but we both knew it would be the last time we'd see each other.

Later that night, after receiving the news that Sarah had passed away, I snuggled with Abigail on the couch. She curled into my side, her silky hair brushing against my cheek. "Open it, Mama," she said, curiously touching the box.

Through tear-filled eyes, I lifted the lid and found the pearl necklace that Sarah had modeled for me four years before.

"It's beautiful, Mommy," Abigail exclaimed, gently touching the shimmering treasure. "But why do I still feel so sad? Sarah said it would help us."

Her question tugged at my heart, but I was prepared. "Well, honey," I said, touching her soft cheek with my fingertips. "This necklace was handed down to me as a reminder of the heavenly necklaces women wear. . . . "

Karen Majoris-Garrison

All Things Are Possible

I was waiting to board my flight from Virginia's Dulles International Airport to San Francisco when I noticed a young family nearby. What struck me was their obvious love for one another. I saw it in the way they spoke to each other, in how they laughed together, and in how they interacted with one another. Trying not to stare too conspicuously, I didn't even realize for a while that the mother was in a wheelchair.

The family patiently waited at the gate with the rest of us. I was in the ladies' room later, when, accompanied by an airline representative, the entire family came in. The husband helped his wife with her bathroom needs as the two little girls stood by the partially opened door of the handicapped stall. Back at the gate, I wondered how a family with such enormous daily challenges could do the seemingly extraordinary with such grace and dignity.

My seat was in the very last row of the airplane; their seats were a few rows in front of me. The obedient, cheerful daughters sat across the aisle from their parents. Both for take-off and landing, the father put an extra strap around his wife's head so she wouldn't fall forward. A couple of times during the five-hour flight, he repositioned her so she was lying across their three seats. He then stood in the narrow aisle and gently massaged her legs.

I introduced myself to him when we were standing in line for the bathroom. I learned that his name was Graham and his wife, Sylvia, was totally paralyzed as a result of multiple sclerosis. The only muscles she could voluntarily move were those in her face. I complimented him on his beautiful family and on his baseball hat, which boasted "World's Best Dad." "A Father's Day gift from my children," he beamed. He told me his family had been in Washington for his mother's funeral and they were now returning to their home near San Francisco.

I was the last passenger to get off the plane, with the exception of my new acquaintance and his family. As I passed their seats, I stopped to briefly chat with them and we even exchanged hugs. I leaned over and kissed the mother on her cheek. As I gently cupped her face in my hands, I said, "I'll keep you and your family in my thoughts and prayers." She sweetly mouthed the words "thank you."

When I returned home from California, I couldn't get this family off my mind. I prayed for them daily, but God seemed to be nudging me to do more. I tried to find out who they were—not an easy task, since the airline wouldn't give me any information. It took four months, every resource skill I possessed, and many wrong numbers before I finally reached the Thompson family.

The father remembered who I was and was surprised by my call. I learned that he managed a trailer park, which enabled him to stay home and take care of his wife and his daughters. His cheerful voice never hinted of a daily routine that would exhaust and discourage the strongest among us.

I asked, "Is there anything I can do for your family from

afar?" I explained, "The Lord has kept the four of you in my heart since our shared flight across the country."

"Well, I'm not sure," he began hesitantly, obviously caught off guard. "I'm trying to make arrangements for a return visit to Virginia, this time for a *happy* reason. One of my nieces is getting married, and my family wants very much to attend the wedding." He told me he had already contacted the one airline that flies non-stop from California to Virginia, asking if his wife could possibly be upgraded to business class if he purchased four round-trip coach tickets. I'd seen for myself how difficult it was for him to take care of his wife's special needs while cramped in the coach section. The airline, however, had said no upgrade could be given. He did have the option, he was told, of purchasing a first-class ticket for his wife for two thousand two hundred dollars.

My mission was born.

Ten months after I met this remarkable family, the Lord had facilitated many miracles.

An airline gifted four round-trip, business class tickets to Virginia. My fund-raising efforts solicited enough money to pay for a handicapped van for the family to use the week they were there. A downtown Washington, D.C. hotel offered two rooms at a generous discount, so the family could sightsee in D.C. for a couple of days before heading home. Special passes to tour the White House were acquired. I knew no one influential of whom I asked favors; all of this happened through prayer.

The day of their trip finally arrived. I met them at Dulles Airport. As the family approached me coming down the ramp at the gate, I felt a lump in my throat. Their smiles stretched from ear to ear. I thought to myself, *How little it takes to make a difference in someone else's life.*

Sylvia, though unable to make a sound, mouthed "thank you" as I hugged her and handed her some flowers.

The girls couldn't stop talking about their wonderful airplane ride.

"We each had our very own movie screen!" one of them exclaimed.

The flight attendants, alerted before takeoff to the special circumstances, had been so moved that one of them quickly went to a store at the airport and bought surprises for each family member. After they had boarded the plane, the girls were each presented with a big teddy bear, the mother a silk scarf and the father a box of chocolates.

We talked non-stop as we headed to pick up their luggage. The driver who delivered the special van met us at the carousel. The Lord was making everything so simple! After loading his excited family into their van, Graham asked if I would come to his niece's wedding, as did his daughters, who were going to be junior bridesmaids. I didn't say "yes" until his sister, the mother-of-the-bride, called me long distance to ask if I would please be their guest.

"You're the angel who made it possible for my brother and his family to come," she said.

"No," I corrected her. "It was the Lord Who made it all happen. I just did what He nudged me to do."

In the church, Graham and Sylvia beamed from the first row as they looked at their two daughters, radiant in their long gowns and with their fancy hair-dos. They suddenly seemed much older than nine and eleven.

I joined their family for the tour of the White House. My husband and youngest daughter met them when we brought dinner to their hotel suite one of the nights they spent in D.C.

Six and a half years have now passed since the Thompsons' magical vacation in Virginia. We've kept in touch via e-mail, snail mail and telephone. I had the joy of being their guest in California for a couple of days. The girls decorated both the outside and the inside of their trailer with colorful welcome signs for me and allowed me to sleep in their bedroom. We went to an amusement park, watched movies together, ate pizza and looked at family photo albums. I watched the family's well-practiced choreography in awe. Chores were done cheerfully without words being spoken. Sylvia's needs were automatically taken care of inconspicuously and lovingly. Parakeets happily chirped from their respective cages. The Lord's presence was everywhere—proving, through Him all things are possible.

Bobbie Wilkinson

One More Chance

*Heaven's the perfection of all that can be said
or thought—riches, delight, harmony, health,
beauty; and all these not subject to the waste of
time, but in their height eternal.*

James Shirley

One night in April 1997, my husband Andrew was having a routine evening at work. It was dark and the day's
warmth had given way to the coolness of a spring
evening. Andy was the supervisor that night for the local
emergency medical services that provide advanced life
support to most of our county. He was hoping for a quiet
end to his shift when a call came over his radio that there
was an unconscious person at the local Kmart. He turned
his truck in the direction of the strip mall and hit the
lights. He would provide backup and support to the team
of paramedics and EMTs that responded ahead of him.

When Andy arrived, a middle-aged man was sitting in
the shoe department of Kmart acting somewhat combat-
ive and confused. The man talked with the ambulance
crew, then became unresponsive and then began

responding again. Within a few minutes, however, he was unconscious and on the floor. When the paramedics placed the heart monitor on the man's chest, they saw on the display what they call a fatal heart rhythm, ventricular tachycardia or V-tach. His heart was beating incredibly fast and not effectively pumping blood to his vital organs. In this state, he wouldn't be able to survive long.

My husband and the team began their work. They quickly administered the prescribed medications and contacted the emergency department physician to give them orders. Soon, however, it was obvious that the medications had failed to work and the man's condition worsened. Their next step was to defibrillate (or shock) him with an electric current to attempt to get his heart back into a healthy rhythm. By all accounts, this man was clinically dead, or would be soon.

After an initial electric shock, the man came around but then deteriorated and again lost consciousness. His heart returned to that awful rhythm. After another electrical shock, he was brought back to consciousness. But instead of calm and compliant behavior, he was confused and belligerent and was obviously angry with them because, he said, they had "brought him back."

The man was transported to the emergency department at the hospital close by, and Andy came home from his shift. He told me how interesting the call had been. He was perplexed that the man was angry with them for saving him, while most people are grateful beyond words.

After that, we didn't think much more of it—that is, until about a month later, when a letter arrived at the emergency department addressed to the ER staff and ambulance crew. The letter was from the man whom they'd rescued in the shoe department of Kmart.

In the letter, he thanked everyone for their love and understanding toward him when he needed them. He said that he had since undergone bypass surgery and had a device implanted in his heart that would keep the rhythm normal, and he was growing stronger every day.

He also apologized for getting angry with the crew when they revived him. The rest of the letter confirmed to Andy why he does what he does. It read:

> *I'll never be fully able to thank you for what you've done for me but will try by moving forward with the rest of my life, making it as vibrant and positive as an example to others who may feel it's okay to ignore their health the way I did.*
>
> *I went to Heaven . . . at least twice! It was a glorious experience and I still revel in the sense of peace and serenity I experienced in those few, brief moments. . . . I now fully understand and accept that it wasn't my time to go to this glorious place. . . . I know enough now not to fear death, but also enough to love and respect life and to seek the plans I know God still has for me here on earth. For the rest of my life, I have the pleasure of living now with more than a mere belief in my Creator and the place He has waiting for us all, but rather with the fact that these things are all very real and are meant for all who choose to follow Him.*

That truth set his life on a course that will change not only him, but all of us.

Audrey Gilger

Mountains of Laundry

When a person is down in the world, an ounce of help is better than a pound of preaching.

Edward George Bulwer-Lytton

After we had been married a couple of years, my husband and I became foster parents. Our first placement was two little boys, brothers, who we were thrilled to adopt a year and a half later. When our sons were two and three, we agreed to take one- and three-year-old sisters into our home. For the following two years we had our own little in-house, full-time daycare.

After the girls had been with us awhile, I attempted to get involved in a Bible study group at our church, but one thing or another always seemed to prevent me from attending. I was feeling a little discouraged, but I purchased devotional tapes and a study guide and thought I could keep up with the Bible study by myself at home.

One afternoon, after I'd put the children down for their naps, I tackled a mountain of laundry that had piled up on the sofa and needed folding. As I was folding, I began discussing my plight with God.

You know, Lord, I've started attending this Bible study and I'm trying to find time for You and everything I need to do, but I just can't seem to find enough time. I've tried getting up before daylight, but one of the kids always hears me and gets up wanting my attention, and by bedtime I'm exhausted. I guess I could study during naptime, but that's the only time I have to get caught up with the housework and laundry. I seem to be able to keep up with most everything but this laundry! Well, I guess You know all about it. You gave me four little kids under three years old to care for, and You know they need clean clothes to wear and You know how much work this takes. I know You understand.

The following Sunday my husband and I were sitting in Sunday school class waiting for the teacher to begin when our family's "adopted grandmother," Betty, came and sat down beside me. Betty was a widow who had raised five children. She was a wonderful woman who was always helping someone, and had personally blessed our family on many occasions.

She leaned toward me and said, "I have a proposition for you."

My curiosity was aroused. "Okay. What is it?"

She sweetly and softly replied, "I really think this is the Lord's idea, but would you let me do your laundry?"

As I sat gaping at her with my mouth hanging open, my mind raced trying to think who I could have told about my laundry situation. I knew I hadn't mentioned it to anyone, not even my husband, Rodney. "Do you know how much laundry I have?" I whispered back as my eyes started to fill.

"Honey, I've raised five kids. Believe me, I know how much laundry you have." She continued, "You know, what you and your husband are doing raising these little children is wonderful, but I know it's hard work. I'm an old woman and I can't watch other people's children anymore, but I can do your laundry. You just have Rodney drop it off on his way to work and pick it up on his way home. I'll wash it, dry it, iron it, fold it; whatever is needed."

Shame on me, because the whole time she was talking, I was thinking, *Oh, Lord, not the underwear! I can't send our underwear to someone else to do!*

Betty was still talking. "Last week I noticed you up on the platform during praise and worship, and you looked very tired. I was thinking about you all week, and then I felt the Lord telling me, 'Ask Ronni if she'll let you do her laundry.'" She finished with, "Now, don't you rob me of this blessing."

I didn't know how to respond. Not wanting to hurt Betty's feelings, I said, "I'll think about it."

Even though I had poured out my heart about how difficult it was to keep up and how I missed my devotional time with Him, I was unprepared for God to actually do something about it. He had given me the task of caring for these little ones, and I was a little put out that He'd taken me seriously when I said I was having trouble keeping up. So I thought, *If I just get a little more organized, I can take care of this myself.*

A couple weeks later, as I walked in and surveyed the laundry room, I sagged against the washer. The mountain of laundry hadn't diminished a bit with my efforts to get better organized. As a matter of fact, it was now bigger than ever. "Well, Lord," I said, "I guess I could send everything but the underwear."

Very clearly, I heard that still, small voice say, "When I ask you for your dirty laundry, I want all of it, even the underwear."

That's when I broke. That mountain of laundry now represented the mountain of pride in my life. Who was I to look disdainfully on a gift offered in love?

As I picked up the phone, my eyes filled with tears, and when I heard sweet little Betty's voice on the other end, my own voice shook as I said, "Betty, do you still want to help me with my laundry?"

My tears quickly turned to laughter at her joyful response. "Bring it on over, honey, bring it on over!"

Our clothes were never cleaner, brighter or less wrinkled than during the two years Betty faithfully and lovingly did our laundry. Then when our little foster daughters were placed in their "forever home" through adoption, we both knew it was time for me to resume the task.

Although she no longer does our laundry, our friendship remains strong. Betty laughed one day when I told her, "I want to be just like you when I grow up."

Veronica Wintermote

2

FAMILY
OF FAITH

The family was ordained of God that children might be trained up for himself; it was before the church, or rather the first form of the church on earth.

Pope Leo XIII

The Little Broom

We can do no great things—only small things with great love.

Mother Teresa

Standing in drizzling rain just yards from the "pile" at Ground Zero, I reflected on what was lost, and what was being found. The frustration of not finding anyone alive for the past several days had clearly demoralized everyone on-scene. Even the search-and-rescue dogs were becoming depressed, having been trained to find living victims.

I thought about all that had happened since I arrived at this horrible scene six days after the Twin Towers fell on 9/11. As a stress counselor and a chaplain in my local fire department, I had felt compelled to take the earliest flight possible from my home high in the mountains of Colorado to this smoking ruin. Upon arrival, what I found was far worse than I had imagined.

When I first walked up to the wreckage of the World Trade Center, I nearly staggered backward. The magnitude of the destruction was far worse than any televised images. My eyes could scarcely take it all in, let alone get my mind around it. I stood in shock at the base of the nearly five-story pile of grotesquely twisted steel girders, pipes, wires, metal ductwork and unidentifiable debris. Acrid smoke and steam rose up from the bowels of the wreckage. The pervasive smell of burning metal, insulation, wires and aviation fuel emanating from the pile burned my nose and eyes. There was another clearly discernible smell, infinitely more disturbing. At times, I could detect an odor of burning flesh, and my heart and mind reeled at the thought of the thousands of people trapped in that hellish pyre.

Around me firefighters and policemen were fighting desperately against time to find someone, anyone, alive in the rubble. Some of these people had labored here since the first morning of the collapse, sleeping and eating only when they had to, refusing to leave the side of their buried sons, fathers and brothers.

Clad in my firefighter turnout gear, the rockers of my yellow helmet emblazoned with the word "Chaplain," I prayed that God would help me to somehow comfort them in this dark hour of grief.

Within a few days after the attack, a tent morgue was set up in front of the World Financial Center on Vesey Street. For several days I worked in the exam room, watching distraught firefighters bring in human remains discovered in the wreckage. I never saw a whole body brought in. As the medical examiners and forensic experts sought clues that might help identify these precious people, I was deeply moved by the tender care and profound respect everyone demonstrated. It was difficult and gruesome work, yet it was a labor of love done not only for the deceased, but also for their families and loved ones. A positive identification would bring eventual closure to their heartbreaking loss.

In a scene I witnessed many times, when the deceased was identified as a firefighter or police officer, an American flag would be unfolded and draped over the stretcher. Several of us in the room would spontaneously reach out our latex-gloved hands to help gently tuck the flag in around the edges. It vaguely reminded me of a mother or father gently tucking a beloved child into bed after a long, tiring day.

The doctors would then step back, look toward me and simply say, "Chaplain?" Stepping forward and placing my gloved hand upon the draped flag, I'd pray for the deceased's family and seek God's mercy on this precious, heroic soul. One could hear the mask-muffled sobs of doctors, police officers and firefighters as we prayed. There in that place of shared grief and sorrow, we were all brothers and sisters.

As darkness began to envelop Ground Zero, the clouds of smoke rising from the debris gave an eerie effect to the huge lights erected at the site. I stood watching the SAR dogs, firefighters and police officers searching through the rubble for any trace of the thousands of people yet missing. In the midst of this scene from hell, I heard the faint ringing of my cell phone inside my rain-drenched fire-fighting jacket.

Answering, I heard a small voice say, "What are you dooo-ing, Daddy?"

It was my five-year-old daughter, Hannah. Born in Nanchang, China, and abandoned by her parents at the tender age of four days old, her only crime was that of being born a girl. Left beside a lonely, dusty road, wrapped in her only earthly possession, a filthy rag of a blanket, she was found by passersby and brought to a government-operated nursery. The first thirteen months of her life were spent there, lying in a tiny crib with only one caretaker for her and the twenty-seven other little girls around her.

Hannah's sweet voice drew me back into a reality that almost seemed a dim memory. She was calling from her "normal" world, where her days were filled with Winnie the Pooh stories and the fascination of watching multicolored birds visit the feeder on our deck, and I ached to be back in her world again.

How could I answer my little girl's question without alarming or spoiling, even in the slightest, her sweet innocence?

Over the blaring noises of Ground Zero I could hear her breathing into the phone, as small children often do, patiently waiting for my answer. My eyes swept over the smoldering wreckage just feet away, where thousands lay trapped. "Honey, some really mean bad guys made a big mess here in New York City, and I'm just helping to clean it up."

There was a pregnant pause. In her sweet, innocent voice, she replied, "Daddy, can I come with my little broom and help you?"

I plopped down in the mud as her words sank in. The effort to choke back sobs made it impossible to speak. Finally, I composed myself enough to mumble something about how important it was that she stay at home and help her mommy clean the messes there. Slipping the cell phone back in my field jacket, I began to cry. Little Hannah had just expressed exactly how I felt at that moment. Whatever training and willingness to serve I possessed, all I had managed to bring to this horrendous disaster was a "little broom" to somehow help clean up the millions of tons of twisted wreckage, shattered dreams and broken hearts. It was as if a fissure in the rubble had opened up under me, and the pile was sucking me down into some dark void of helplessness.

The loud metallic clanking of one of the cranes dragging a huge chunk of twisted metal out of the rubble pulled my broken heart out of the wreckage of my own dark broodings. Scrambling to my feet, I wiped the tears with a grimy glove and slowly walked back to the makeshift morgue tent near the World Financial Center. The medical and support teams there were enduring the horrifying task of processing and cataloguing the thousands of body parts we were finding in the rubble. A weeping firefighter chaplain would once again take his "little broom" there for awhile, seeking to comfort and encourage, trying to sweep away a little of the filth of that horrible place from their souls. A "little broom" can do *something* useful and make a difference if made available. Even a little girl from China was smart enough to know that.

Bruce Porter

A Time to Dance

Be faithful until death, and I will give you the crown of life.

Revelation 2:10

She pulled me off the picnic bench where I sat chatting with some of our elderly relatives at the Minnesota family reunion that warm July afternoon. The fiddler played a two-step, and she swung me into a Lindy. I looked around, wondering what people must think of these two old ladies dancing together. But it didn't worry Gail, my younger sister, one bit. She was enjoying herself as though she was seventeen again. I wondered where she got her stamina as I huffed back to the picnic bench after the music stopped.

Gail's extroverted, sanguine personality contrasted with my introverted, melancholy one. She made life fun and interesting.

The phone call came in October. Gail had colon cancer. I traveled from Tennessee to Minnesota to be with her as she convalesced from surgery. As we prayed together and asked God to heal her, I closed my eyes. A peace came over me, and I had a vision of people dancing, swirling long, colorful scarves over their heads. It was a celebration of some sort—perhaps a wedding. Then I knew Gail would get well and that she would dance again the way she loved to do.

In the days that followed, my sister indeed got stronger. She didn't get sick from the chemotherapy, another indication that she would get well. Her recovery progressed and, though her back started to bother her a bit, she didn't let it hinder her plans to travel. She asked me to accompany her to visit relatives in Pennsylvania, where we enjoyed walks in the quiet woods. She stopped me as she listened to a cardinal and looked for its bright flash of red in the green lacy treetops. The new life of spring burst forth everywhere.

We visited historical sites. She posed as one of the signers of the Constitution at Independence Hall in Philadelphia. She visited Gettysburg. She even rode in an Amish buggy pulled by a horse when we visited Lancaster County. It was as if she was filling her senses with life itself. The pain in her back grew worse, however. It was time to go home.

Tests revealed that the cancer had spread to her spine and her liver. Two painful surgeries and radiation treatments failed to stop the insidious intruder. Summer slipped into August. Gail was sent home to die.

To comfort and pray for her, I offered to move into her home, determined to care for her as long as she needed me. She and her husband were relieved and grateful. The journey through the valley of hope and tears had begun.

The medication nauseated her. Unable to eat, she lost weight. In spite of her discomfort, she laughed at past experiences we shared growing up together on our parents' farm in Stacy, Minnesota.

"Remember the time a couple of teenage boys we didn't want to see drove up the driveway?" she recalled as I rubbed her back. "We snuck out the back door and ran to the privy! Dad talked to the boys for almost an hour before they finally decided to leave, and we were free to leave our hiding place!"

"I remember," I chuckled.

"Well," she said, "the experience helped make me wise."

"How's that?"

"It helped give me good judgment," she said.

I carefully rubbed the scars on her back from the tumor surgery. "And how did you get your good judgment?"

"From learning about bad judgment—like following you out to that horrid, stinking hiding place!" The gleam in her eye masked the pain usually there.

We both laughed, savoring the camaraderie always present between us.

We prayed together every morning and night, asking God for His healing touch. She would sing praises to Him accompanying music from a CD or tape, then slip into a peaceful sleep.

The autumn days were filled with Gail's physical care. Because the cancer caused nerve damage, she needed a walker to support her steps. She was determined to keep her dignity as long as she could, and although it was painful for her to do so, she insisted on walking to the bathroom rather than using a bedpan. She walked to the deck and sat in the warm, pleasant afternoon sun. Her strength seemed to wane each day, however, and visits to the deck became fewer and fewer.

Soon she was too weak to leave her bed. One day I bathed her and dressed her in a purple gown. "You look like a queen," I said, admiring the royal color.

"I am a queen."

"And who's the king?" I asked.

"Jesus!" she smiled and fell asleep.

Each day that followed, she insisted I dress her in

purple. Then she fell into a coma. Five days later she went home to be with her King.

Now she's dancing with Jesus, swirling long, colorful scarves over her head. I miss her very much and often wish she were dancing with me, but it's okay. He's the better partner.

Virginia Cheeney

God Has a Plan

There is a time for everything, and a season for every activity under heaven.

Ecclesiastes 3:1

It was the day after Christmas. The snow on the rooftop had the requisite number of hoof prints, and all was cozy as we slept inside our warm flannel sheets. But when the phone rang at 4:30 A.M., any sense of comfort flew up the chimney. I became ice cold, and my heart started pounding. Phone calls that early in the morning are never good.

My brother, Jim, was on the line. "What medication is Mom on?"

"Just some high blood pressure medicine, I think. Why?"

"She's having a heart attack."

Our mother? Having a heart attack? It couldn't be happening. She was the healthiest eighty-four-year-old lady you could imagine. She ate heart-healthy salmon eight out of seven days a week and never touched anything deep-fried. Physically fit, she didn't know that twenty-five-pound vacuum cleaners are perfectly happy in closets. She thought hers should be exercised regularly, hoisting it up and down several flights of stairs.

Four years earlier, when she was a mere spring chicken, age eighty, she noticed a leak on the ceiling in the house where she lived with our father for forty-eight years. She hired a handyman to fix it. He was up on the rooftop when a thunderstorm began rumbling. Mom donned a well-worn jacket, climbed out the second-story window at the top of the stairs, shimmied over to the handyman's side of the roof and began helping him nail down the shingles. When a neighbor saw this, he shouted up to her, "Do your children know what you're doing?"

"No," she scolded him, "and don't you tell them!"

We eventually found out and tried to reason her out of such future activities. Getting on the rooftop, a la Dancer and Prancer, was reasonable, as she defiantly explained. "The handyman is sixty-five years old and has health problems. I didn't want him to get sick when it started raining."

Two years later, we asked Mom to consider living with one of us kids. She decided to move three hundred miles to be near me and my family, but "Only if I can have my own house." We agreed, with the stipulation that she stay off the roof. We bought her a house with no inside access to the roof—just in case.

As she settled in she declared, "It's about time I start a new chapter in my life. The good Lord has a plan to provide for us. He never gives me anything I can't handle with His help." Then she warned, "Just promise me you won't tell anyone here my age. I don't want my new friends to think I'm old."

It didn't matter. Her actions at her Monday-Wednesday-Friday exercise class at church fooled them anyway.

So when the phone rang that December 26, I was baffled why this Wonder Woman was having a heart attack. But, as she trusted, the good Lord provided a plan. My brother had heard Mom taking aspirin in the bathroom outside his bedroom door. He was wide awake when she said, "I think I'm having a heart attack." Instead of being in her own home where volunteer fire and ambulance services would have taken her to a hospital twenty minutes away, she was at my brother's, where the paramedics arrived in just three minutes.

Faster than Santa can swoop down the chimney, the emergency crew strapped her to the gurney and transported her to a hospital rated to have the best cardiac care in western Chicago just ten minutes away. She was in surgery before you could sing, "Grandma Got Run Over by a Reindeer."

Mom is wise beyond her eighty-four years: "God has the right plan, even when we can't see it." A plan to help push heavy Hoovers, scale rooftops and save my mom at Christmas time.

Jean Palmer Heck

The Key Ingredient

*Delight yourself also in the Lord,
And he shall give you the desires of your heart.*

Psalm 37:4

The family piano was now gone, and with it, a part of my life. Oh, I knew it had to go when my parents died. It and everything else in the home where they'd lived for nearly a quarter-century.

"Sure, you can have the piano," I told my sister. Her two children could take lessons on it. Single at the time, still working my way through graduate school, I realized I couldn't keep the behemoth player piano my parents bought secondhand early in their marriage. The "player" part no longer worked, and its paper rolls were brittle with age.

But as my sister and husband rolled the piano into a moving truck, so went something that had brought me comfort in the excruciating grief of losing both parents within six months.

The wall in the dining room where it sat for years looked sadly bare. I dragged my parents' old, wheezy vacuum cleaner from the coat closet and attacked the dust matted on the wall and rug. How many hours had I spent here as a child, practicing scales and recital pieces? Now, living temporarily in my parents' home while I cleaned it out, I'd returned to the keys to play and sing hymns of hope and comfort.

I never considered myself a pianist. I'd quit piano lessons in sixth grade because my tiny hands barely stretched an octave. I could play hymns, but advanced pieces needed big hands. So I switched to violin, which I played through college.

But I always found a piano somewhere to practice. After college, I got involved in a church's music ministry, enabling me to use the sanctuary instrument. During a two-year mission stint, for several months my tiny apartment "stored" (to my great delight) a piano belonging to fellow missionaries. The clockwork of Bach inventions, the passion of Beethoven and the heart-stirring melodies of hymns brought me joy and satisfaction.

After mission service, I moved thousands of miles away as I worked my way through graduate school. A piano of my own remained out of the question. Electronic keyboards were coming out, but their keys just didn't respond like a real piano. Besides, I needed every dime for my education.

Sometimes I'd sneak into the music building and find a vacant practice room to play its piano. But such were hurried times, and the instruments were like strangers. Then my parents died, and my life went on hold as I moved home to settle their affairs.

With my parents' piano gone, I still had that violin. But I had little desire to play it. I bought a secondhand guitar for thirty dollars, but never got good enough to play and sing at the same time. My hands were more at home on a keyboard.

Life moved on—and I finished graduate school and found work. I furnished a small apartment and played my violin in a church orchestra. I still yearned for a piano.

But God was at work. A young man came into my life and asked me to be his wife.

"I've been talking with my parents," he told me a few weeks before the wedding. "They want to give us something they no longer need. They think you'd enjoy it."

I wept when he told me: their piano.

Isn't that just like our loving God? He truly delights in supplying the desires of our hearts.

Jeanne Zornes

Triple Wedding Ring

"Tell me the story about Granddad riding horseback in the Oklahoma Land Run, Mom," I begged. "And about Grandmother walking behind the covered wagon all the way from Nebraska with you in her arms."

At the turn of the twentieth century, I was five years old, and my mother, Fynes Lavern Fleming McGill, patiently wove fascinating tales for me as she tucked me into bed. These memories inspired Mom to find the elusive Triple Wedding Ring quilt pattern to make one like her mother's. No one seemed to know how, so Mom took a picture of the quilt and mailed it to a quilting magazine with a request for the pattern.

Instead of receiving the pattern, she got ninety requests from other readers to send it if she ever found it.

Decades later, a woman in Nebraska sent the pattern to Mother, who felt obligated to send the coveted pattern to all who'd requested it. She bought extra large sheets of tracing paper and patiently duplicated the pattern and directions and mailed all ninety copies. As she addressed envelopes and applied the postage, she stopped often to rest and massage her now terribly arthritic fingers.

"After all the years of searching for the pattern, I'll never get around to making this quilt at my age," she sadly told her cousin Fern, visiting from Iowa. "My arthritic fingers won't allow me to quilt anymore."

"I'll be happy to make it for you," Fern offered, knowing how much Mom had her heart set on having that quilt. Nine months later Fern called. "I've got enough scraps to make a second quilt for your daughter. I'm centering the flowers in each piece. You're going to love it."

And indeed I did.

I cherish that quilt today. It was my thirtieth wedding anniversary gift from Mom. We used it as the backdrop behind the rose trellis in our garden ceremony on the farm when we renewed our wedding vows. The minister explained the significance of the quilt and Mom's passion to create it when he explained exchanging triple vows. "Not only to each other," he reminded us, "but to God, who binds you together in His everlasting love. The Triple Wedding Ring is so much stronger than the Double. When couples commit their lives to God first, His perfect love flows through both of them to hold their union together and they become one in Him."

Just before Mom's death in 1989, my sister was visiting when Mom's phone rang. It was a woman inquiring if we'd ever found the Triple Wedding Ring quilt pattern Mom had asked for in the magazine fifty years earlier.

So I took out tracing paper and tediously copied Mom's well-worn pattern and directions once again and mailed them to her.

A reminder of His vital role in making our marriages heavenly.

Arlene Purcell
as told to Judy Howard

In Good Hands

The Lord is not slow in keeping his promise, as some understand slowness. He is patient with you, not wanting anyone to perish, but everyone to come to repentance.

2 Peter 3:9

The phone rang early. Hal, my husband, answered it before it rang again.

"Yes?" he said. "Oh . . . I see." By the tone of his voice I knew it was the phone call we'd expected and dreaded.

We'd watched Hal's father, Harold, grow weaker since his heart attack in January. Dad's bypass surgery eight years earlier had given us far more than the five years doctors had promised. Then Dad experienced several smaller heart attacks. His lungs began filling with fluid. Doctors had reached the end of what they could do for him in the hospital and transferred him to an extended care facility.

With his needs beyond what care we could give and because he lived an hour and a half away, the most we could do was visit him as often as possible. Since we couldn't help him physically, the best care we could give was to care for his soul.

Hal and I had become Christians fifteen years earlier, and we wanted to share our faith with his family. His mother, Grace, had taken Hal and his brothers to church when they were young, but his father never went. Grace quit attending after Dad's first heart attack. Did she stay home to make sure Dad was okay after his quadruple bypass? Or had his heart attack shaken her faith? I didn't know.

Give us an opportunity to tell Dad about you, I prayed to Jesus. *He must decide whether he will take you as his Savior, but please don't let him die without a clear opportunity to respond to you.* I had prayed similar prayers for years, but when Dad became sick my urgency increased.

Hal hung up the phone. "Dad died at 3:30 this morning."

Lord, I prayed silently, *did he have the opportunity I asked for?*

Hal and I had both looked for that opportunity to tell Dad about Jesus, but we saw none. With each visit, Dad seemed less willing to talk to us at all. He just stared at the television. When we tried to start a conversation, he pressed the "up" button on the volume control. The more we tried, the more he increased the volume. The urgency I felt inside increased as well.

We asked a hospital chaplain to visit Dad. He did. We asked our own pastor to visit. He made the trip. A pastor from Mom's church visited too, but the result was always the same. Up, up went the volume on the TV. I didn't know what else to do but pray.

And now Dad was gone.

According to my faith, those who accept Jesus Christ as Savior are ensured an eternity in heaven with Him. However, those who refuse this gift of salvation spend eternity separated from God. I still hoped somehow God

had answered my prayer and had helped Dad understand, but had He? I didn't know.

We buried Dad in the veterans' portion of the cemetery.
Mom, a veteran of World War II herself, made her own final
arrangements at the same time. But none of us knew how
soon she would need them.

The week after Dad's funeral, she started showing signs
of illness. One day, a neighbor found her on the floor, incoherent. Doctors diagnosed Mom with a cancerous tumor
in her stomach plus lymphoma. She was hospitalized and
we resumed the endless trips to visit.

Mom was too weak to live alone, and her sons discussed
their options, each offering to care for her. But it became
clear her needs exceeded what any of us could give. The
best we could do as her caregivers was to let professionals
help. She moved into an extended care facility. The chemo
weakened her so that she didn't speak anymore. She
began having small strokes, then a major stroke. And
there we were, the week of Christmas, laying Grace to rest
beside her husband.

We invited everyone to gather at our home that
Christmas. As we quietly celebrated the birth of Jesus, I
not only wondered about Harold, I also wondered if Grace
had a true understanding of Jesus Christ. How I wished I
knew.

The new year dawned, and we all felt emotionally and
physically drained. Nevertheless, the work of dealing with
Harold and Grace's estate lay before us. Each of us sorted,
separated, donated, gave away or sold their belongings. We
fixed up their home for sale, painting inside and out.
Finally, six months later, Hal and I set the few remaining
items in the driveway for one last garage sale.

Neighbors, Christine and Alfonso, stopped by. "You
know, we visited your dad in the nursing home," Alfonso
told us.

"No, we didn't know that," Hal said.

"One afternoon I told Christine, 'We need to go see Harold.' We went right then. When I walked into his room," Alfonso said, "his face lit up! He was so happy to see us. So I just started telling him about Jesus."

"Really?" Hal asked, glancing at me.

"Your Dad said he wasn't ready to go," Alfonso said. "I told him, 'I'm not saying you're going to die, but we all need to be ready.' I explained to him about Jesus and then asked if he'd like to ask Jesus to be his Savior. He began to weep and said yes, so I led him in a prayer."

"We had no idea! When did this happen?" I asked, incredulously.

"Well," Alfonso thought for a moment, "he died early the next morning."

"I prayed with your mother, too," Christine added. "When the ambulance came for your dad, I stayed with her. I asked her if she was sure she'd go to heaven when she died and she said no, so I prayed with her so she could be sure."

"Your parents are in heaven," Alfonso declared.

I know.

Dianne E. Butts

Potato Salad and Picnics

*Woman is the salvation or the destruction of
the family. She carries its destiny in the folds of
her mantle.*

Henri Frederic Amiel

Life is like potato salad; when it's shared it becomes a
picnic.

When my three children were young, my husband Roy
and I were very busy. He was working on his master's
degree while working three jobs and I had three jobs of
my own. There was very little time that wasn't crammed
with stress, busy-ness and term papers.

"Can we go on a picnic, Mama?" my six-year-old daughter, Becky begged. "Please."

I had said no so many times in recent months, I decided
the usual Saturday morning chores could wait. To her surprise, I agreed. I prepared a few sandwiches and filled a
cooler with ice and drinks and called Roy at work. "Meet
us at the college pond for a picnic at twelve o'clock sharp,"
I said excitedly. My eleven-year-old twin sons loaded the
cooler and the picnic basket in the trunk, and off we went

to spend some quality time together as a family. I glanced at the kitchen counter just before heading to the car and spied a package of stale hamburger buns. I thought about the family of ducks living at the pond. We stopped and picked up a bucket of fried chicken at a fast-food restaurant on the way.

Becky and I spread the tablecloth on the cement picnic table while Brad and Chad tossed a football back and forth. In no time flat the ducks joined us. Becky squealed with delight as the ducks begged for breadcrumbs. About the time I got the lunch spread out on the table, Roy arrived on the scene. We joined hands and bowed our heads. As the wind blew and the ducks quacked, he thanked God not only for the food but for our family.

That was one of the happiest meals we ever shared together. The gentle breeze God sent our way caressed my face, as the sunshine warmed my heart. The meal was graced with giggles and laughter. We felt a closeness that had been hidden by work and school-related responsibilities for so many months. Once the food was consumed, Roy and the boys skipped rocks on the lake. Becky continued to feed the ducks, and I sat quietly on the picnic table, thanking God for blessing me with such a wonderful family.

Too soon, Roy had to go back to work. The kids continued to play together while I watched. I put the many things that I needed to do on the back burner of my life and simply enjoyed sharing the day with my children. Seeing the joy on each of their faces made me smile.

When we got into the car to return home, Becky crawled in the front seat with me. "Here Mama!" she exclaimed. She was holding a tiny yellow wildflower. Happy tears came to my eyes as I reached out and took it from her. When we arrived home, I put the tiny flower in a toothpick holder and placed the remaining food into the refrigerator.

That night as I tucked our children under their covers, I kissed their cheeks and realized what a wonderful life I had.

"Thank you for the picnic," one of the boys whispered.

"My pleasure," I whispered back.

As I walked out of the room it dawned on me that even the busiest lifestyle could become a picnic when it's shared with the ones you love.

Even though the kids have now grown up and moved away from home, I can still remember how I felt that day while sitting on the picnic table.

Maybe today would be a good time to cook potato salad, call all of my grown kids, feed some hungry ducks and throw a few rocks into the lake. Since life is like potato salad, let's make it a picnic.

Nancy B. Gibbs

Peaceful Coexistence and the Bogeyman

Blessed be the hand that prepares a pleasure for a child, for there is no saying when and where it may bloom forth.

Douglas Jerrold

When we were five years old, our parents, Gladden and Carmen, read bedtime stories to my twin brother Norman and me. Together we recited our prayers and were kissed goodnight. After this comforting ritual, I would snuggle down in my cozy bottom bunk bed with Norman on the top bunk, and we'd drift off to sleep.

Then suddenly, "OOOOOOOOOH! It's the bogeyman, and I'm going to get you!"

The booming, eerie voice terrified me. It sounded like Norman, but my fears always stopped me from getting out of bed to verify this suspicion.

Sometimes I would challenge the bogeyman and yell, "I know it's you, Norman!" But then the bed would shake and the wailing became even louder and more frightening.

My terror reached a point of no return. One night I tearfully called for Daddy to come and rescue me. I expected Norman to be punished on the spot, but that was not my father's style. He was a teacher, a man of faith, nonviolent reconciliation and consensus. He usually discussed issues with us and, more often than not, got us to work out our own problems.

So my father came in and I tearfully poured out my tale of woe. The top bunk was very quiet. I think Norman was awaiting his fate, but my father merely patted me on my shoulder and left the room. Both Norman and I were too stunned to speak or move. I was painfully disappointed not to be rescued and have the guilty severely punished.

A short time later my father returned with a small picture in his hand. He taped it to the underside of the top bunk where I could see it. It was a picture of Jesus as a Shepherd holding a baby lamb. Daddy knelt down beside my bed and whispered, "You can give your fears to God, and He will protect you and always be with you. You needn't be afraid of the bogeyman or that the upper bunk will shake and fall and crush you." Then he kissed me and turned off the light.

The next night the usual bedtime ritual was followed, and I had my eyes on my Shepherd and the lamb. When the lights went out, the bogeyman was out in force. "OOOOOOOOOH! It's the bogeyman, and I'm going to get you!"

With a quivering voice I announced, "God will protect me." Surprisingly, my fears began to slip away. But the scary noises increased and the bed began to shake. Strangely empowered I repeated my statement, adding, "I am not afraid!"

This went on for one or two nights, and then that old bogeyman surrendered. My relationship with my brother shifted a bit after that. He still teased me because that's what brothers are supposed to do, but with a little more respect.

My father never said a word about the incident. But once in a while when he tucked us into bed, he would wink at me and nod to the photo of the Shepherd and the lamb.

Sylvia Boaz Leighton

Money!

God only looks to the pure, not to the full hands.

Laberius

Our family was Christmas shopping in the clothing department of a large department store when our nine-year-old son, Bradley, shouted, "Money!" Rolled up with a rubber band was a substantial amount of cash, apparently dropped unknowingly by its owner. The money had rolled under a display table, and it was by sheer luck that my son saw it at all.

He was so excited about his find that my husband and I hated to rain on his parade with a gentle reminder. "Somewhere, someone else is very sad about losing this much money," his dad told him.

I added, "Yes, and the person who lost it may have saved for a long time and is frantically looking for it now."

After a short discussion of who might have lost it we asked him, "How would you feel if you had lost the money?"

"I think I'd be sad and maybe even sick to my stomach," he admitted.

I asked, "Do you think you should keep the money or turn it in to the store manager?"

It wasn't an easy decision for a nine-year-old. He frowned. "Turn it in."

When the lady behind the desk at Lost and Found asked, "How can I help you?" I nudged Bradley forward to speak for himself.

"But, Mom, what if no one ever comes to claim it?" he asked.

I gave him a smile and stepped forward to explain about the lost money. "Do you think if the money isn't claimed it could be given to our son, who found it?"

The desk clerk had watched Bradley struggle with changing his mind and readily agreed.

We left his name and address, and the clerk wrote a quick note. Then, using the rubber band, she attached the note to the money and placed it in a lockbox.

When we retold this incident to others, many called us naive. "Surely the store manager or some other employee will keep that money," people would say. In fact, the general consensus was that we were "fools" to encourage our son to turn the money in. His neighborhood friends teased Bradley, chanting, "Do-gooder! Do-gooder! You're nuts!"

He just shrugged it off and said, "It wasn't my money." His dad and I were so proud of him.

Two years later a letter came in the mail addressed to Bradley. It was from the department store, which was now going out of business. The letter stated that they had found a roll of money in their vault with Bradley's name and address on it. A notation said it should be sent to him if not claimed. Attached to the letter was a check made out to Bradley with a note from the manager:

Dear Bradley,
I do admire you so much for making such a grown-up

decision at age nine. I remember your struggle and know it wasn't easy. It took a person of strong character to turn in that money. There are many adults who would struggle with such a decision. The money was never claimed and so I am pleased to honor your request. The money is now yours!

She made a smiley face with the words "enjoy" and "have a ball" under it.

It would be a wonderful story if it ended right here, but there's more.

Twenty years later Bradley had a son born prematurely. Little Nathan weighed only two pounds and suffered a stroke when two days old. My son was laid off, job searching and short of money. Times were bad all around for him and his young wife. Bradley left the ICU and went to the hospital chapel and prayed for his son's life. On his way back to ICU, he stopped at a vending machine for a cheap snack. He deposited his coins and retrieved his selection, then coins began to pour out like a slot machine paying off a jackpot! Bradley collected the coins in his shirttail and marveled at his luck. Just when he was thinking about counting his loot he remembered his childhood experience. He knew what he had to do. He had just prayed for a miracle for his son. He knew, however, this was not the miracle he needed. Perhaps it was a test from above.

"Well, God," he prayed, "I figure I need all the points I can get right about now. My son's life hangs in the balance and the outcome is in Your hands. This isn't my money. You've seen me through till now and I'm counting on You. Please, God, give me a strong, healthy son."

Then he walked over to the nurses' desk carrying his shirttail filled with coins and emptied them on the counter. "Can you return this to the vendor, ma'am?" he asked.

The wide-eyed nurse was astounded. "Are you sure you don't want to just keep this? Most people would."

Bradley just grinned. "I don't know how much money is here . . . but I'm certain that my reward will be much greater by far."

He was correct. That was six years ago. Little Nathan is now healthy and happily in kindergarten and the joy of our lives . . . God's ultimate payoff!

Christine M. Smith

Charlie Brown Meets Baby Jesus

A happy family is but an earlier heaven.

Sir John Bowring

For years I had carefully placed the little plastic Nativity scene under the Christmas tree. It had been purchased along with our other meager decorations the first Christmas we were married back in 1962. My husband was finishing his fourth and last year at college, and money was tight. Each year as Christmas approached, I looked longingly at the beautiful wood and ceramic crèches, wondering when there would be enough extra money to purchase one.

Finally the day arrived. Our sons were eleven and fourteen, and we had recently moved into our newly built house. I watched the after-Christmas sales and there it was, nothing elaborate, not a large crèche, but it was wood and ceramic with 50 percent off the original price. We made our way to the local department store with all the other bargain shoppers, purchased the crèche and carefully packed it away until the following Christmas.

Several weeks before the next Christmas, we brought

the box from the basement and arranged the crèche in a place of honor in the center hall where, as I went from one part of the house to another, I could enjoy my treasured gift. An angel on the top watched over Mary, Joseph and the baby Jesus. Jesus lay in the manger with outstretched arms, surrounded by wise men, shepherds and animals.

One day as I hurried by the crèche, something caught my eye. I stopped to look and there beside the manger, looking down at the baby Jesus, was a rubber figure of Charlie Brown. *Charlie Brown!* Charlie Brown from the beloved *Peanuts* cartoon series.

I was quick, much too quick, to question the boys and say, "Get that thing out of my crèche." I knew instantly our youngest son, Mark, had been the culprit as he looked at me with his boyish grin.

Charlie Brown disappeared. Christmas was over and the wooden stable and ceramic figures were lovingly packed away.

As Christmas approached the following year, the crèche was again displayed in its place of honor. It was the first thing holiday guests saw as they entered the front door. It was the last thing we saw each night as we turned off the lights and headed up the stairs to bed.

Several days before Christmas as I passed the crèche, I was again surprised. There gazing down at the baby Jesus was not only Charlie Brown but on the other side of the manger stood another little rubber figure. *Linus!* Linus, blanket and all, stood looking into the outstretched arms of Baby Jesus.

For some strange reason as I beheld this, I was not upset as I had been the previous year. Maybe the crèche didn't belong to me alone. Maybe Mark, with his childish prank, was showing he loved it as much as I did. Maybe this young boy was mature beyond his years, knowing the baby with his outstretched arms was for everyone.

That afternoon as I watched my children get off the school bus and head for the house, my heart overflowed with love for them. I smiled when I mentioned that Charlie Brown had once again mysteriously appeared in the crèche and now Linus had joined him.

As the years went by, I never knew when Charlie Brown and Linus would make their mysterious arrival, but Christmas after Christmas they showed up, looking down into the outstretched arms of baby Jesus.

Mark left for college, but each Christmas Charlie Brown and Linus came home for Christmas break, too.

Then came marriage and the move away from home. Still Charlie Brown and Linus continued to find their way into our crèche each Christmas.

Last Christmas I stood back with tears in my eyes as Mark bent over the crèche with his little daughter, Savannah, helping her quietly and carefully place Charlie Brown and Linus beside the baby Jesus when they thought I wasn't looking.

As the crèche was carefully packed away in its now-torn tissue paper and aging box, I smiled to myself, secure in the thought that the tradition of Charlie Brown and Linus would continue. And secure in the knowledge that those outstretched arms of the Christ Child welcome us all to the manger.

Jean C. Myers

3

ANSWERED PRAYERS

A good man's prayers will from the deepest dungeon climb heaven's height and bring a blessing down.

Joanna Baillie

One Mother's Dream

Mother love is the fuel that enables a normal human being to do the impossible.

Marion C. Garretty

For as long as I can remember, I dreamed of holding a baby. When I was a child, she was an infant-sized doll. If I could sit still, I was allowed to hold my baby sister, then, three years later, my brother. In summer, I rocked a large zucchini with button eyes from Grandma's garden. When the neighborhood gang played house in our backyard, I was always Mom—and a bit bossy! Acting as Mother Mary in the annual La Posada at church, I felt honored to be carrying Baby Jesus.

As I grew older, with each romance I dreamed of the day when I would hold a baby and birth a family. I wept barren tears in my mid-twenties during years of discerning a celibate religious vocation, and later while in a relationship with a man who didn't want to marry. I held babies I loved deeply . . . first a goddaughter, then a nephew, all the while smiling with joy, wondering when my time would come. I continued to dream and started to pray.

At thirty-one, the dream began in earnest. Together with Jim, my new husband—literally the man next door—I imagined the day we would hold our child, fantasizing perfect names and even beginning to purchase necessary baby gear. Month after month after month, tears and blood flowed like clockwork. I held another nephew, then a niece, then a second goddaughter. Well-intentioned friends said things such as: "Just relax." "Get away for a romantic weekend." "If you adopt you'll get pregnant for sure." "Fall on your knees and pray more." As if I hadn't already prayed, and tried everything I could think of! I was angry and sad. In prayer, I let God know it. After all, I was working in church ministry serving the Lord. I deserved my dream. I began to wonder if I was paying a price for past sins.

But the God I encountered in prayer was suffering with me, not condemning me. Barrenness has a powerful precedent in scripture. Stories of Sarah, Rachel and Elizabeth brought me renewed hope. I just knew a baby and family was God's good and creative dream in me. How could it be denied? I heard God's word in Psalm 46: "Be still and know that I am God." Yet, year after year my healthy, strong, vibrant body betrayed me.

Jim and I spent considerable time contemplating fertility treatments, sperm donors, domestic and international infant adoption, and our limited finances. When a notice in our church bulletin listed a phone number with a request for foster adoptive parents, we just wanted to eliminate a choice we didn't think was a fit for us. Thus, one hot July evening, we sat on our porch with a caseworker from the local foster adoption agency. The three of us sat on our deck, overlooking a Colorado lake with a little rowboat moored on the shore where Jim spent most leisure time fishing.

As our conversation progressed, the caseworker asked, "Are you certain you want to adopt an infant?"

I replied, "Yes."

A little later in the conversation, the same question. My answer remained, "Yes."

Finally, again, "Are you certain you want an infant?"

I looked into her eyes. "What are you thinking? That's the third time you've asked me the same question."

"Well," she answered, "if you were to adopt an older child you could continue working." I just stared at her.

"And," she continued, "I know a seven-year-old boy in town who loves to fish and desperately needs a strong father and forever family."

I didn't move. The next thing I knew my six-foot-five husband was towering over us, practically shouting, "That's the right age for me!"

I sat stunned. Birds chirped in the trees. I listened to my heart beat wildly.

So be it.

One month later, just in time for third grade, our son-to-be spent his first night in our home.

Nothing prepared me for parenting a little boy who had lived in nine foster homes. The warm fuzzies I had anticipated were nonexistent. Somewhere along the way I neglected to comprehend that foster children like Justin already had birth parents, a family and past experiences that shaped their lives. Bonding and attachment might not happen, maybe couldn't. I discovered my own worst behaviors were not unlike Justin's: anger at not being listened to, not having my needs met. Odd that as an adult I had the same feelings as the child in my home.

I slowly learned to understand the gift of being a lifesaver for a young boy—and he becoming a lifesaver of sorts for me, too, as I grew into fuller maturity, discovering within myself reservoirs of patience and wisdom. My prayer was simple: to love him as Jesus.

Together we learned the safety of boundaries. We talked

about feelings, listened to one other. Justin began to grow with our focused, consistent attention, meals and bedtimes. Learning about Jesus, he discovered he could be loved no matter what. I felt happiness that he felt safe enough to throw a temper tantrum. He explored personal interests, caught fish and gained confidence. Through prayer, I learned to love him as if I had birthed him myself. God softened my heart and taught me generosity.

One afternoon after an emotional meltdown, Justin asked if he could sit on my lap. Though his legs and arms were a bit long, I snuggled him closely against me. Looking beyond my shoulder, he cautiously asked, "If you had been my birth mom, what would you have done?"

Realizing he wanted to hear a different version of his own tumultuous childhood, I said softly, "I would have held you every day, rocking you just like this, and told you stories, real and imaginary. You would have known you were safe and loved, no matter what." I stopped talking, feeling the weight of his body against mine, then continued, "And you know what? We can still do that, even though your elbow is poking my side!"

We chuckled together and after a minute of rocking, the air hushed. He turned, looking me straight in the eyes, and asked, "Could you tell me a story now?"

My blinking eyelids pushed back tears. Smiling at him, I began: "A long, long time ago, a little girl dreamed of being a mom and holding a little boy on her lap. . . ." His hand gripped mine tightly. Breathing slow and steady, he listened intently, never taking his eyes from mine.

In the coming months Justin often asked to sit on my lap, and we discovered how much we both needed each other. Later that year, after his legal adoption, I received an unexpected valentine: "Dear Mom, Thank you so much for taking care of me over all these years and making sure that I have food to eat and that I have a roof over my head. I also love having a very loving and caring person such as you."

Not words I ever expected I'd receive from a child. But still more powerful to me than an actual, "I love you, Mommy," which I suspect I'll never hear.

Justin is now in his teens and an only child. I have learned the fierce love that I am certain Mary shared with her son two thousand years ago. Jesus has taught me to welcome and love the orphan. Just last week, at five-foot-nine, Justin gave me a hug, and looking down at me, asked, "Do you remember when I was small enough to fit in your lap?"

I smiled a "yes" into his eyes and offered a silent prayer of gratitude to be living a mother's dream.

Pegge Bernecker

Cantaloupe Moon

When I consider your heavens, the work of your fingers, the moon and the stars, which you have set in place, what is man that you are mindful of him, the son of man that you care for him?

(Psalm 8:3-4)

"We have an accidental cantaloupe ripening in our flower garden," my neighbor Frank said. "Why don't you bring Aurelia down tonight and help us harvest it?" Frank and his wife Gloria were two of the many people praying for our daughter, whom my husband Dean and I had recently adopted from Romania. There had been no fresh fruits or vegetables at Orphanage #3 in Bucharest, only a thick plot of crabgrass thriving in a neglected courtyard. In contrast, the children of Orphanage #3 were far from growing like the proverbial weed. Labeled "irrecuperable" by the orphanage psychiatrist, five-and-a-half-year-old Aurelia weighed just twenty-seven pounds.

As we set out for Frank's house that evening, I exclaimed, "Aurelia, look! A harvest moon!" Hoping to add to Aurelia's vocabulary, I added, "Do you know what color that is, Aurelia? It's orange!" Aurelia hardly noticed. She was busy riding the bike Dean had specially equipped with oversized sneakers attached to the pedals.

Frank's garden was the jewel of the neighborhood. Roses, lilacs, irises—everything he planted looked like a photo op from a seed catalog. His cantaloupe plant was no exception: The khaki-colored melon huddled underneath an abundant, curling vine. With Frank's assistance, Aurelia bent down to cut the cantaloupe from the vine. It was a beautiful melon—and I couldn't resist inserting another teachable moment.

"Aurelia, how does it feel?" I asked. She balked at holding the melon, so I showed her how to touch the netted rind with one finger. "Rough," I said, listening to her repeat the word after me. Aurelia inhaled the musky fragrance of the cut cantaloupe, but she refused to scoop out the seeds or taste the fruit.

"Oh well," I said to no one in particular on the way home. "It *is* a beautiful harvest kind of evening. Just look at that moonrise!"

Safely home at last, Aurelia parked her bike before looking up and noticing the nighttime sky for the first time. Pointing heavenward, she thrilled me with two simple words: "Cantaloupe moon."

Lori Williams

The Birthday

Every thread of gold is valuable. So is every moment of time.

John Mason

"Hurry, Mom, hurry! Blow out the candles!" my four-year-old daughter, Abigail, shouted, tugging on my shirt. "Make a prayer," she reminded, her brown eyes alight with childish wonder.

"Make a prayer?" her grandmother asked. "What's that?"

"Silly Grammy!" Abigail laughed, covering her mouth. "We say prayers instead of wishes! It's easy!"

The lights dimmed and the candles flickered. Several witty birthday cards on aging were propped beside the cake. Just last month, my older brother refused to celebrate his fortieth birthday. He had not wanted to be reminded that he was getting older. I closed my eyes and breathed deeply. How many people, including myself, did that each year?

My daughter slipped her hand into my pocket, her tiny fingers finding mine. I rubbed her soft skin and sighed.

Memories of my friend, Susie, flooded me. Mother of two and married for over twenty years, Susie had been young and vibrant. She'd had a welcoming grin, a kind heart—and breast cancer. Violently sick from chemotherapy, she had lost her hair and begun a journey of pain and endurance.

Her husband, desperate for a medical breakthrough, had arranged experimental procedures, but nothing worked and her condition worsened. Time passed, but Susie refused to give up.

Those who knew her best began to doubt her life-and-death decisions. "Why is she doing this to herself?" they'd often asked. "She and her family are going to have to accept the inevitable. She's going to die. She should stop the treatments and live the rest of her days as best she can. Can't she see that?"

I had joined together with a prayer partner, and we had diligently lifted Susie in prayer from the onset of her cancer. Everyone who loved Susie wanted what was best for her. Some chose the "live your remaining days free of medical services" approach. Others continued helping her find new alternatives. Whatever their advice, Susie never wavered from her path—doing whatever she had committed to do in order to beat the disease. She continued medical treatment though her doctors told her there was little hope.

During Susie's struggle, at night when I cradled my newborn son, I often thought of her family that would be left behind if she died. Maybe it was because of how I loved my own children and husband that her battle affected me so greatly.

Looking at life through Susie's eyes, a new humility and appreciation for each new day surrounded me. When my husband kissed me as he left for work, I'd linger in his arms a little longer. Every night, I'd kneel beside my children's sleeping figures and study their angelic faces, not wanting to take one second for granted. Soon, I began to ache for Susie, and during that time I realized why she'd continued on with such passion.

Susie knew the secret of life. And that secret, simply, was life itself.

She wanted another opportunity to laugh and smack her husband's hand as he pinched her when she walked past. She wanted to witness her daughter's high school graduation and her son's first prom. She wanted to see the glory of another sunrise and wanted to be in the world when her first grandchild entered it. Life was not a mystery but a miracle. And Susie knew that, right up until the moment when, on a crisp winter day, she died.

"Mama," Abigail said, pointing to the candles. "Hurry, they're melting!"

My husband, holding our precious son, Simeon, caught my eyes from across the table. He kissed the top of Simeon's head, then smiled at me. Butterflies fluttered in my stomach. Those whom I loved most were near.

Because of Susie's zest for life and faith in God, I've never seen birthdays in the same way again. Anxiety didn't flood me at my first wrinkles. And since Susie's death, I've never bought an insulting birthday card again. Instead, I've embraced the joys and trials of getting older. After all, each birthday is one more year that I've experienced life's many jewels, ranging from my children wrestling with my husband to me being awakened by a bird's morning song.

"Hurry, Mama! Hurry!" Abigail pleaded. "I'll help you blow them out!"

My son giggled, waving his hand at me, and my husband winked. "Let's do it," I told my daughter. We filled our cheeks with air and blew out the candles. The smoke traveled upward.

"Look, Mama! Look!" Abigail shouted, pointing a finger towards the ceiling. "The smoke's carrying your prayer to heaven! It's gonna be answered!"

Bending down, I cupped Abigail's beautiful face. Her eyes were beaming, and I inhaled the sweet scent that was hers exclusively. "It already has been, honey," I whispered, thanking Jesus for another year. "It already has been."

Karen Majoris-Garrison

Table of Plenty

Bless us, O Lord, and these your gifts,
which we are about to receive
from your bounty,
through Christ our Lord. Amen.

Catholic Prayers and Devotions

When our family sits at the table for a meal, I am reminded of how blessed we are to give grace, eat, drink and share our assemblage under one roof.

There was a time in our lives when internal circumstances led to our family being separated from one another.

Many summers ago, when our daughter was five years old, my husband and I decided to disunite after thirteen years of marriage. We both felt more affected by the *worse* than the *better*.

I filed for divorce, obtained legal guardianship of our daughter and ventured to a town about fifty miles north of the city where my husband resided.

It was not an easy time because I had been a stay-at-home mom for several years, and had very little money. We stayed with relatives of my husband's for a while. Then we moved into an apartment over a cake shop, which was one block from where my daughter attended school.

Meanwhile, my daughter and I began visiting a large church in the center of town. The more we visited, the more determined I was for us to return there.

One Sunday, as I listened to the angelic voices of the choir that echoed from the rear balcony of the church, the Holy Spirit touched my heart and soul with such magnitude that I felt compelled to become a member.

I wanted my daughter to be baptized in this particular faith. I also wanted her to grow in the knowledge that, although her parents were apart, we dearly loved her and, most importantly, so did God.

During the same period I obtained an education grant and enrolled in a computer class so I could find a job to support us. It had been years since I was in a classroom all day, so it took all I had to concentrate and persevere, but I knew that with God's help it would be done.

Each day before I drove my daughter to school and hurried to my class, I prayed, "Dear Heavenly Father, please help me find the strength and courage I need to get through another day. I pray that You will wrap Your loving arms of protection around my daughter and me, so that we may be reunited by the end of the day—alive and well. Amen."

As my spirituality grew, so did the positive factors in my life. I was blessed with an internship during the two semesters I was a student. I wrote an essay for the Soroptimist's Club and won an award.

By Thanksgiving, there was much to be thankful for: our new friends, and the kindness they gave to us as mentors, neighbors and parishioners.

I was receiving child support payments and was thankful to God, the state and my estranged husband for the help. He had always been a responsible and devoted father, and I could tell by his phone conversations that God was also at work in his life. For the first time in many years, I sensed in him a genuine sensitivity and concern for my total well-being.

One night at bedtime, I overheard my daughter pray, "God—please let me see my daddy on Christmas, and let my mommy and daddy be together again. Amen."

The prayer brought on a flow of emotion that I had tried desperately to suppress. As I silently sobbed, I repeated her prayer.

The next day my husband phoned to let me know he had shopped for the presents our daughter had requested for Christmas. At that point, I invited him to join us at the apartment for the holidays.

When I hung up I had ambiguous thoughts about seeing him, and wondered if I had been too impulsive. While I was pleased that his presence would be an answer to our daughter's prayer, I was also worried that it would have the potential to evoke an upsurge of negative feelings between us again.

The church asked if it could provide my daughter and me with Christmas gifts. I turned them down, not because I was proud or ungrateful, but because I felt God would provide us with the gifts for which we had prayed.

On Christmas, my husband and I communicated without blame or consternation. We laughed about things that no longer had any significance, and calmly discussed everything that did. We related to each other with greater respect. This time there was clarity in our individual purpose, credulity within our joint understanding and unity in our mission as parents. Our family of three shared in the spirits of hope, joy and gratitude that holy season.

As the months progressed into the next year, our daughter had her first communion. After the sacrament, a photo was taken of our family outside the church. In the picture, there is a statue of St. Joseph with his arm extended toward us, in a surrounding halo of light. I perceived the anomaly in the picture to be a sign that God was still answering our prayers, and that He wanted us to be a *real* family again.

After almost two years of a second courtship—which included commutes, a wealth of letters and phone calls, bouquets of flowers, restaurant dinners, counseling and church visits—my husband and I rebuilt our marriage. This time, we based it on faith, love, respect and patience.

The day before school began in the fall, my daughter and I moved back to the city and reunited with my husband as a family—in our new home.

Sure, there are still some challenges, but they don't seem as insurmountable anymore. We live one day at a time, grateful to God for all blessings great and small, and for His forgiveness of our failings.

We give you thanks, almighty God,
for these and all your gifts
which we have received
through Christ our Lord. Amen.

Stephani Marlow James

A Change in Plans

In his heart a man plans his course, but the Lord determines his steps.

Proverbs 16:9

"Please God, help me. I can't live through another Mother's Day." Heartbroken, Tammy longed to hold a baby and feel its soft skin against hers. She longed to hear a newborn's cry in the middle of the night. She longed to be a mother.

Two years ago on Mother's Day, she and Chris were elated because the baby growing inside her was already eleven weeks old. They were hopeful that this time she would go full term. But later that day their dreams were shattered. Waves of nausea and painful cramps overcame Tammy. Fearing the worst, they called the doctor. He confirmed their dreaded thoughts. It was a miscarriage—her third.

Now, a year later, Tammy struggled with memories of fertility drugs, surgery, frustration and disappointment. The verse Jeremiah 29:11 came to her mind: "For I know the plans I have for you, declares the Lord . . ." She swallowed back tears. "God, what is your plan for me? I am forty years old and don't have a lot of time. I pray that a baby is part of Your plan for us."

The emotional ride she had been on for three-and-a-half years came to an end after two attempts at artificial insemination failed. Adoption seemed their next viable choice.

With a renewed sense of hope, Tammy and Chris began the adoption process. Physicals, paperwork, FBI checks, written testimonials, a home study and a profile of them had to be completed before they could be considered. Finally, when it was all done, Tammy breathed a sigh of relief and prayed that God would bless them with a baby soon.

A couple of months passed without any news from the adoption agency. Feelings of doubt crept into Tammy's mind until finally she received a call at work from the caseworker. Would they take a newborn with potential health problems? Feeling uneasy about the circumstances, Tammy and Chris tearfully declined, wondering if they'd ever be picked again.

In a few weeks, Tammy received a package in the mail from an old friend of Chris's family whom she'd never met. Inside was a diaper bag filled with necessary baby items and a note:

> When we were planning to adopt our first child, someone gave us a diaper bag. When I heard about your situation, I wanted to do the same thing for you. With each of our children, we were away from home when we received the call saying we were parents, so the diaper bag came in handy. Put this in the trunk of your car and you will always be prepared.

What a gift of hope, Tammy thought. She tucked it away and prayed she would need it soon.

Nearly nine months passed since they first contacted

the agency. Finally they got another call. This time the agency had a pregnant woman due in a few weeks! This time Tammy and Chris said yes, they wanted to be considered. Since they were leaving the next day to spend Mother's Day weekend with her mom and dad, Tammy gave the agency her parents' phone number.

Friday morning, while preparing for their five-hour trek to her parents' house, Tammy remembered the diaper bag. Feeling a little foolish for planning weeks in advance for a baby that might not even be theirs, she tossed it in the truck.

They arrived at her parents' home to find Tammy's dad pacing in the front yard, awaiting their arrival. He raced over, and before they got out of the truck, he exclaimed, "Get in the house. Get on the phone. Call the adoption agency. You guys are parents!"

Shaking, Tammy called the adoption agency, and they all listened in disbelief on the speakerphone. The baby had arrived early, and the birth mother had chosen them that morning to be the newborn boy's parents. If they were interested, they had to drive four hours back toward home early the next day to meet the birth mother and get her final approval. There were still no guarantees, but if they were not there by 10:30 A.M., they wouldn't have a chance.

That night Chris and Tammy hardly slept. Was this baby God's plan for them? Were they making the right choice? What would happen to their lives now? Would they be good parents? They held each other and prayed. A peacefulness filled them and they slept soundly for a few hours.

Early the next morning, with the diaper bag in hand, Tammy and Chris headed to the hospital to meet the birth mother and the caseworker. It was hard for Tammy to sit still. She wanted to be considerate of the birth mother's feelings, but she wanted so much to see the baby. She could hardly believe that if the birth mother consented, their son would go home with them that day. Finally she heard, "Would you like to see the baby?"

The caseworker led the happy couple to the room while the birth mother left to shower. They quietly approached the bassinet. Tammy's heart melted when she saw his tiny little face. She gently picked him up and held him close, touching her tear-covered cheek to his soft, warm one. Chris embraced them both. She knew at that moment this was their son.

That evening at home, after their family and friends left, Tammy and Chris lay together with Luke nestled between them. They soaked in the events of the day—it was still so unbelievable. They joked about not having a crib, just a diaper bag. Tammy smiled at Chris, then at Luke. She realized this was God's plan all along. She closed her eyes and knew tomorrow, her dream of a perfect Mother's Day would come true.

Kerrie Flanagan

Daddy's Guardian Angel

For He shall give his angels charge over thee, to keep thee in all thy ways.

Psalm 91:11

My son commutes two hours to and from work each day and has to leave extremely early each morning. He never seems to get enough sleep, so I help by driving Airianna, his five-year-old daughter, to school.

One day she and I were discussing the importance of wearing a seat belt. I reminded her that recently a seat belt had saved her daddy's life when he was in a rollover accident.

"Your daddy always wears his seat belt," I told her. "With a seat belt and a prayer to God you are doubly protected. Every day Grandma says a prayer for his safety. I ask God to send his guardian angel to ride along with your daddy to watch over him and keep him safe while he drives."

She thought about this for a minute, then said, "Grandma, why couldn't the guardian angel just drive . . . and let Daddy sleep?"

Christine M. Smith

And the Answer Is . . .

Jesus looked at them and said, "With man this is impossible, but with God all things are possible."
Matthew 19:26

When my sons were growing up, I enrolled them in vacation Bible school and I always signed up to teach. As they outgrew Bible school, I transferred my teaching skills to adult literacy programs. But when I heard the plea that more VBS teachers were needed, I called in and added my name to the roster. I certainly had the experience, and besides, it would be fun to be with children again. After I was assigned a class of eleven three-year-olds, I attended the appropriate workshops. I spent a week making elaborate lesson plans and constructing the visual props provided by the leader's book, incorporating the church's "Climbing Faith Mountain" theme.

The night before vacation Bible school began, I prayed, "Dear God, thank you for the opportunity to teach these little ones about you. With this prayer, I'm ready."

Well, I thought I was ready.

It had been many years since I'd stood in front of a

group of little ones, so imagine my surprise to rediscover that they ran everywhere, leaping and laughing, brightly colored sandals slap-slapping against summer-tanned heels. With our combined efforts, my teen helper and I managed to corral their energies and herd their attention to the story mat.

We sat in a lopsided circle, busy hands folded and nestled in laps. Our first story-lesson up Faith Mountain was one of obedience. I told of God's request for Abraham to move his family and livestock to a new place. We stood and I led my group from one side of the room to the other, "baaing" and "mooing" in imitation of Abraham's sheep and cows as we trudged along.

Concrete examples will reinforce what I've taught them, I thought and mentally patted myself on the back.

We settled back into our circle. "Abraham had the faith to obey God's word," I said as I ended our story.

At the close of the morning, I asked, "Who had the faith to move his family and livestock?"

"God!" eleven cheerful voices shouted.

I smiled and shook my head no. "Abraham."

"Abraham," parroted the serious, elfin chorus.

Our story for the next day, "Joseph and His Many-Colored Coat," was about trust. I explained that when Joseph was taken from his family and found himself in prison, God still watched after and protected him.

At the end of the second morning, I gathered my charges and asked, "Who trusted and prayed for his safety and protection while he was away from his father and brothers?"

"God!" they sang loudly.

Again I shook my head. "Repeat after me," I said. "Joseph."

"Joseph." They were just a little out of unison.

Day three brought us a story-lesson of strength. "God told Joshua to lead the Israelites around the walls of

Jericho and blow their trumpets, and the walls came tumbling down." We marched like little infantrymen around and around the mat. We stopped, opened our mouths wide and shouted out trumpetlike sounds, and then collapsed into a large heap onto the floor. Bodies rolled and legs kicked in jubilation.

I righted myself and studied each sweaty face. "Who was strong enough to make the walls of Jericho fall down?"

"God!" They shrieked and raised miniature fists above their heads.

I stood and retrieved the picture of the trembling walls. My finger singled out a man with a trumpet. "Joshua!" I said loudly.

Urchin faces lifted upward. "Joshua!"

For Thursday I built an elaborate pallet, complete with a blanket and a little boy puppet, to help tell the story of Samuel. Squeals erupted and hands clapped as they watched the boy spring up and down to answer God's voice booming out Samuel's name.

"Samuel was a good listener." I narrowed my eyes and took in each stare. "God wants us all to be good listeners."

We ended yet another morning. I swallowed hard and ventured, "Who was a good listener this morning?"

"God!" Their voices bounced off the walls of the room.

My heart sank. "Sam-u-el," I said, enunciating each syllable.

Eleven pouty mouths formed the name "Sam-u-el."

On the final morning of vacation Bible school, I doubted that I'd taught my group anything as we assembled for our last story-lesson.

"God loves and cares for us so much that He sent His son Jesus to teach us about that love. And even though Jesus went to heaven, He'll be back one day." I paused and finished with a smile. "In the meantime, remember, God is the answer to our questions in life."

What? What was that I'd said? "God" is the answer?
Hmmm. Maybe my three-year-olds hadn't been giving me
the wrong answers all week after all. . . . Maybe I'd been
asking the wrong questions.

I began anew. "Who did Abraham obey when he was
asked to move?"

"God!" they yelled.

"Who did Joseph trust when he was in prison?"

"God!"

"Who gave Joshua the strength to make the walls of
Jericho fall down?"

"God!"

"And who spoke to Samuel?"

"God!"

Finally, I said, "Jesus is the Son of—"

"God!" we said together.

The three-year-olds knew all along the response that
the seasoned teacher had forgotten. Who is the answer to
all our questions?

"God!"

Janice Alonso

Eskimo's Gift

Give what you have. To someone it may be better than you dare to think.

Henry Wadsworth Longfellow

Howling winds whistled through the electrical outlets, making an eerie sound in my tiny apartment. Crystallized snow as far as the eye could see was the norm in Churchill, Manitoba—polar bear country. The one-hundred-degrees-below-zero blizzard whipped around the old army barracks, converted to apartments. I was a nursing instructor teaching Eskimo teenagers a nurse's aide course.

One day after class in September, I'd said to beautiful sixteen-year-old Anita, "I'd sure like to get a pair of mukluks and some mitts. Do you know where I can get some for winter?"

"Yes, my mother . . . she make you some," she beamed.

"Really!" I replied, delighted. Sure enough, a month later, she brought me a beautiful pair of mukluks, made with sealskin uppers and moosehide soles, along with a pair of sealskin mitts. They were not exactly fashionable, but beautifully beaded, and I wore them with pleasure.

They didn't cost much, either, not like the expensive leather knee-high boots in my closet, bought on the spur of the moment in Montreal before I came to this howling wilderness. As I emptied my wallet, the salesman guaranteed they would keep me warm, but they were unsuited for this weather.

Now I could hear Anita's tinkling laughter just outside my door, like wind chimes in a soft breeze. She was early. I'd wondered if anyone would show up tonight.

A hesitant knock. Anita, a sloe-eyed, raven-haired beauty, walked in and sat down on the floor. She shivered, and I did too. Her ebony eyes twinkled. She was serene even at her age, and I was drawn to her bubbling personality and simplicity as she spoke.

It was then I noticed her tattered sneakers, frayed and yawning open at the toe. But she never mentioned her frozen feet. She sat cross-legged, her toes peeking out at me. I thought, *How can she stand it in this cold? Her feet must be frozen!*

But she chattered on and on about her childhood when everyone in the north cared for everyone else. She told me that when an animal is shot, enough is left for the next hunter, just in case they didn't get anything. She learned caring at an early age.

When the other students were no-shows, she told me about her wonderful faith in God. "He answer prayers," she grinned.

It was then I sensed a nudging in my spirit. *Give her those boots in your closet.* I ignored the idea. After all, they were much too expensive for such a young girl. She wouldn't appreciate them. Mukluks were much more serviceable up here because the soft soles easily slithered over the crystallized snow. So I continued to rationalize as I thought about my precious boots.

But the nudging persisted, and I had no rest until I

stood up and opened the closet. There they were, sitting there unused and useless. Fashionable. Warm with sheepskin lining. Beautiful. I loved them. I bit my lip as I remembered that God loves a cheerful giver, and I handed them to her.

"I think these are yours," I said.

"Thank you. I pray that Jesus give me boots!" she exclaimed in her staccato English.

She pulled them over her feet. They were a perfect fit, of course; they were hers, after all. For a fleeting moment I wanted to switch the mukluks for those beautiful boots, for she had no idea of their value. But I resisted.

The wind continued to howl outside, and we continued to share with one another the significance of faith in God. When she left and plodded out across the snow, I stared out at the mounting storm, and a thrill permeated my spirit knowing Anita's feet were as warm as my heart.

Arlene Centerwall

Caroline's Compassion

*In praising and loving a child, we love and praise
not that which is, but that which we hope for.*

Goethe

When my daughter, Caroline, was very young, we
started saying a prayer every time we heard a siren from
an ambulance or fire truck. It's a quick prayer, just, "God,
please be with the people the ambulance (or fire truck) is
going to help."

I always initiated the prayer, and sometimes she would
even whine, "I don't want to say it this time."

I just reminded her that someone was in need, and that
if we were in need, we would want people to pray for us.
I thought it was a good way to help her learn about compassion and how, as Christians, we love and care for
others, even if we don't know them personally.

It's the same reason, I told her, that we pick up a few
extra items at the grocery store and deliver them to our
church's food pantry. And it's the reason we prepare care
packages for missionaries and bag up clothes she has out-
grown to take to a local ministry helping the poor.

But when she started kindergarten in 2001, I realized she might not fully comprehend the compassion thing.

When her class was collecting canned goods at Thanksgiving to benefit a local mission, we looked in our pantry to choose something to donate. She didn't want to give away the corn or sweet peas, because those were her favorites.

"Let's take the black beans and . . . here, kidney beans . . . yuck!" she proclaimed.

I realized that, to Caroline, this was more about cleaning out the pantry and getting rid of the foods she didn't like than it was about helping the needy.

Rationalizing that she was only five years old, we took the cans of "yucky" beans and off we went to school.

I was rather surprised to pass another mom in the hall that morning, carrying two huge bags laden with groceries.

"Ashlen insisted that we bring all of this," she told me. "I tried to pick out a few cans, but she just kept reminding me that the people were hungry and that we needed to give them more."

"That's so sweet," I told her, with what must have looked like a big fake grin on my face.

Actually, I was thrilled that her daughter was so kind, but I had to wonder why mine, apparently, was not.

Through the holidays, I was determined more than ever to teach my daughter about compassion. I told Caroline about all the monetary donations during the season, and we spent extra time focusing on the gifts we were going to give others, rather than what we might receive. We made extra deliveries to the food pantry, took flowers to the local nursing home and baked cookies and brownies for a few of our elderly neighbors.

One day at the grocery store, we saw a huge box for donated toys for underprivileged children.

I pointed the box out to Caroline and told her people were bringing toys to be given to children who might not otherwise get Christmas presents.

"Maybe we could bring something for the box," I suggested.

"Well, we could buy some toys, and if they are not something I like, we could bring them here," she told me, matter-of-factly.

Oh, boy. I realized we still weren't quite there yet. In earnest, I turned to God. I asked Him to help me find ways to teach Caroline to be more compassionate, and I asked Him to open her heart to better understand the importance of loving and helping people.

A couple of months later as I rushed through the house picking up toys and putting away laundry, I peeked in Caroline's room and noticed her sitting on her bed, head bowed and hands folded.

"Dear God," she said, "please be with the people the fire truck is going to help."

In all my busyness I had not even heard the siren.

But she did.

Frances Pace Putman

Power of Prayer

*For the ears of the Lord are on the righteous,
and his ears are open to their prayers.*

1 Peter 3:12

As a faithful member of my church, I was asked to be president of our children's organization of 120 children from two to twelve years old. Although I had a degree in elementary education, I felt too young and inexperienced to have such a huge responsibility. This would be much different than teaching. I would supervise and lead teachers of all the age levels, making sure the kids' spiritual education was the best it could be. I accepted the position, but felt overwhelmed. I didn't know where to turn for help. I prayed fervently for direction, knowledge and courage. When I was invited to attend a Christian Leadership Seminar, I knew it was what I had been praying for and would help qualify me to handle the challenge ahead.

Personally, I had been facing another challenge. My marriage was just not the way I had pictured it as a young single girl. I had two boys ages four and six, my husband worked long hours to provide for us, and I was juggling the demands of a young family, a part-time job, and volunteering at school and church. There never seemed to be enough time, especially for our relationship. I was disillusioned and discouraged. Every night as I knelt in prayer, I begged for answers as to why this marriage was so tough. I desperately needed to know what to do to make it better, and was sure God would show me the way. Night after night I pleaded for help.

The day of the leadership seminar arrived. My friend Janet and I walked into the hall, surprised to see 120 people already seated. We worked our way toward the front and found two seats about a third of the way back from the podium. The first speaker, Stephen Covey, would talk about leadership. Janet and I were excited to learn and be inspired to better serve the children in our church.

Stephen Covey started with a brief description of leadership and some of the traits we needed to be good leaders. He then started to talk about his wife and their marriage. He detailed how they met, married and were now trying to raise several children. He talked about how difficult relationships can be at times when we are in them for the long haul.

My friend Janet squirmed in her seat, seemingly annoyed and nervous, but I was glued to every word he said. He was telling *my* story. Janet finally leaned over and whispered, "He's off the topic. I sure wish he would get back on track."

I gave her an understanding smile but silently hoped he would stay with *this* topic.

I listened intently as he continued talking about his relationship with his wife. He said that one day she came to him and said she didn't love him anymore. Though he couldn't explain why, he answered her, "Yes, you do." He said he didn't know how they had gotten to this point in their marriage, but suspected it wasn't too unusual for most marriages to experience these times. They had married when they were quite young and didn't know each other very well. He joked that they had gotten married because they liked strawberries—but strawberries were in season only two weeks out of the year!

Laughter rose spontaneously from the crowd. I didn't laugh. I related too well.

Again my friend Janet complained, "He's off the subject. I'm not learning anything about leadership."

I sat quietly, believing he had been sent that day to answer my prayers. I was so moved that I could hardly speak.

When he concluded, Janet and I bid farewell and went off to separate classes. I was full of emotion as I started to cross the courtyard of our church in the direction of my next class. My knees even felt weak as I walked, and I contemplated going home instead. Then I looked up and saw Stephen Covey rapidly approaching me. He was likely hurrying to his next class, so I moved to one side. So did he. I moved again. He moved directly in front of me. Then he enthusiastically took my hand and shook it. Looking directly into my eyes he said, "We were communicating last hour, weren't we?"

Without another word, he just kept walking.

I stood totally stunned. I could hardly breathe. A warm and comforting feeling surrounded me like the hug from a loving Father.

I walked to the parking lot, my heart full. I got in my car and drove home with a renewed sense of reverence and determination to make some changes in the way I thought and acted. I recognized how much I must be loved. Not only did my Father in heaven hear my many prayers, He sent one of his servants to answer them.

Suzanne Vaughan

An Unfolding Miracle

You are the God who performs miracles; you display your power among the peoples.

Psalm 77:14

My friend invited me to go with her to the opera. Since I had never attended an opera before, I was excited to experience it, and so that evening I drove to the Seattle Opera House and parked my car a few blocks away. Strangely enough, I had a premonition as I locked my car: *This is the last time I will see my car.*

I promptly dismissed it and walked toward the opera, anticipating a glorious evening.

As we walked to our cars after the opera, I felt blessed to have experienced such beautiful music, incredible voices and colorful costumes. My friend found her car but, to my horror, my car was nowhere to be seen. We spent almost two hours driving up and down the streets of Seattle where I thought I had parked, searching for my 1997 Honda Civic. My mind started racing. *What did I leave in my car?* My laptop, my day planner, client notes, training books, my Bible, basketballs from my church. My heart sank deeper and deeper. I couldn't afford a new car —not now! Not when I was thinking about buying a new home. And then I realized that there was a possibility that I had left my house keys in the car. My friend, not wanting to panic me any more than I was, calmly suggested that I find someone to watch my apartment, since my home was now at risk.

Earlier that month, my pastor had begun a sermon series on the book of James. "Consider it pure joy, my brothers, whenever you face trials, because the testing of your faith develops perseverance." That morning, I had written in my journal:

> *January 20*
> *Father, I lift You up and praise You as Lord of lords,*
> *and King of kings. You are a God who intimately cares*
> *about me . . . trials bring perseverance so that I may be*
> *mature and complete, not lacking anything.*

My friend graciously offered to let me spend the night in her home. "I just know that God will do something through this," I said. My hands reached in the pocket of my coat and there were my home keys, safe and sound. I had put them in my coat pocket that day. God does care.

> *January 21*
> *I am trying not to lose hope about recovering my car.*
> *. . . I can't verbalize how I feel, I only can rest that You*
> *know, You care, and Your Spirit will be present. Father,*
> *I pray for Your help, guidance and grace today.*

I reported the car stolen that day to the police. The policewoman was encouraging. "When we recover your car, we will call you."

"When?" I said with a surge of hope.

"These cars usually are recovered in a few days, unless

of course this car was taken by a gang that steals cars for parts. They seem to favor Honda Civics."

My heart sank once again.

The next few weeks were spent trying to get my life back on track. I rented a car, began the process of buying a new laptop, and started living my life without those things that were so much a part of my life.

> *January 23*
>
> *I feel that this isn't just a random occurrence. . . . It is a tremendous teaching opportunity—Lord You are so good! You love me so much that You will use anything and everything to help me be conformed to Your Son. Oh Jesus, I love that You love me. I love that Your fingerprints are on this situation.*

I decided to write down all the things I learned spiritually, personally and professionally from this situation. I was amazed as I looked at the list: Despite the loss, I am surviving. People matter more than things or even my business. God uses people to show His tender love. Losing a car and material things was nothing compared to what the tsunami victims lost. God loans things to us, but everything ultimately belongs to Him.

Weeks went by. I bought a new laptop, a new day planner and was just about to buy a new car when the call came: "This is the Seattle police, and we would like to talk with you about the recovery of your vehicle."

I was in shock; the next day I was planning to go with a friend to look for another car. We drove to pick up my vehicle, and there it was! There didn't seem to be any outward damage. My friend couldn't contain herself any longer, and she ran to the car while I went to pay the cashier. Minutes later, she burst into the towing office. "I see the bags in the back!" I burst into tears. We headed to the car, the car that I thought was lost for good, and to our amazement everything in the car was in the exact condition as I had left it! There was my Bible and day planner in the front seat, all my bags, including my laptop in the back seat.

God unfolded a miracle that reminds me of His faithfulness.

Jan Dwyer

Desperate Prayer

Then he spoke a parable to them, that man always ought to pray and not lose heart.

Luke 18:1

My daughter Lori, fully clothed in winter attire, prepared to take Clancy, one of her two black Labs, out for their Sunday evening walk. She had promised him that if the rain stopped they'd stroll down by the creek, his favorite destination.

Clancy and Duke had been there for Lori time and time again. They were there when the neighborhood ruffian climbed a tree to peep into Lori's bedroom. He learned firsthand that Clancy certainly was not his best friend. All he left behind was his telltale baseball cap beneath the tree, dropped as he scampered for home with Clancy on his heels.

Twice daily, in the darkness of cold winter mornings and evenings, Lori fed her horses and Toughie, the yellow barn cat. As she trudged knee-deep in the snow to the barn, Duke and Clancy eased her loneliness with their comical actions, bounding and barking between

mouthfuls of snow. For their unselfish loyalty, unequivo-
cal love and companionship, Clancy and Duke expected
nothing in return but a pat on their heads, Lori's praising
soft voice and a dish of Dog Chow.

Lori's relationship with Clancy became stronger when
Duke developed arthritis. Now gray-faced, he could no
longer take part in all their activities, such as playing stick
or taking long walks. Too many winters and trips through
the deep snow had taken their toll; those swims in the icy
creek didn't help either.

Lori looked out the kitchen window and noticed it had
quit raining for the first time in several days. She pulled on
her down-filled jacket and laced up her heavy boots.

Clancy, along with Duke, was lying on the back porch—
sleeping bundles of black Lab, love and loyalty. Lori
nudged Clancy gently and spoke enthusiastically, "Come
Clancy, we're going for a walk before it gets too dark."

Needless to say ol' Clancy only had to be asked once.
He almost knocked her down in his effort to get out the
door before her. She smiled at his joyful enthusiasm. Duke
gave them a Lab smile but remained on the porch.

Lori and Clancy started their walk along the road,
deserted as usual, in the direction of the nearby creek.
They had gone only a short distance when black clouds
began to roll in and darken the sky. Once more it began to
spit rain.

She yelled at Clancy, who had bounded ahead to the
bridge that crossed the creek. "Come on, Clancy, we have
to head for home." Clancy, busy chasing a mouse, paid her
no mind.

Lori yelled again, "Come on, Clancy, we have to head
home, no swim for you today."

Clancy leaped off the bridge and into the tumultuous
water. Lori raced to the bridge, calling his name all the
way. Under normal circumstances, his dive into the

stream would have held no consequences for this strong-swimming Lab. But these were not normal circumstances. The stream had become a torrent, due to the rapid run-off from the nearby mountains. High water raged through a barbed wire fence that crossed the creek; the forceful water swept Clancy solidly up against it. He struggled to swim toward shore, but the more he struggled, the more entangled he became.

When she reached the bridge, Lori saw Clancy impaled against the barbed wire fence, struggling and whimpering in desperation, trying to free himself. Lori took one look at this frightful scene and instantly jumped into the swiftly flowing stream. Her heavy boots and down jacket imme-diately began to pull her down into the deep icy water, leaving her gasping for breath. In a matter of seconds she also was impaled on the fence next to a struggling Clancy. She grabbed him and held his head up with one hand and grasped the wire with her other.

She knew they had to get out of the freezing water before hypothermia set in. With the frigid water draining her strength, Lori knew she had to either let go of Clancy or risk both of them drowning. "I can't let go of Clancy, God," she prayed, "But I can't hold on much longer. *Please,* I need your help!"

At that moment, a pickup truck appeared, approaching the bridge.

Lori prayed once more in desperation, "Dear God, please help us!"

The truck neared . . . then crossed the bridge, causing Lori's heart to drop in despair. Then it stopped and backed up onto the bridge again. Two men emerged from the truck and in seconds they ran down the embankment, yelling, "Hold on there! We'll be right down."

One grabbed the fence and reached out his hand. New strength surged through Lori as she swung Clancy over so the man could reach him. He grabbed him, then passed the dog up the bank to his buddy. Then he reached out once again, this time for Lori. She thrust her free hand and he pulled her out of the water—soaked jacket, heavy boots and all.

Crowded in the pickup on the way back to the ranch, Lori asked her rescuers, "How did you ever see me in the water?"

"I really don't know," one said. "We just decided to take this road instead of our usual route. As we were talking, I happened to glance out my window, and I saw your blonde head above the murky water—lucky you."

But Lori knew it wasn't luck that stopped their truck on the deserted road. It was God answering her desperate prayer.

James A. Nelson

Asking Too Much

And all things, whatever you ask in prayer, believing, you will receive.

Matthew 21:22

"To a fabulous day!" my client said as our glasses clinked in celebration. After three days of signing more than one thousand books to honor nurses and promote his company, I was as delighted as he in their success. This favorite client always gave me the royal treatment. After several scrumptious dinners at some of the finest dining establishments in New Orleans, we wound up this last night of the convention at Pat O'Brien's piano bar.

The five of us joined more than one hundred revelers in singing everything from the "Wisconsin Fight Song" to "Roll Out the Barrel." Finally we sang my requested favorite, "Old Time Rock & Roll," then merrily gathered our things to leave.

At the street side, an O'Brien's attendant placed our infamous Hurricane souvenir glasses in protective boxes and plastic carrying bags. We'd taken cabs to the convention center a dozen times in the past few days, and we easily hailed another to transport us to our hotel. We could have walked, but Bourbon Street after dark is not a positive place to be.

So, with coat, purse and bag in hand, I wedged into the cab with my companions.

"Where to?" the cabbie asked in what I guessed to be a Caribbean accent.

At least this cab has a meter, I thought. I'd heard myths about New Orleans cabs. "Anyone can slap a sign on their car and call it a taxi in New Orleans," someone had teased. I had to admit that I'd found the cabs' authenticity and professionalism to be as diverse as their drivers.

Within ten minutes we were at the hotel. I grabbed my coat and bag and headed to the lobby. I stopped cold. "My purse!"

I ran to the driveway. Our taxi had already disappeared into the wee hours of the morning.

We frantically tried to remember the company name on the taxi or any identifying details. "Red" was our only clue.

The hotel security guard phoned the only company he knew to have red cabs. No answer. After reassuring hugs from my client companions, I was escorted to my room by the uniformed attendant. He used his passkey to let me in since my room key was in my purse—along with my travel wallet, airline ticket, cash, credit cards, airline travel cards, cell phone, driver's license and camera.

I got ready for bed, flopped onto it and started to pray. "Please God, let me find my purse," I muttered over and over and over again until I fell asleep.

At the crack of dawn I began dialing every cab company in the Yellow Pages. The few who answered had dismal news: Cabbies do not return cabs to the stations, they drive them home. By law, all lost items must be turned in to the Taxi Bureau at City Hall within forty-eight hours. Discouraged, I called the bureau the minute they opened, and a polite lady took my information.

"From your experience, what do you think my chances are of ever seeing my purse again?" I asked.

"I'm guessing 95 percent of lost stuff is never turned in," she admitted.

I wished I hadn't asked.

I whispered an all-too-brief prayer of thanksgiving as I retrieved my hidden passport and "emergency cash" from my suitcase. At least I could get home.

Clinging to my briefcase, I caught yet another cab—no red ones in sight—and met my client at the convention center to sign another hundred or so books. I faked cheerfulness through our final lunch together. I barely picked at my sandwich, my stomach too busy tying knots to eat.

As I hailed a final cab to the airport, I saw a red one pulling away from the curb. In heels, I ran and flagged down the driver. No, he hadn't heard about my lost purse. No, he didn't think it would be useful to take my home number. No, he didn't think I'd ever see my purse again, in spite of the one-hundred-dollar reward I offered on the spot.

From the airport, I called my husband Mark to instruct him to cancel the credit cards. When I heard his voice, I choked back tears. "How could I be so careless? I've lost everything I need to travel for a living!"

Mark assured me we could replace all the lost items and promised to hug me long and tenderly when I returned to his arms that night.

I hung up and began my feverish prayer in earnest. "God, I always brag about how You take care of me on the road. You've held airplanes when my connecting flight was delayed, retrieved the leather jacket left at airport security, and sent the only parking lot shuttle I'd ever seen the one blizzardy night I needed it. I only missed one plane in ten years, and then, when I went to the rental car counter at midnight, there was only one man in line—a Good Samaritan driving to my exact destination. The only time the airlines lost my luggage, You had it delivered to my hotel by morning. After all You have done for me, and since losing my purse was my fault, is finding it asking too much?"

I went to a café to see if my queasy stomach could tolerate soup, and continued my pitiful prayer. "It seems like I'm always yammering on and on all day long, thanking You or asking You for something, Lord—everything from parking spaces to bridesmaid dresses. Is finding my purse against these odds asking too much?"

It was way past my bedtime when I finally returned home to Mark's long and tender hugs that night.

At 1:30 A.M. the ringing phone jarred me out of my deep sleep. I panicked when I grabbed the phone and heard her. "Mom! What's wrong?"

"Honey," her voice was thick with sleep. "A taxi cab driver from New Orleans just called me." She sounded confused. "He said he has your purse. He says to reach him by calling your cell phone tomorrow."

I didn't know whether to laugh or cry with relief. I briefly recounted the story to Mom, and in her typical, faith-filled fashion she said, "Honey, never be surprised when God answers your prayers."

She was right, of course. You can't ask God for too much.

LeAnn Thieman

Ask and ye shall retrieve.

4

GOD'S HEALING POWER

Now Jesus went about all Galilee teaching in their synagogues, preaching the gospel of the kingdom, and healing all kinds of sickness and all kinds of disease among the people.

Matthew 4:23

Grace

Whoever welcomes children in my name welcomes me.

Mark 9:37

My husband, seven-year-old son Colin and I sat down to breakfast on a Saturday morning in the spring. It seemed a typical start to a weekend, eating our cold cereal interspersed with discussion of chores to be done and the upcoming soccer game. However, my husband and I knew that this was to be a memorable meal. I began the discussion with my common phrase, "Colin, we've got something to tell you."

"I know, I know," he replied. "You love me!"

My husband and I chuckled. "Of course we do, but there's something else we want to tell you," my husband began. "You know how you've been praying for a baby brother or sister?" Colin's eyes began to grow wide in disbelief.

I continued. "Well, we just found out from the doctor . . . I'm pregnant!"

Colin's jaw dropped, he got out of his chair, and began jumping up and down next to the table. A barrage of questions followed. "Will it be a boy or a girl? When will it be born? Where will it sleep?"

The months passed by, my belly growing noticeably bigger. Colin would often sit next to me on the couch as we watched a television show, his hand on my belly, ready to feel his baby brother or sister kick. Sometimes he would follow a goodnight hug with a "belly kiss" for his baby sibling.

Colin would also imagine what life would be like. "Mom, if it's a boy," he said one day as we were driving home from school, "I could teach him how to play soccer, like Uncle Pete taught Uncle Matt. We could wrestle too!" He obviously was setting his sights on a brother.

The day finally came when we'd find out if Colin could look forward to having a sports buddy or a teatime buddy. (Despite my efforts at promoting gender equality, he emphatically claimed, "Girls are just not as good at sports as boys.") It was a hot June day in Colorado, and Colin was outside playing with his neighborhood friends when we arrived home from having the ultrasound. Colin came bursting into the kitchen, not giving us a minute to savor the moment. "Well, what is it? Is it a boy or a girl?"

I looked deep into his eyes, wondering how he'd react. "It's a—girl!" His eyes darkened for a millisecond and I sensed a glimmer of disappointment. "Oh." He paused, then smiled. "I'm going to have a baby sister!" He then ran out of the house to share the news with his friends.

But all was not right with his baby sister. In the weeks that followed, we shared other news with him—she had Down syndrome. We chose not to share the more painful news that our baby, Grace Ann, had developed fluid in her lung and brain cavities. While she might live to term, it was more likely, given the amount of fluid, that she would die in utero. For the next two months, we lived in a state of uncertainty. We were praying for a miracle, and at the same time, wondered what life would be like for our baby if she did live to term. Meanwhile, Colin was modifying his dreams of the future. He talked about how Grace might need to come to his room at night to feel protected from a loud thunderstorm. We smiled as he was beginning to assume a "big brother" identity, yet we also grieved, wondering whether he'd get the chance to assume the role.

At seven months, every mother's worst nightmare came true: Grace stopped kicking. The ultrasound confirmed my worst fear—a still body and no heartbeat. An induction delivery was scheduled for the following week. We agonized over when and how to tell our son that his baby sister had died. We decided to err on the side of caution by telling him after the delivery. He knew there were some complications, as I was going to the hospital before the due date. In his mind though, this just meant that he'd get to see his baby sister sooner.

The next day he came to the hospital. He was very quiet as we explained what had happened. He then left the hospital room with his dad and went for a snack in the lounge. Colin asked many questions and wanted to see pictures of Grace. As children often do, he shared his first impression when he saw the photo. "I don't mean to be mean, but she looks kinda weird!"

The days that followed were a blur of mourning mixed with a sense of purpose—that we honor our baby girl with a funeral and involve her big brother in the event. Colin seemed poised and confident in his black suit as he wheeled her casket from the altar to the limousine and carried her tiny casket to the gravesite. It was his moment, his brief chance to guide his baby sister, although not in a way that we ever imagined.

After the funeral we tried to maintain Colin's routines. Each night, as we had every night, we sat together on his bed and said our "thank you" prayer. Colin sometimes interrupted with questions. "What's it like in heaven?" "Can Dad cut the word 'Grace' in the backyard grass with the lawn mower so I can see her name from my bedroom window?" "Why can't we bury her body in the backyard since she's part of our family?"

After a few nights, it seemed Colin was finished asking questions. Perhaps like us, he was gradually beginning to accept the situation.

But one night, after ending his prayer with the usual, "God bless Colin, God bless Daddy, God bless Mommy, God bless Grace," Colin stopped. "Wait!" he said. "Why are we saying 'God bless Grace?' Why are we praying for her when she's already in heaven? We should say 'Grace bless us.'"

And so we do. Every night we end our prayer with "Grace bless us." We know she's guiding her parents. She's guiding her big brother, even if he thinks girls can't play sports as well as boys!

Margaret Berg

Hope

Who, contrary to hope, in hope believed.

Romans 4:18

Scott and Janice had tried for many years to have a baby, and when their son, Scotty, entered the world, our church celebrated right along with them. Soon, however, the doctors diagnosed Scotty with serious heart problems.

Rallying behind the young family, our church supported and reminded them of God's promise never to fail or forsake His children. Nine months passed, and Scotty's doctors determined that he needed open-heart surgery. His chances of surviving the operation were slim, but without it, his chances of living past his first birthday were slimmer.

Throughout his ordeal, one thing had become amazingly clear about Scotty: He absolutely loved the color yellow. Whenever he'd catch a glimpse of the bright hue anywhere, he'd squeal in delight. Even his nurses added a touch of yellow to their uniforms when caring for him.

Sadly, Scotty's operation wasn't a success, and the attempt to save his little heart failed.

His parents, grief-stricken, escaped to a friend's vacation home soon after the funeral. Weeks passed but the gaping wound left by Scotty's absence remained unbearable. One evening at sunset Scotty's parents walked along the beach. As they clutched each other's hands, they felt the dark realization that Scotty's tiny fingers would never again be clasped between theirs. Too heavy a cross to bear, they felt alone in their grief and prayed there on the beach for a glimmer of hope to dispel the darkness.

And then, along the water's edge, it appeared: A bright yellow bird landed between them as they walked. Neither had ever seen such a bird before. It didn't scurry or fly away but continued to scamper between them on their bare-footed journey in the sand.

The bird's comforting presence filled them with peace, the peace granted to believers in 1 Thessalonians 4:13–14: "But I would not have you be ignorant, brethren, concerning those that have fallen asleep, lest you sorrow as those that have no hope. For if we believe that Jesus died and rose again, even so God will bring with Him those who sleep in Jesus."

After they'd made it back to the beachfront house, the bird remained, seemingly studying them for a few moments, then lifting its wings and heading upward towards the sky.

While watching its graceful flight, they imagined Scotty, in the presence of God, soaring high above the clouds and making his way to that incredible yellow ball for a warm kiss upon his chubby cheek.

Hope had come to them: a yellow bird messenger fashioned by the Creator's own hands.

Karen Majoris-Garrison

Lifted by Love

*The bin of flour was not used up, not did the jar
of oil run dry, according to the word of the Lord,
which He spoke to Elijah.*

1 Kings 17:16

We never dreamed that Garrett would be anything
other than a perfectly ordinary boy. The brown-haired,
brown-eyed tornado that tore through our home seemed
to have enough energy for a dozen boys! Every time we
turned around, Garrett popped up, full of questions and
ideas, and always on the move.

By the time he was seven, though, Garrett began to
stumble and fall when he ran, and even sometimes when
he was walking. His teachers noticed a change in his
ability to keep up with his schoolwork, although he
seemed to be as smart as ever. He got sick more easily and
was always tired. We knew something was going on, but
nothing could have prepared us for the shock of the doctors' diagnosis. Garrett's symptoms were due to a rare
genetic syndrome called ataxia-telangiectasia (AT), a disease that causes progressive neurological deterioration,

immune deficiency and sometimes even cancer in children. There was no cure. Nothing we could do could take away this disease from our son. We dreaded the thought of standing by helplessly, watching him struggle a little more each day to speak, to walk, to do so many of the things we took for granted. Where could we turn for help? We felt alone and terrified at the obstacles we faced.

But Garrett was not alone.

Many other children were fighting the same battle—more than five hundred just in the United States. When we contacted the National Organization to Treat AT we were told about a study being conducted at Children's Hospital in Philadelphia. They invited Garrett to participate in the experimental treatment at no cost to us other than the expense of our transportation. Johns Hopkins in Baltimore, Maryland, also had a research program for AT and wanted Garrett to visit their clinical center for evaluation. This was both good news and bad. Our home in Portales, New Mexico, was a long way from Philadelphia and Baltimore, and Garrett would have to make five separate trips in a span of only a few months.

Like Garrett before his illness, I had always felt strong and independent. My husband worked hard to support us, and his income had always been adequate for our needs. Now, though, we had a challenge that exceeded anything we were prepared to face. We couldn't afford to fly our entire family to the East Coast even once! Philadelphia and Baltimore might as well have been on the moon. I called everyone—Social Security, welfare and other government organizations—trying to find out how we could get help with flights, meals, car rental and all the other prohibitive costs.

As many times as my husband and I worked through our budget, we couldn't squeeze out even a fraction of the money we needed. Our minds and hearts felt numb with the heartbreaking disappointment. We tried to pray, but our faith seemed to have grown as weak and frail as Garrett's thin little legs.

Again, God reminded us that we were not alone.

"Let's set up a fund for Garrett," my friend Tammy suggested. "We can write a story for the local newspaper and let the rest of the community know what's going on."

"Would they really print his story? And if they do, will anybody read it?" I asked with great skepticism. It had never occurred to me that other people in our town might be willing to help Garrett. I had always thought that this burden was ours alone to bear.

"Of course they will! And you just wait and see. I think you'll be surprised how much people care. Besides, what do we have to lose?"

A few days later, the newspaper printed the story and donations began to trickle into the bank. Little by little, the people in our community sent in enough to cover every one of the expenses—for the first trip. When we were ready to leave, we went to the bank and withdrew all the money.

Thank you, Lord, I prayed. *At least we can make one trip to Philadelphia. That's better than not going at all. We'll take this journey one step at a time.*

We returned home with a little better understanding about Garrett's illness, but no idea whether we would be able to continue the treatments. When we called the bank, though, we were amazed to find that the donations had continued to come in! By the time we needed to make arrangements for the second trip, we had just enough to pay all our expenses. Once again, we withdrew the entire amount.

The third and fourth months were the same. Our bank account filled up each time we had to make a trip, like the cruse of oil of the widow of Zaraphath in 1 Kings 17, whose handful of flour and little jar of oil never ran dry. We were even able to make the fifth trip to visit Johns Hopkins!

Today, at twelve years old, Garrett is as full of joy and enthusiasm as any other boy his age. Just one of his smiles can warm my heart for a whole day. But we know that until a cure for AT is discovered, he will never be able to walk without leaning on us.

Like Garrett, I've learned how much I need someone to lean on, too. I know better now than ever before that God is always there for me. He has also taught all of us that we can lean on the love of others; they will answer His call and be there for us just when we need them most, lifted by love.

Pat Dodson and Candy Gruner

He Took Care of Me

For it is written: "He shall give His angels charge over you, to keep you."

Luke 4:10

A heart transplant! I was sure that the doctors must be wrong. For all my fifty-eight years, I had never even spent one night in the hospital. Now, they were telling me that my heart was so damaged that it had to be removed! How could this be?

And, how could I work full-time, shovel snow, rake leaves and have recently planted over seventy tulip and hyacinth bulbs with a heart that, as the doctors now explained to me, was "falling apart"?

My weight, blood pressure and cholesterol were all normal, but the EKG results during a routine annual physical showed that my heart was not only severely damaged, but that sometime in the recent past I had actually suffered a massive heart attack. This was so hard to comprehend since the only time I'd ever remembered being sick was when I had the flu several months before. And shouldn't I have felt some pain if I had suffered a heart attack? The doctor explained that what I thought was the "flu" was probably a massive heart attack. To make my condition even more serious, a cardiac catheterization showed an orange-size tumor silently growing on my heart. The doctors told me I was dying. To save my life, their first choice was a heart transplant. A second option was a life-threatening, near impossible surgery to remove the growing tumor and try to repair my damaged heart. I was in a state of shock. I couldn't make this decision alone. I turned to God to help me.

Now, I was never one to formally pray, but my connection with the Lord was always through simple conversations. So I talked to God and asked him to show me the way. I began to think about my husband Luke, who had died of cancer eleven years before. I told God that this was the first time I had to face a crisis without my husband, and I was afraid. It had always been just the two of us, and when Luke was alive, he took care of everything. I knew if he were with me, he would have put his arms around me, made me feel safe and guided me in the right direction. I told God that I missed Luke now more than I ever did.

Though the doctors recommended the transplant, there was something unexplainable drawing me to learn about my other choice. I was told it was a complex operation and that there was only one heart surgeon in the area who would even try to attempt it. A feeling came over me, and I had to know who he was and where I could find him. When I further questioned the doctors, I was told his name was V. Paul Addonizio, M.D. He was Chief of Cardiac Surgery at Abington Memorial Hospital in Abington, Pennsylvania, a suburb of Philadelphia.

The name sounded familiar; then it all came back to me. A year before Luke was diagnosed with cancer, he had needed emergency heart surgery. Was this Dr. Addonizio the surgeon who had saved my Luke's life? I remembered how very much Luke had respected him and called him a straight shooter. Luke used to tell people that he was lucky to have had him be the surgeon to operate on his heart. After all these years, could this be the same doctor? The towns weren't the same, the hospitals weren't the same, but the names were.

Even though over eleven years had gone by, when Dr. Addonizio walked into my examining room, I recognized him immediately. How could I have forgotten the face that saved my husband? And now I was hoping that he could save me.

As he carefully explained the complicated surgery and how he would have to remove most of my heart to eliminate the aneurysm, then patch and remodel my heart to rebuild it to its normal shape, I couldn't stop thinking that Luke had sent Dr. Addonizio to save me, just as he had saved him.

I left Dr. Addonizio's office and on my way home I thanked God, because for the first time during this horrible nightmare, I felt at peace and no longer alone.

My procedure was to be the world's first of its kind, using human skin from the skin bank, because of its strength and resistance to infection. I was petrified on the morning of surgery. As I lay on the hospital stretcher in the holding area waiting to be wheeled into the operating room, I told God that my life was in His hands—and Dr. Addonizio's.

Once in the operating room, Dr. Addonizio gently took my hand and said, "I truly believe there is a guardian angel looking over you." And as I went to sleep, I felt Luke, my guardian angel, by my side.

As I recovered, I learned the operating room was silent when Dr. Addonizio touched my fragile heart to make his first incision. It instantly ruptured and fell apart in his hands. I guess the Lord was there to catch the pieces. The walls of my heart were as thin as tissue paper and, had I not had this surgery, it would have exploded in my chest and I could not have survived.

Today, I feel better than ever. I'm back to work and gardening, feeling blessed that God sent Luke to take care of me just like he always had.

LindaCarol Cherken

The Healing

*H*ave mercy on me, O Lord, for I am weak;
O Lord, heal me, for my bones are troubled.

Psalm 6:2

Maria's arrest record for prostitution was her claim to fame. She had been a "frequent flyer," in and out of the hospital for drug-addiction-related maladies, so this admission would probably be no different than the previous ones, I thought. She would be hydrated and medicated and followed by the medical residents, then sent on her way until the next visit.

My usual routine on the night shift was to get the nursing report, then make a quick check on each of my patients before mixing the medications. I call it my "drive-by," introducing myself, locking bed brakes, sniffing out a potential problem that could rapidly snowball into a crisis. Making a mental note of each patient's needs helped me prioritize the care to be given, so the initial assessment is invaluable.

Assuming Maria's stay would be the same as always, and knowing she was familiar with the routine, I breezed into her room with the intent of an exchange of smiles and hand waves. But rounding the corner of the curtain separating the two beds, I found a very different Maria from the ebullient woman I had known. In place of a bold, laughing chatterbox was a somber, pale figure lying quietly in the darkness on the unrelenting hardness of the plastic hospital mattress. A wan smile replaced the usual hearty greeting, and my senses immediately went into full alert.

Was she in pain? I knelt by her bed and questioned her. Oh, yes, she was in pain, but not the kind most of us know. She told me that her newly diagnosed cancer was a fast-moving type for which there was no cure. Her pain was in her soul.

When my care for the other patients was complete, Maria's room was where I could be found, listening to her tale of countless men and drugs, which took her away from ugly reality. Her children had been taken away from her, but, oh, how she loved them. She said she was "no good," and they deserved someone who could care for them, but not a day passed that she didn't miss them. Now, as she approached the end of life on Earth, she was turning to face the demons of her past. How ashamed she felt!

Her sorrow was seemingly insurmountable as she repeatedly told me what an awful person she had been. I allowed her to talk herself to sleep, and prayed for the wisdom to know what to say. This pain was more excruciating than any I had ever encountered. What could I say that would be of any help? I didn't want to be an empty talking box, reciting platitudes that meant nothing.

I carried the vivid memory of her anguish home with me, and after a few hours' sleep, I searched through my collection of spiritual readings, and found exactly what I needed.

When I returned to the hospital, I gave her a poem

about Jesus forgiving Mary Magdalene, and I spoke about God's unconditional love for her, Maria. Unrehearsed words crossed my lips in an endless procession, and I passionately poured out my heart. She read the poem. Once. Twice. Again. Then, the tears trickled down her cheeks, and she reached up and hugged me tightly.

"This is me in the poem. My mother has been telling me about Jesus for so many years, but I wouldn't listen. Now, you are telling me the same thing. He loves me no matter what I did? So, it must be true. I have to find out more about Him."

Speechless, I returned the hug. When I checked her later, she was sleeping with the poem clutched tightly in her hand.

My assignment was changed for the rest of the week, and Maria and I didn't have the chance for any more talks. I did put a Bible on her bedside table while she napped, and, on the day of her discharge, I stopped at her room to say good-bye. She was sitting up against a bank of pillows, Bible open in her hands, peacefully absorbed in the printed text. She flashed a smile when I walked in. "You gave this to me, didn't you? I just know it was you! You'll never know what it means to me." She was going home to live with her mother for her remaining time and to make amends with her children.

I never saw Maria again. My part in her life was fleeting, and certainly was not in the official nursing care plan, but I was reminded once again that the Great Physician uses all of us to do His work in many ways.

Irene Budzynski

Emergency PA

A wise physician is a John the Baptist, who recognizes that his only mission is to prepare the way for a greater than himself.

Arthur S. Hardy

I was working as a physician's assistant in a rural emergency department in Lake Placid, New York, in the mid-1980s. At the time I was in my late twenties and about five years out of residency training. The local ambulance was staffed with basic-level EMTs, so they would call for assistance from us when they had a serious case that might require prehospital advanced life-support skills.

One April morning before dawn, the nurse woke me up in the on-call room. I was dispatched to the scene of an accident only a few blocks from the hospital. When I arrived I found a young man in his thirties lying on the road, struck by a car. He was obviously seriously injured with multiple fractures and internal injuries. He had not suffered any head trauma and was fully aware of his horrible situation.

I recognized him as a patient I'd seen several times in

the ED when I had treated him or his family for minor problems. I remembered him telling me several weeks earlier that he was getting his life together for his family; he had gotten a new job and had begun running in the mornings before work to lose some weight. He was jogging when he was hit.

I began to examine him. He looked at me with an expression of dread and said, "I'm dying."

I looked him in the eyes. "You're not going to die, I won't let you."

At this point in my life, I was really hitting my stride. I knew my job well and was supremely confident. I basked in the respect of the nurses, physicians and other PAs. People would say, "In chaos and trauma, it's Mark you want. He's the best in an emergency." I believed it too. I thought it was totally about how smart, how fast, how good I was with my hands. I knew I could pull most anyone out of the sausage grinder alive.

The snow fell lightly on this icy morning. With great difficulty I established an IV and helped the EMTs prepare this man for a quick "swoop and scoop" to the ED.

As we rushed into the trauma room, I realized I was beginning to lose him. Shouting orders for more blood, I worked feverishly to establish two larger IV lines and intubate him. He continued to deteriorate. I put in a central line and began pouring fluid directly into his heart.

Then he arrested.

I worked the team of EMTs and nurses, pulling every trick out of my bag. Despite everything I did, I felt him slip away through my fingers.

About this time the on-call physician showed up. He evaluated the injuries and our efforts and ordered us to end the code. I looked at him. "What are you doing? I'm not quitting!"

He said, "Mark, it's over. Let him go."

I walked out of the room into the hall and saw the family talking to the town priest. I turned the other way and headed to the on-call room to get myself together before facing them with my failure. I was devastated. The guilt and sense of failure rushed over me like a wave. If only I were smarter, faster, better, he would be alive.

I felt a hand on my shoulder. I turned around to see the priest standing there. He looked at me and said, "You people in medicine take too much credit when it goes well and beat yourself up too much when it goes badly. Some things are out of your hands." And then he walked away, back to the family.

In this moment of epiphany, I realized for the first time that it is not I who is the center of the universe, it's God. My role is to do the best I can do. The outcome will be decided without me.

Mark Ippolito

A Purpose in Death

The horrific news of my husband's death immobilized me. Matt was riding a moped in downtown Cagayan de Oro in the Philippines, where we were missionaries, when a jeepney bus veered out of traffic and hit him.

Numb with grief, I made arrangements for his funeral. It is customary in the Philippines for Christians to hold Services of Hope at the church each night preceding the burial. These meetings are a combination evangelistic and memorial service with beautiful singing.

While I was standing at the first evening's Service of Hope, trying bravely to greet all the people who had been affected by Matt's death, a thought came to me. One person had been forgotten—the driver of the jeepney.

I knew Philippine law stated that if someone causes another person's death, the guilty party is jailed until the matter is fully investigated. According to the law, if a victim's family asks for the prisoner's release, it will be granted. I spoke with one of the church leaders, who volunteered to go to the prison the next day and sign papers stating that I wanted the driver released.

The next night at the service more people came to express their condolences. A man with his head held low made his way to where I was standing. Without a word, he gripped my hand. Tears streamed down his face. I knew he was the driver of the jeepney that had killed Matt.

I motioned to a church member who knew several dialects, and with his help I told the driver I did not hold him accountable for Matt's death. "I'm happy for your release from prison," I said, trying not to cry.

The driver's eyes widened. His lips parted in a smile so brilliant I couldn't help smiling back. "My husband was a Christian," I explained. "He loved the Filipino people so much that he chose to live here to tell them about God's love." Then I added, "Would you like to learn more about God's love and forgiveness?"

The man shook his head and then left the church. I didn't expect to see him again.

The next night at the last Service of Hope, the man again approached me, this time accompanied by his wife and three sisters. All four women sobbed noisily on my shoulder, crying their gratitude for their loved one's release from prison.

The jeepney driver and his family attended Matt's funeral the next day. Matt's parents told him that they too forgave him and believed that God had a purpose in Matt's death.

The driver and his family began attending church regularly, bringing a jeepney filled with people from his barrio. On the day they eventually accepted Jesus into their lives I thought, *Only He could take a vessel like a jeepney that had brought death, and use it to bring people to Him.*

I praised God, and I knew that in heaven Matt was praising God too.

Peggy Littell
As told to Kayleen J. Reusser

My Network

*For by grace you have been saved through faith,
and that not of yourselves, it is the gift of God.*
                                                        Ephesians 2:8

I have always known that building a strong connecting
network was the secret to my career and business success,
but I never knew it would help save my life.

On a Thursday at 5:00 P.M., my doctor called. "Sarah—
the routine chest X-ray you had this morning revealed a
tumor—between your heart and lung—it's the size of an
orange—you need to have a CAT scan ASAP."

A fear I had tried to deny seized me. Twelve years ago
my brother had died of Hodgkin's disease. Four years
later, my mother died of it, and on the day of her funeral
my sister was diagnosed with the same cancerous demon.
All three had tumors in their chest—like me.

My panicked mind raced as fast as my fingers on the
phone pad. Knowing we'd need pre-approval, my husband, Fred, and I spent the entire next day, Friday, trying
to convince my insurance company to approve this desperately needed test.

They finally agreed at four o'clock and we rushed to get it done that evening, only to be told that the radiologist couldn't read it for a day or so. We wouldn't know anything until Monday morning.

I knew that these lymphatic tumors could double in size in seven days! Waiting three was not an option. I did the only thing I knew to do in times of crisis. I prayed. "Please, God, connect me with the right people to help me."

Suddenly a friendly client came to mind whose stepfather repaired radiology equipment for the hospital where my CAT scan was done. I knew it was a long shot. But after one phone call, he drove fifteen mile in a blizzard to meet us at the hospital and introduce us to the doctor, who then spent an hour showing us the scans of my fast-growing tumor. He said I needed a vascular surgeon to perform the biopsy confirming the cancer type. There were only a handful of these surgeons in town.

On our fourth call, we found one who took my insurance and agreed to do it on Wednesday. Our relief was short-lived—twenty-four hours later I was bumped off his schedule for a week due to an open-heart case that took priority.

Once again we turned to my network for help. We called an old friend and colleague of my husband's, an internal medicine doctor in Denver whom we hadn't talked to in five years. She immediately called a vascular surgeon, who agreed to see us that afternoon. Forty-eight hours later, I was on the operating table having my biopsy. However, again it was a Friday—no results until Monday afternoon.

Yet again, we turned to my network for help. We called a friend in San Antonio who had a friend who was a pathologist in Arkansas who told us what to say and do to get the on-call pathologist to come in and meet with us.

Forty-five minutes later, on a snowy, cold Saturday

morning, Fred and I were looking through a microscope with the pathologist showing us my tissue biopsy confirming classic Hodgkin's lymphoma.

When we met with my doctor on Monday morning, we told him what my cancer was . . . he hadn't even seen the report yet!

After three surgical procedures, a nuclear PET scan and several other diagnostic staging workups, three weeks after my diagnosis, my chemotherapy began.

For five months, over seventy people in our network—including clients, coworkers, colleagues, friends, neighbors and parents of my children's classmates—brought meals to our home during my chemo weeks. I'm the only person I know who gained twelve pounds on chemo!

My two daughters decorated a three-ring binder to hold over 250 cards, e-mails and letters I received from my vast network. The cover simply read, "Mom's Cancer Blessings." I dragged this thirty-pound book with me to chemo every week for five months to read the inspiring and uplifting words from my network of encouragement.

My network also connected me to over one hundred prayer chains throughout the world. I will never really know how many people prayed for my recovery, but I can tell you I felt the power of prayer. I'm convinced I would not be in remission and completely cancer free today without them—and my Divine Connector!

Sarah Michel

A Voice in the Woods

*Jesus said to her, "I am the resurrection and the
life. He who believes in me, though he may die,
he shall live."*

John 11:25

I remember the first time I got close enough to smell
his cologne. We were playing "pass the orange" at youth
group. He stepped up to me, brushed his cheek against
mine and began to move the orange awkwardly from
under my chin to his without using his hands. I could
feel his breath and the scent of his Old Spice. He intoxi-
cated me. He was shy and mysterious, maneuvering
around my neck, millimeters away from my lips, smiling
up at me sheepishly. I wanted to kiss him right there in
front of everyone. *Dear God, just an inch higher, let me kiss
you!* He was beautiful. Long brown hair, bell bottoms and
Beatle boots that made him look hip and mysterious. I
must have written his name a hundred times. I kissed my
pillow at night, pretending it was him. And when
"Crimson and Clover" came on my radio in the darkness,
all I could think about was Mark. I had fantasized about

him for two years and he didn't even know it.

Now he was lying in a casket. It was the first time I had ever been to a funeral or seen a coffin. I took a step back in horror. He lay so frozen. The church filled up quickly, and I made my way through the crowd to the front. I tossed my song down on the music stand. I had never written a song for a funeral before. Getting through it without crying was going to be the challenge. His coffin was right in front of me. Two men wearing carnations closed the heavy lid as his parents sat down in the front row. The cheerleaders in the back sobbed and clung to each other. When a teenager dies, girls come out of the woodwork to help grieve the moment. Looking back, I think every adult in that place wished they could have allowed themselves to show their feelings as openly as those girls did. He deserved it, and someone needed to weep for him. Weep loud and long and without apology. He was the first boy I ever loved. Now half the sophomore class was waiting for me to sing his eulogy.

I glanced at the front row as I sang and saw his mother's face, hanging on my every word. His sister broke down, hiding behind her long, black hair. She was off to college next fall. I noticed a chain around her neck with Mark's high school ring dangling from it, as if they had been going steady. Girls are like that with their brothers.

I strummed the last chord on my guitar and sat down behind the casket. The minister stood up, pale and thin-lipped.

"God had a reason to take him," he began. "He had only sixteen short years on this Earth, but God had a reason."

I stared down at my lap, refusing to look at this clergyman I was beginning to hate. *You're a liar*, I thought. *God wouldn't kill Mark. The drunk driver killed Mark. God wouldn't do that.*

He rambled on about God needing Mark in heaven, as the two women in Mark's life, his mother and sister, squeezed each other's hands until their knuckles turned white. His little brother sat there, staring straight ahead in a JC Penney's suit that was too big.

Norma Peterson ended the service on the organ as the casket was wheeled down the center aisle and then loaded, like air freight, into the back of the hearse. The limo drove off to the cemetery, and the rest of us stood in front, chatting about nothing. Marge Sherman took a smoke break, and some of the football players stood with their hands in their pockets, talking about Saturday's game. I couldn't handle it. This was it? That's all? I couldn't process it. I didn't know what to do.

So I ran. I ran down the hill to my house; ran across my yard to the woods at the end of my street. I ran through the purple flowers and wild onions, to the thick of the woods near the stream. I stopped breathlessly by the water, wrapped my arms around a huge tree and sobbed into the bark, sobbed from somewhere so deep, I couldn't open my eyes for a long time.

Then I looked around at this magical chapel in the woods I had stepped into. I felt calm. Honeysuckle filled the air, and a ladybug landed on my arm. I bent down and picked one of the white lilies that covered the forest floor. I grabbed an armful of purple stems until I held a whole bouquet. Standing there in the dappling sunlight, a voice spoke to me. It came from inside my own heart, but it was louder than the rush of the water racing in the creek beside me.

"I didn't kill him. I only resurrected him."

I noticed a butterfly hovering over the water, gold and black wings sparkling in the sunlight. All around me was life: flowers, hummingbirds and bees buzzing in the orange daylilies. It was then that I realized how wrong he was, that minister. God didn't "take" Mark. God didn't bend down and kill this boy and break his mother's heart.

I carried my flowers to the edge of the water and let them fall. They twirled down into the rushing stream, and then spun down a waterfall. The last petal floated out of sight, and I stood back and felt something, someone, behind me, covering me with a warmth that I had never felt before.

"God, take my flowers to Mark," I whispered. "Comfort him."

And in that moment I knew that He would, because He had already comforted me.

There would be times in the future when I would attend other funerals; tragic deaths and untimely losses that made no sense. People would rationalize with the same idea of a Supreme Being who cut down innocents in the middle of their prime. "God took him," they would say.

And I would answer unwaveringly: "God doesn't kill people. Years ago He told me so. And I believe Him."

Carla Riehl

Hold On to Hope!

A life of hope is focusing not on the problem but on the solution, not on loss but on what needs to be done, not on the past but on the present and future, not on death but on life.

Dr. Grace Adolphsen Brame

I'm going to die!

The words pierced my soul. I dropped the telephone and replayed the conversation in my mind.

"Kathy, your AIDS test . . . it's come back positive!" my doctor blurted out.

In shock, I stared out the window. My worst nightmare had come true. In June 1986, I was a nurse working in the emergency room when an accident-related trauma patient was wheeled in. We cracked open his chest to perform internal CPR. My bare hands were wrist-deep inside him; back then no one wore gloves. Despite our best efforts, he died minutes later.

Later that night, we found out he had AIDS. My own heart skipped a beat as I looked down at my hands and remembered a minor cut on my right index finger.

After the dreadful call, I rushed to the hospital to meet with the doctors. My head was spinning. I couldn't think. My hands shook so, I could barely grip the steering wheel.

This just can't be true. Why me? I'm a nurse—trying to help a patient. I'm only twenty-six years old—I'm not ready to die!

The doctors ran additional tests to confirm the positive results. My nightmare continued. Two weeks later, the confirmatory tests also came back positive. They notified the Centers for Disease Control (CDC), which was also concerned—I was the first healthcare worker in America to test HIV-positive from an on-the-job exposure.

Since its discovery in May 1981, AIDS was thought to be a guaranteed death sentence. Most AIDS victims did not survive more than a year. Speculation was rampant, but no one really knew all the ways it could be spread.

No, this can't happen to me, I thought angrily. *I can't handle it! What am I going to do?* It was more than I could bear.

Reluctantly, that night I sat down and told my family. My mom and dad were supportive.

But my boss said sympathetically, "Kathy, if this gets out, this hospital will shut down. I'm sorry, but you can't work here anymore."

That weekend, I shared the shocking news with my church. To my amazement, some members turned away from me. I overheard one say, "You know AIDS is God's punishment." Other members whispered, "Should we touch her?" They were afraid.

I stopped eating. I stopped sleeping. One night in a graduate school class, as I wrestled with my own demons, my professor announced a film, *Living with AIDS.* Sitting in the classroom in disbelief, I watched young people at the prime of their lives waste away in hospitals. My classmates talked in horror of the disease. Little did they know my secret.

That night I determined I was not going to die the slow, agonizing death of an AIDS victim. I was not going to waste away. I could not! I would not!

I would choose how and when I would die.

After class, I started driving, my mind racing for hours around a track called "regrets." Regrets about not spending more time with my family and friends. I was always too busy, too stressed. Regrets about not taking the time to find out who Kathy Dempsey was. Finally, I found myself in the parking lot of Chattanooga's most famous hotel. I was about to add to its legend. I sat alone in my car that dark, drizzling night with a bottle of sleeping pills in my hand. I was a nurse. I knew what it took. . . .

Three knocks on my car window jolted me back to reality. It was Robin, one of my friends, appearing from out of nowhere. "Kathy, are you okay?"

I rolled down the window and asked incredulously, "How did you find me here?" With tears streaming down my face, I despairingly shook my head, "No. I am so scared and lonely."

Robin climbed into the car beside me. We talked. We cried. We prayed. For hours she repeated, "Kathy, hold on to hope."

God's message got through, and I finally went deep inside and harvested the hope to go on.

Three months later, I received another phone call from my doctor. "Kathy, I'm not sure how to tell you this." My heart stopped beating again. "But your tests, all eight of your tests, have come back negative. The CDC says you don't have AIDS now!"

There was a long silence. I took a deep breath and hung up the phone. *I'm going to live! I'm going to live!* No words had ever felt so joyous! I felt like a thousand-pound weight had been lifted from my chest. I remembered my regrets; now I could do something about them. I fell to my knees, thanked God, and promised myself from that day forward, "I will not live my life the same way again."

Some people call it a medical error; I call it a miracle. What a gift! I thought my life was over and now I had it back. It was like a VCR, and I got to push "rewind."

Now, any time I think I can't handle something and I'm about to throw in the towel, my mind returns to that lonely night in the car when God sent His messenger to stop me and remind me. No matter how difficult the situation, I need only to hold on to hope!

Kathy B. Dempsey

5

THE LEAST OF MY BROTHERS

Assuredly, I say to you, inasmuch as you did it to the least of these My brethren, you did it to me.

Matthew 25:40

Recycling

Our deeds determine us, as much as we determine our deeds.

George Eliot

Since I had a truck with a trailer hitch, I was the one volunteered to haul the aluminum can trailer to the recycling center after our Bible study on Saturday mornings. It wasn't that big a chore; it took a couple of hours at the most, and sometimes one of the guys from the group rode along with me.

After a couple of trips, the procedure became routine. I would drive up to the scale, weigh my load, back up to the pit and help shovel the aluminum cans out. The attendant would make a few notations, hand me a slip of paper, I'd go back to get weighed again, then take the slip to the cashier. The total was tabulated, the deductions taken and they'd write me a check. Simple enough.

After a few times though, I started having a little problem with their notations and deductions. It was completely guesswork by the attendant, and I had no recourse as he deducted for non-can waste, non-aluminum cans and, of course, my favorite: water content. If it had been raining and the cans were wet, this was usually the largest deduction. The recycling center seemed to think that empty cans could just absorb water, substantially adding to the total weight and our deductions. I had a hard time believing this, but I tolerated it because any money received was a gift to our church fund and graciously accepted. I trusted the Lord could handle any injustice on their part.

One Saturday morning, it was raining and cold—what many would call a raw day. I wanted to wait for another Saturday to haul the cans, knowing how the deduction system would work against us, but the trailer was full. As I suspected, there were no volunteers to ride along this dreary day, so I hooked up and headed down to the center, doing my duty for church and God.

Everything was pretty much normal when I got there. This early Saturday morning, with the cold wind and rain, was especially slow. When I backed up to the pit, the usual attendants were not to be found. After a minute or so I went ahead and started to unload the cans myself, as I had many times before.

About this time a rather large fellow with a cigar and an attitude came around the corner. "What's going on here?" he barked.

I could tell by his white shirt and nametag that he was the supervisor. Poor weather and Saturday morning had combined to deter his help from coming in, so he had to man the station himself, he said. He made it quite clear that he was not happy to be there and seemed determined to make sure I was not happy either. I quickly determined I should simply stay out of the way and make a quick departure.

After we finished unloading, he whipped out the check sheet and started making deductions. He didn't miss a one. It seemed he could find little good with our load of cans as he continued his checkoff. I regretted making a run this day, but it was too late to turn back. When he got to the water deduction, he was especially critical and the deduction cost us dearly. When he finished, he turned to me and asked the name of our organization so he could list it on the sheet.

"Corpus Christi Catholic Church," I said.

He stopped in his tracks. He looked up from his sheet and asked, "What church?"

"Corpus Christi."

He pulled the cigar from his mouth and asked in a gentler tone, "Is that the one by the mountain?"

I replied that it was, a bit surprised that he would know it because it was far from there and few outside of its locale would know much about it.

Standing in the cold wind, he began to tell his story. "When I was in jail, my family needed some help making ends meet. My wife checked with a bunch of organizations for help paying the rent and buying some food for my family. All of 'em turned her down—except you. Yours was the only place that'd help us." I could see tears in his eyes.

His voice choked, "Thank you." At that he reached over and pulled me to him in a bear hug. I'm no small man, but I felt like a child in his embrace. If he could have seen my face as he squeezed the air out of my lungs with his huge arms and his big heart, he would have seen the tears there for him. After a solid slap on the back, he finally released me. I stepped back, breathless, unable to speak. But that was not a problem for him.

He tore the worksheet out of his book and tossed it away. "Let's see here," he said as he filled out a new one, quickly going down the list, checking no deductions. Scrawling Corpus Christi in big letters, he signed it and handed it to me with a big smile and another "Thank you."

After weighing the trailer on the scale again, I took the sheet up to the main desk. The cashier looked at it a little suspiciously but didn't say anything, noting the supervisor himself had signed it.

I drove away feeling warm and happy, knowing our recycling fund had grown a good bit larger that day—more money to help families in need.

Richard Duello

And When I Was in Prison, You Visited Me

Surely goodness and mercy shall follow me all the days of my life.

Psalm 23:6

I tried not to stare as several dozen female inmates entered the gym one by one, some in white, some in maroon jail suits. A gray-haired woman walked with a cane in small, steady steps. A blond with six inches of brown roots patted her very pregnant belly. Another smiled effusively, revealing only three or four teeth. One seemed so young—barely twenty. Her scrubbed-clean face and simple ponytail didn't hide her natural, model-like beauty.

They sat silently, despondently, in the last of four rows of semicircled folding chairs. "Come on up," Tom coaxed as he walked down the aisle shaking hands with everyone. An Asian girl stared at the wall. A Hispanic woman rhythmically kicked the chair in front of her with her toe. "Here's a front row seat!" Tom beckoned. I watched his approach with them intently. I'd never visited a prison before—never dreamed I would. So why had I chosen ministering to women in prison as the charity for *Chicken Soup for the Christian Woman's Soul*?

I had a feeling I was about to find out.

"How many of you have read *Chicken Soup for the Prisoner's Soul*?" Tom beamed, and waved a copy of the book he had coauthored. A dozen women raised their hands. "What was your favorite story?" He pointed to the inmate with a three-inch tattoo on her wrist. "Ivy's Cookies," she said with what seemed to be a rare smile.

I couldn't believe it. There were 101 stories in the book. How could she have chosen that one?

"It's one of my favorites, too," Tom said, nearly dancing with delight. "Why is it your favorite?"

"Because this teenage girl took cookies to prisoners like us and they wouldn't talk to her. They treated her all mean and ignored her, but she just kept bringing cookies every week. Then at the end of the story when Ivy is older, one of the prisoners' daughters brought cookies to her at her home. That was so cool." The young woman blushed.

"Well, we have a special surprise for you here today," Tom said. "The author of that very story, 'Ivy's Cookies,' is here with us, and she's going to read that story to you!"

Some inmates smiled brightly at the news while two African Americans sat stoically.

It was Candy Abbott's first prison visit too, yet she stood in front of them and began reading her story with all her heart. She emphasized how Ivy Jones had questioned herself about why she kept coming to the prison week after week when the inmates clearly didn't appreciate or care about her. Then an evangelist came to the prison and ordered the inmates to make a circle and thank God for one thing. Candy went on to read about the lopsided, silent circle and how one prisoner finally said, "I want to thank Ivy for the cookies. Thank you, God, for Miss Ivy bringin' us cookies every week." Then one by one, the prisoners each thanked Ivy for her weekly visits. Candy concluded the story and closed the book. "We have another surprise visitor for you today," she said proudly. "Ivy is here!"

Many inmates gasped and most clapped as Ivy walked from the second row to the front of the room. "We've never done this together before," Candy explained.

Ivy reminded me of the evangelist in the story as she addressed them. "I didn't know what I was doing when I was that teenager visiting the prison. I was scared, but I prayed to God to show me what to do and He did. And He'll show you what to do too. Just ask Him!" she proclaimed. If you need strength, ask Him for strength. If you need hope, ask Him for hope. He'll give you what you need just like He did me."

"Amen!" someone shouted.

"God disciplines those He loves." Ivy looked into each of their eyes and added softy, "And He must love you very much."

The model look-alike's face reddened. She fanned her hand in front of her face as if to wave the tears away.

Ivy completed her brief sermon to the applause of the inmates, and then Tom came forward again. "There is a new *Chicken Soup* book called *Chicken Soup for the Christian Woman's Soul,* and part of the money from the sales of that book will go into a special fund to buy copies of it and *Chicken Soup for the Prisoner's Soul* to give to incarcerated women. We plan to send some to you after the first of the year." A few inmates clapped; many whispered with excitement; some sat motionless, expressionless. "We have a final surprise for you today—the coauthor of *Chicken Soup for the Woman's Soul,* LeAnn Thieman." Most of the women clapped with enthusiasm, but a few sat scowling with their arms folded across their chests.

Until that moment I hadn't a clue what I was going to

say. I'd trusted God would answer my prayer and give me the words. "It seems we have a theme here today," I began. "Apparently God uses baked goods to help do His work on Earth." Some chuckled. Most smiled, except for those with the folded arms. "Twenty-five years ago I bought a dozen cupcakes at a bake sale to help support the orphans in Vietnam. That's all I ever intended to do for them, but God had a bigger plan. He just used those cupcakes to trick me into helping Him!" In one long deep breath I rattled off my story of how I joined the organization to help support the orphans, how my basement became the state chapter headquarters, how we had decided to adopt a son from Vietnam, how I agreed to go bring six babies back to their adoptive homes, and how, when I got there, I helped bring out three hundred as a part of Operation Babylift. The room broke into applause. When I told them the part about a baby boy crawling into my arms and heart and family, a collective sigh filled the gym. "I was not and still am not anybody special," I explained. "I was raised a poor Iowa farm girl with seven brothers and sisters and I wore hand-me-down clothes. I'm living proof that God uses ordinary women to do extraordinary things."

Tom stood behind the group and stared me right in the eyes. "Why did you pick a women's prison ministry for the charity of this book?"

I looked at the old woman with the cane, at the pregnant woman rubbing her belly, at the tattooed woman and at the one with few teeth. I breathed past the lump in my throat. "Because a lot of good is in this room." A tear escaped the model's eyes. The black women unfolded their arms. The Asian woman looked me in the face. I continued. "I know something very bad happened to put you here, but I know you have a lot of good in you."

"Amen," the voice came again.

Tom hugged me long and hard as I headed for my seat. Then he introduced his wife, Laura, a frequent companion on his prison visits and coauthor of the *Chicken Soup for the Volunteer's Soul* book. "Everybody has a story to tell," she said warmly. "And yours isn't over yet—you can still choose the ending." Many heads nodded in unison.

Tom lightened the mood. "Just like in 'Ivy's Cookies,' let's all circle up," he cheered. To my amazement, the women followed him to the side of the gym and formed a circle, holding hands. "Now let's say one thing we are thankful for," Tom urged. "I'll start. I want to thank God for letting me be here with you today."

A woman with long graying hair spoke first. "I'm thankful for the people keeping my children strong while I'm in here."

"I want to thank Ivy for coming today—and next time, will you bring us cookies?"

"I want to thank Tom and Laura and Candy for coming here today when I'm sure they got better things to do."

"I want to thank LeAnn for donating money from that book so we can get a copy someday. Those stories give me hope."

The model spoke. "I want to thank God for sending me to prison. If He didn't love me enough to send me here, I'd be dead."

"Amen."

"Everyone take one step forward," Tom instructed and we inched ahead. "Now another step forward," he said with a giggle. "And another." We jammed in closer together. "Now that's a big Texas hug!"

There I stood with my arms wrapped around forty women prisoners, all smiling, all hugging. Indeed, a lot of good is in this room.

LeAnn Thieman

The Wrong Person

*I the Lord have called you in righteousness, and
I will hold your hand.*

Isaiah 42:6

Rick's face shone with wonderful news. "Robin, the Lord
wants us to continue with our honeymoon for a long time!"

In utter joy, I hugged him.

"He called me to the mission field." His eyes filled with
purpose. "India is in my heart." My arms fell to my side.
*What about me? I thought we would pastor a small country
church in the States—near a mall.* Had he heard God's call
correctly?

Soon I received my call—from his mother. "Robin, when
God called Rick to the mission field, he called you too."

She began making plans to return our wedding gifts
"since you will not need them anymore."

I gritted my teeth. I would inform Rick when his parents
were not around. I was not going to India. "Lord, you have
the wrong person," I said.

I was not going when I had my shots and my passport
picture taken.

As we lent our car to my best friend, I still was not going. While we bought our new luggage, I was not going. As I resigned my teaching position, I asked for a new application. As we sold all our earthly possessions at a yard sale, I was not going. I felt happy at our going-away party, for I was staying.

Sitting on the overseas flight to India, I planned on turning around the moment the plane set down in Iran to catch our connecting flight. The only thing I had to do was inform Rick of my decision. I was not going to be a missionary. I wanted my house inside the safe perimeters of a white picket fence with clothes in dresser drawers and clean sheets on the bed. The Lord simply had the wrong person.

But when I looked into the wonderful blue eyes I fell in love with, I couldn't bear the thought of leaving him. Rick and God were a package deal. Just where did I fit in? Was I limiting God from working in my life? Did my attitude scream out, "This far and no further, God"? How did that translate in my marriage?

Changing planes in Iran, we learned the Shah was fleeing the country to save his own life. I wanted to flee with him to save mine. The Iranians were in revolt. I understood the feeling. While Americans were at the airport trying to get out, we were at the airport trying to get in, like salmon swimming upstream.

I decided to break my news to Rick during our two-hour layover. My speech was prepared. My courage gathered, I was at last ready. Rick would soon learn I was returning to the States and my dog. While standing in line, handing my boarding pass to the flight attendant, I opened my mouth to tell him I was not getting on the plane. Just then the announcement came: The airport was now closed due to the revolution. Rick looked rather startled, so I decided to postpone my own startling news for a less stressful moment.

As we drove up to the Commodore Hotel in Tehran, I couldn't help but notice all the large tanks with cannons pointing toward it. My refuge was the bull's-eye.

Okay, I would tell him a little later. I still had time. Perhaps after he had his morning devotions; scriptures always perked him up.

The next day was Sunday. Rick directed, "Get ready for church."

"Church? We are in a Muslim country." I shook my head at him.

"I am sure there is a Christian church somewhere. Let's go find one."

"There are people out on the streets shooting Americans!"

"Don't make excuses, Robin. Just get ready."

After looking through the phone book, we found a Christian church, and it was only twelve city blocks away. No cabs were available, so we walked.

Shortly after arriving, I decided I would pass Rick a note during church saying I was not going to India. Only first I had to use the restroom. Slowly, I circled down the cement steps and found the room at the end of a long, dark hall in the basement. I locked the creaking door behind me. Ready to rejoin my husband and the lively congregation on the floor above, I tried to unlock the door. It would not budge. I twisted it. I pulled it again and again and again.

"Help!" I cried hysterically into my hands. I surveyed the small room, searching for a window to make my escape. There was none. Three-foot walls of stone surrounded me. I envisioned a revolution taking place on the street above my head while I remained locked in the water closet below. How long would it take for Rick to notice I had been gone too long? He might get sidetracked praying for someone infirmed and forget about his reluctant wife.

As I pulled and pushed the bathroom door I muttered, "God, if Rick's plan is the center of Your will, why am I so miserable?" Was I fighting against Him as hard as I was against the lock on the door? At that moment, I surrendered totally to Him. I quit pounding and pushing and rattling and struggling. His will was now my will, no matter where it took me—to America, to India or to Niagara Falls.

God had called Rick during a church service; He called me in the restroom under the street.

I pressed the lock one more time and it flew open. "Lord, as easily as this lock opened, please allow me to do Your will. Help us leave this country for India."

Arriving back at the hotel as giggly honeymooners, Rick and I heard the airport had miraculously opened for only two hours. Our jet awaited us on the tarmac. It was heading east, toward the rising sun. Amazingly, my courage and prayers began to take root.

Stepping out into India, sights, sounds and smells I had never imagined enveloped me; some delightful, some frightening, but all wonderful.

In the mission field, I learned the true meaning of being a child of God and the wife of a committed Christian man. Missionaries and marriage both require teamwork. God and Rick and I were a team.

I had been the right person all along.

Robin Lee Shope

Putting On the Boots

There is a strength of quiet endurance as significant of courage as the most daring feats of prowess.

Henry Theodore Tuckerman

"A twelve-year-old girl is in desperate need of a home because both of her parents have been sentenced to prison."

As soon as this call came on the church prayer chain, my heart went out to her—within two days, Nikki came to live with us. She'd been knocked around from place to place, being rejected over and over. Some families had kept her for a few days, some for a few weeks. Nikki's self-confidence was zero.

But God began to do a miraculous work in her life, slowly convincing her He had great plans for her future. About a year later, she heard about an organization called Teen Missions, which offered short-term mission assignments to teenagers. She applied, got accepted and everything was in motion for her trip to Africa. She was so excited, I thought she'd burst!

The first thing she needed to do to prepare for this great mission assignment was to get a pair of big, high-top construction boots and wear them every day to break them in. She ordered the boots, then sent out her missionary support letters to raise the $5,000 to go.

The response was paltry.

She refused to put on the boots. They sat in her closet for three solid months with the tags still on them. Without clear signs of support from God and others, she wouldn't take a step.

As it happened, right around this time I was scheduled to speak at a women's conference, so Nikki decided to make bookmarks to sell at my book table. She designed one that involved cutting, ironing, gluing, hole punching, threading and tying a bow. She sat for hours cutting fabric until there was a purple indentation in her hand and tears streaming down her face.

"Why don't you stop now?" I urged.

"No," she declared, "I'm going to do this!"

I knew at that instant she had "put on the boots." Yet I could see she still felt discouraged and ill-equipped.

The next day, I reminded her that God had called Gideon to fight a tough battle, but Gideon didn't think he was good enough for the job. I told her, "Gideon said, 'God, I can't do what you're asking me to do! I'm just a kid. Besides, I'm from a lousy family. You better pick someone else.' None of that mattered to God," I reminded her. "In fact, God loves to pick the most unlikely people to do His work. The Lord eased Gideon's worry by posing a very simple question, 'Am *I* not sending you?'"

I explained to Nikki, "It's not about the one who's going, it's about the One who's sending. If God is sending you, you can go in complete confidence."

That day at the women's conference, she raised $742— most of it in $1 donations. Some ladies donated $5, $10 or

$20, shoving the money into her boots, which were set up on my book table.

When we returned from the conference, we filled our house with giant posters proclaiming Who's Sending You? Over the next several months, Nikki made almost four thousand bookmarks and raised $5,000 at my conferences around the country.

She demonstrated her faithfulness by "putting on the boots" for the One who was sending her.

Donna Partow

"I'm thinking about becoming a
biblical archaeologist because I really dig religion."

Waiting at the Fence

I love these little people; and it is not a slight thing when they, who are so fresh from God, love us.

Charles Dickens

Late one December afternoon, my husband and I boarded a plane with several other couples from Atlanta and headed to Nicaragua to deliver Christmas presents to children at several orphanages there. After landing, we went to the mission house and organized our gifts, excited and eager to get to the orphanages the next day.

The next morning we loaded onto a school bus and headed to our first stop, Moises Orphanage for boys. As our bus rambled along, our host instructed us to start playing with the boys as soon as we arrived, then he would call us all together, share the Christmas story and let us give the gifts. Anticipation was high, and we were a bit nervous when we saw the chain-link fence that separated Moises from the road.

We drove up a wide dirt driveway surrounded by several small blue-green cinder-block buildings. Boys of all ages were running around, and their faces broke into big grins when they saw our bus.

I was excited to be at Moises. As the mother of two sons, I was very comfortable around boys. We poured out of the bus and the games began! But I felt as if the Lord was saying, "Wait just a few minutes. There is someone I want you to meet." I waited, and then I saw him—a shy little boy, about eight years old, hugging a pole, quietly observing all the activity. I went over to him and said the one word I knew in Spanish, "Hola!"

He smiled, but didn't let go of the pole. Then I tussled his hair and tickled him a little bit. He began to laugh, so I grabbed a ball and tossed it to him. I'd never met a boy yet who could resist a ball. We played catch for a few minutes, then he gently took my hand, led me to a concrete wall and motioned for me to sit down. He snuggled right up to me and we just sat there, smiling at one another. I pointed to myself and told him my name. "Miss Dean."

He looked up at me with his big brown eyes, smiled and pointed to himself, and said, "Martinez."

At that moment, he captured my heart.

We sat there a few minutes, then he jumped up and tossed me the ball and we were playing catch again. Then again he took my hand again and we went back to the concrete wall. He motioned for me to sit down, and he crawled up in my lap.

My heart started to break. I thought about how much I loved holding my boys and that Martinez didn't have a mama's lap to crawl into. I held him close. He gazed up at me and smiled, then buried his face in my shoulder. I hugged him even tighter, and my heart broke a little more.

Martinez got up and motioned for me to follow him. I did, and he indicated that I should stop and stay where I was standing. I smiled as he ran full speed ahead into one of the small cinder-block buildings and then came running toward me with something in his hand—a beat-up and battered Wiffle ball bat. He had such pride in his eyes. I was humbled and broken knowing that at my house we would have thrown that bat away, yet it was obviously Martinez's most prized possession.

We played ball for a little while, until it was time to gather together for the Christmas story. Martinez sat in my lap, and we smiled at each other as the Nativity story unfolded in pictures. Then it was time for the presents! The children were as excited as we were. Martinez's name wasn't called until almost the end. There were more children at the orphanage than we thought, so all he received was a shirt and one little Matchbox car.

He smiled and examined the car, then we went out to the dirt playground where he drove it along imaginary dirt roads as I laughed. I heard something said in Spanish and knew it was time to leave.

Martinez grabbed my hand and walked with me toward the bus. Very abruptly, he stopped and jumped into my arms, hugging me with all his might.

Choking back tears, I prayed, "Lord, this is so hard! I love this little guy. He has such a kind nature about him. He is so smart and sincere. I'd take him home in a second."

Martinez got down and took my hand and we continued toward the bus. When we got to the door, he hopped back up into my arms and looked at me with tears in his eyes. I held him tight and told him that I loved him, that I would always pray for him. I knew he didn't understand English but with my whole heart, I knew he understood.

I got on the bus with Martinez's eyes locked with mine as I went down the aisle to find my seat. Our eyes remained locked, and he followed the bus as it drove down the wide dirt driveway to the chain-link fence. When we got to the fence, Martinez wrapped his fingers through the wire and stared at me the entire time—until the bus drove out of sight.

I slumped down in my seat, and cried out, "Why Lord? I want to take him home with me. I love him. This really hurts. Why did you want me to meet Martinez?"

And ever so sweetly the Lord spoke to my breaking heart: "I want you to tell others that I am Martinez. I am the One with My fingers wrapped through the chain-link fence. I'm waiting to play with them, to snuggle up close to them, to jump into their arms and hold onto them with all My might because I love them so much. I am waiting to take the beat-up and battered things in their lives and make them prized possessions. My eyes are looking with excitement, longing with anticipation for them. I am waiting. I am waiting."

Dean Crowe

God's Gentle Man

*The best portion of a good man's life is his little,
nameless, unremembered acts of kindness and
of love.*

William Wordsworth

I was checking out a construction job site in one of the
poorer sections of town at lunchtime, so it was deserted
of the few workmen there. At this point just three walls
were up on the building, which sat back and isolated,
away from the main thoroughfare. I was taking a few
measurements when a fellow casually walked up from off
the street. At first glance I could tell he was not a work-
man, so I eyed him cautiously while asking politely if I
could help him.

He said, "I just started in a new job, and I'm waiting for
my first paycheck. My wife and little girl and I are staying
in a motel. I worked all night and when I got back to the
room they told me that if I don't have payment for tonight
right now, they're gonna make us leave."

I asked if he had checked with welfare and charity agencies for help. He replied he had, but they were slow in

coming up with any money. After waiting a long time that morning for a return phone call, he felt he had to do something, so he started walking and asking for help.

As a Christian man, I like to think of myself as someone who will help those in need, but in Atlanta these kinds of requests are not uncommon. So sometime back my wife and I had decided that we would give to specific charities qualified to help such families, so that when we were confronted by such requests, we had an answer ready.

I expressed to the gentleman a simple "No."

His response was surprising. "Thank you," he said kindly, and turned and walked back out to the street.

Normally I would not have given it a second thought, but today this was not the case. Maybe it was his response, maybe it was his story, maybe it was the Holy Spirit, but something pulled at me to rethink what had just transpired—that maybe this time my response was wrong; maybe this gentleman had not just wandered up but maybe he was sent to me. It was out of the way, I was the only one here, and he was the only other person on the job site.

I tried to soothe my conscience with my self-righteousness, telling myself that I already help such people, that I cannot just give to anyone who shows up with a sad story. Believing that a certain amount of stewardship goes into handling our gifts normally justifies my reluctance to give to those who just walk up on the street and ask for money—but not this time.

I stayed on at the site for a few more minutes, finishing up what I had come to do, but the presence of this gentleman and the wrongness of my response kept gnawing at me. Finally, as I got into my truck to leave, I turned to what some of my friends had taught me—I prayed about this. Then I thought, *Let's check this out. Let's see if there really is a place nearby where he could rent a room for a family; if so, he'll be there and then I'll know I should help.*

After driving down the street in both directions and not finding any such place, I convinced myself that I was right, it was all just a story to get some cash and I could leave now knowing I had done right. So why did it feel so wrong?

Finally, after stopping once again in a parking lot, I put God to the test. "Okay," I said out loud, "if You want me to help this gentleman then You show him to me. If I see him I will help him."

Convinced I had solved the problem, I started to pull out onto the street, squeezing between two buildings and pulling out across the sidewalk to see oncoming traffic. I looked right—nothing was coming. I looked left—and right into the eyes of the gentle man looking into my truck window. I'm sure he saw the shock and amazement on my face as he looked in at me in puzzlement. It took a second or two to regain my composure, but I finally found the button to lower the window. "Still need help?"

"Yes."

"Where's this place you're staying?"

"Just down the road."

"Get in." It was a short ride and I had to make a few turns, but sure enough there was the motel, just as he'd said. As I drove up we saw his wife and daughter sitting in the lobby.

He said, "After working all night and walking all morning, I'd given up and was on my way back to get them when you picked me up."

I gave him what cash I had, enough for one night and a meal for his family. He thanked me profusely, then said, "What can I do for you?"

I just said, "Keep me in your prayers, as I will you."

Little did he know he had already done more for me than I for him.

Richard Duello

6

MIRACLES

Every believer is God's miracle.

Gamaliel Bailey

Lisa

A miracle is a work exceeding the power of any created agent, consequently being an effect of the divine omnipotence.

Robert South

Eight years ago my big sister received a last-minute invitation from the Lord. Lisa was snowboarding on New Year's Day when she stopped in her tracks. Her boyfriend came up behind her and asked if she was all right. Lisa said, "I saw a vision. Oh my gosh, I saw a vision!" She immediately went into a seizure and was rushed to the hospital. She had suffered a dual cerebral aneurysm which resulted in a stroke. Within twenty-four hours she was brain-dead.

When I received the call from my mother to get to the hospital as quickly as possible, my throat closed up so tightly I thought I would never breathe again. I didn't know what to pray for. I couldn't even think. I was paralyzed with pain and anguish. All I could do was ask the Lord to get me to my sister's side, quickly and safely.

I endured my journey from my home in Alabama to my

sister, hospitalized in her home state of New Jersey. Once all the family members were assembled in the hall, it began to snow. Lisa adored the snow.

I've never experienced deeper heartache than when my parents walked me into my only sibling's hospital room and I saw her body supported by machines, her mind and spirit gone. With irreversible brain damage, she had no possibility of regaining the ability to move, think and feel. My sister had left this world, and I couldn't bear it.

I asked my parents to leave me alone with her. When they stepped out of the room the floodgates of my grief burst into gut-wrenching sobs. I asked her lifeless body, "Why? Why? Why did you leave me?" In the midst of my sobs, I yelled, "I need you!"

Miraculously, my sister's head turned left, then right, signaling, "No, you don't."

I stared in awe and disbelief! But deep inside I heard God saying, "I am here. I will take care of you. Lisa is home now, with Me. Be at peace because we are at peace. With My new angel, we will look after you and always be with you."

Stunned, I yelled out for my mother and father. I called for everybody to come into Lisa's room. But it never happened again. She never moved again. The message was for me.

The next time I went into her hospital room by myself, I walked over to her head. As I stood there, looking at her body, thinking about what had happened previously, something different happened to me. Lisa's presence, her spirit or essence, gathered on my right shoulder. I could feel her there, like an angel on my shoulder, looking at her body with me, letting me know that she was with *me*, not her body; she was free, she was home and she was happy.

When I told this to Mom, she smiled knowingly. "When I stood beside her, rubbing lotion on her arms and hands, in my mind I actually heard her say, 'I'm free, I'm free and I'm so happy, Mom, don't be sad.'"

I called to tell my husband about this, and he recounted how he had tucked our four-year-old son Jeffrey in for the night. Hours later, Jeffrey woke calling, "Auntie Lisa, Auntie Lisa!"

I couldn't believe it. "And Grandpa too," my mom told me later. "He can't or won't explain it.... All he will say is that he felt Lisa visiting him."

It seems God's newest angel was making her rounds!

We stayed with Lisa's body for the next five days, and it continued to snow ... and snow ... and snow. The Lord celebrated Lisa's arrival with what became known in the Northeast as the Blizzard of '97. It was a fitting send-off.

I still see and feel Lisa's presence. When I am in need of comfort and guidance, He is there and she is always nearby. She visits me in dreams, and I feel her with me when I need her and least expect it. I'm so blessed to still enjoy and learn from my big sister, God's angel, making rounds.

Stacie L. Morgan

One Miracle After Another

*God encourages us in our every affliction, so
that we may be able to encourage those who are
in any affliction with the encouragement with
which we ourselves are encouraged by him.*

2 Corinthians 1:4

She was only nineteen when she asked to work with us.
We always welcomed good, energetic people to help in the
afternoons at our childcare center. Alicia, a pretty, smiling
blonde who loved children, was a sophomore at the local
college.

The entire three-year-old class received lots of loving care
from Alicia, but she took a special interest in those with special needs. When Ken, our little ADHD boy, had trouble
focusing on a task for any length of time, Alicia brought in
activity books and devised games to challenge him. When
Hannah, our Down syndrome child, came, Alicia learned
simple sign language so she could communicate with her in
the same way her special education teacher did.

Alicia was a special young lady who wanted to please
everyone. Despite going to school in the mornings and

working in the afternoons, it was hard for her to say no
when anyone asked her to do something else. One staff
member asked her to babysit long hours, sometimes "forgetting" to pay her. Another wanted her to sell Mary Kay
products in her "spare" time.

One afternoon in April, Alicia came to work even
though she had been sick all day and hadn't had anything
to eat or drink. As she went to her classroom, she passed
out in the doorway, flat on the floor.

Devon's dad was there and helped us move Alicia to a
quiet corner. He stayed with her while I rushed frantically
to call her mother. Mrs. C. wasn't aware that Alicia was
sick and had missed her morning classes. She rushed to
the center and took her home. We all assumed she had
some sort of virus and would be fine.

I was in total shock and disbelief when the phone call
came the next day: Alicia was in the intensive care unit of
our trauma hospital. She had shot herself that morning
while her parents were out for breakfast. Doctors were not
optimistic about her survival. *Why?* I wondered, heartbroken. *Why would our sweet Alicia, who was so kind and loving
and giving, attempt to take her life?*

When I went to the hospital, Alicia was in a coma and
on life support. Her parents felt there was no hope. If she
lived, there would be no quality of life. She would not be
able to walk or talk; she might never be aware of her surroundings. I prayed with them, asking God to heal her,
asking Him to comfort them and give them hope. Alicia
was too precious; she had too much to give to die so early.

On Monday, a couple of teachers asked if we could get
together and pray for Alicia. We agreed to meet at six
o'clock, after working hours, when there would be no
interruptions. I expected no more than three or four to
come, just those who worked directly with her. Before our
meeting, I called Mrs. C. to ask about Alicia. She said the

situation was very grim. The doctors thought they should take her off life support the next day—there was no hope for her survival. I cried, "Oh, please don't do it. We're getting together to pray for her tonight. Please don't do it yet!" How amazed I was when at six o'clock not three or four, but every one of our staff members came to pray. As a "family," our hearts were broken. Rick, our administrative director, asked a parent who was a pastor to tell us about suicide and grief. He talked as though Alicia were already dead. As he spoke, everything in me cried out, "She's not dead! She's not going to die!" I said to the group, "Let's stop talking about death. Let's pray now that she will live."

Several staff members prayed aloud. Miss Connie prayed the most beautiful prayer imploring God to reach down and touch every part of the brain the bullet creased, every cell that was damaged, and to heal Alicia from the inside out—body, mind, soul and spirit. Miss Amy started singing "Amazing Grace." We all joined in and sang songs of praise, knowing that nothing is impossible for God.

The next day Mrs. C. called. "The most amazing thing happened last night! Alicia opened her eyes! The doctors want to keep her on life support for a while now."

Rejoicing, I asked, "What time did Alicia open her eyes?"

"Six o'clock."

Every day, each of us prayed for Alicia, our parents prayed, people all over the city prayed with faith that she would be healed.

Miraculously, Alicia came out of the coma, but progress was slow. Doctors still had no hope she would have any quality of life. Several weeks later, Mrs. C. called me at work. "Miss Frances, somebody wants to talk to you."

I heard a soft, small voice on the phone. "Miss Frances, this is Alicia." I wanted to laugh. I wanted to cry. I wanted to raise my hands in praise and fall on the floor in awe!

Day by day Alicia got a little better. She was transferred

to Shepherd's Spinal Clinic, where she learned to talk and walk again. While she had no memory of any events surrounding her "accident," she remembered the children in her class and asked about them when I went to visit.

One miracle followed another. Three months after the accident, Alicia went home for her twentieth birthday. Only weeks later she drove alone to downtown Atlanta for therapy each week. Then miracle of all miracles—she, who would never be able to walk or talk, came back to work with us the following summer.

Yet the greatest miracle is still in process. Only four years after the accident, Alicia went back to college, earned a bachelor's degree in special education and is now enrolled in graduate school to work with deaf children. Although a slight speech defect remains, Alicia has the most radiant smile! She still has no memory of the accident or why she pulled the trigger that day, but she knows that God has healed her from the inside out. She knows He has a special plan for her life, that He saved her so that she can help others with the same kind of help she received from Him.

Frances Griffin

The Accident

*The angel of the Lord encamps around those
who fear him, and he delivers them.*

Psalm 34:7

This was the call every parent dreads. I picked up the
phone to hear our sixteen-year-old daughter, Whitney, in
absolute hysteria. She'd had a head-on collision in a busy
Dallas/Ft. Worth intersection, six hundred miles away. To
make things worse, she had our two- and three-year-old
nieces she was babysitting in the car with her.

"Are you hurt?" I kept asking.

"Just my wrists, because of the airbag, and my head
hurts and my shoulder hurts and my back . . ."

"What about Abby and Hallie?"

"They're absolutely fine. They're eating snowcones right
now on the sidewalk. Dad, this is my worst nightmare!"

I stayed on the phone and did my best to calm her as
the police and emergency medical technicians arrived and
began treating the injured. The other driver, trapped in
her car, had to be freed from the mangled mess of metal by
the Jaws of Life.

Finally I spoke with the attending police officer, the EMT and anyone else who would listen to my long-distance plea for help. They treated Whitney at the scene of the accident, Abby and Hallie were without a scratch, and the other driver was taken in an ambulance to a local hospital. Whitney's car was totaled.

As the police were investigating the accident, the officer's first question was, "Who was driving this gray car?"

"I was," said Whitney.

"Well, how did you get out of the car?"

"I don't remember. All I remember is the crash, the airbag deploying, and then my two little nieces and I were standing on the sidewalk."

"I don't see how that's possible," replied the officer. "The impact of the crash has jammed the front doors, and the rear doors were childproofed. You couldn't get out of this car from the inside."

We thought this was curious, but were so absorbed in the trauma of it all that we didn't think about it too much.

In the days after the crash, we learned Whitney's injuries were painful, but not life threatening—one broken wrist, the other badly sprained, a whiplash injury and a large contusion where the seatbelt had grabbed her. Abby and Hallie were literally and miraculously unscathed.

A few days after the accident, their mom, Julie, asked Abby if she remembered the crash and, recalling what the police officer had said, asked her if Whitney had gotten them out of their car seats.

Abby recounted the impact in great detail, then replied, "No, Mom, the angel opened the door and then Whitney got us out."

In one of our many conversations with their parents after the accident, this is the sentence that stopped us in our tracks. Julie said to my wife, "We really don't talk about angels in our house. In fact, I didn't know Abby really even knew what an angel was."

We do. Psalm 91:11–12 says, "For He will command His angels concerning you to guard you in all your ways; they will lift you up in their hands, so that you will not strike your foot against a stone."

Yes, we know, now more than ever before.

Dick and Mel Tunney

The Almost-Missed Miracle

It's never too late to be who you might have been.

George Eliot

"The photo of your daughter has arrived. Come right over!" announced our adoption agency on the phone. Within minutes, we were driving, drunk with anticipation, our hearts dancing out of our chests, toward this magnificent moment.

After fifteen torturous months of waiting, we glimpsed our first look at the thumbnail-size, black-and-white photo of the little girl from China destined to be our daughter. "She is," I sighed, "a black-and-white portrait of innocence."

"She has a cleft palate," the worker reported. "There will be no way to determine the severity of her condition or how many surgeries she might need until you have her examined." He asked, "Will you accept this match?"

My mind floated back to the intense crucible we had faced in our journey to adopt. Halfway through the process, the Chinese government shocked us by decreeing that families who had children didn't qualify to adopt a healthy child. With two teenage children, this new twist meant we could only adopt a child with special medical needs. And we wouldn't know the "minor" medical condition until we were matched.

I felt betrayed by this change of contract. I remember collapsing in the newly pastel-decorated nursery, drooping like the pink bunny in the rocking chair next to me. I wept over the injustice. It had been hard enough at our ages to rally the courage to adopt a *healthy* child and to ignore the raised eyebrows and disdainful comments about our plans. Our trek through the minefields of fear had intensified exponentially. Admittedly not the nurse type, I imagined all kinds of horrible medical conditions we might face. What a slap in the face in the middle of a path already fraught with uncertainty and raw emotion.

"I just want my baby!" I cried, trying to grapple with both fear and fury. I wasn't up to handling the emotional nausea and extra financial burden that I sensed was shadowing my adoption fantasies. There were hundreds of thousands of healthy abandoned girls in China needing families. Why this ridiculous red tape, I fumed. I halfway understood why several families dropped out of the process at this point, disgusted by this new obstacle. "God, help me process this," I agonized.

I traced the heart steps that had brought me to this juncture. I pondered the raw facts that had moved me in the beginning. The "one child" law for population control had caused a holocaust of baby girls in China. Everyone wanted a son for financial security and to carry on their family name. Girls that escaped abortion and made it through the birth canal faced another horror: total abandonment.

Rocking with the bunny on my lap, my self-pity began to diminish as my focus turned outward. I pictured new mothers throughout China, just hours after cutting the umbilical cord, being forced to do the unthinkable. I imagined their tears as they secretly and gently laid their bundled little girls somewhere out in the open, hoping that the cries of their delicate offspring would be heard . . . that someone would deliver them to a government welfare institute. Their desperation engulfed me as I envisioned them giving their final kiss.

"How could I turn back now?" I avowed. "Some precious, tiny girl has miraculously survived the gauntlet of life thus far and awaits my loving arms. . . . Will I, too, forsake her because she's not perfect?"

Even my young teenagers understood that love required sacrifice. To help us raise the money we needed, they joined my husband on an excruciating, 101-mile walk across Death Valley, getting sponsors per mile. "We didn't mind the blisters and pain, Mom, as long as we thought about rescuing our little sister," they reported, having grown up a year in just one week. "We walked through the valley of death to give her a chance at life."

Rehearsing all of these moments brought my struggle with selfishness and fear to an end. My husband confirmed our direction. "Maybe we are the only way this little girl can ever get the medical help she needs," he tenderly concluded. His selfless words calmed the remaining storm inside me. Perfect love had cast out fear. Quitting now would only hurt our daughter; she was the one being imprisoned by these restrictions. And love isn't love if it doesn't pay a price. Didn't I learn that from Jesus?

"Yes!" I blurted out loudly to our agency worker. "Absolutely!"

I was elated that we had settled the issue months earlier.

"You'll fly to meet her in two weeks, then," he announced to our utter shock.

Our hearts nearly stopped when we spied the Chinese nannies filing into our Nanchang City hotel lobby, carrying little bundles. All ten anxious families in our group had paced the halls for the last hour in anticipation of this thrilling delivery. We'd all waited, pregnant with a dream of a daughter for well over a year, but this last hour of labor was the most acute. This labor of the heart in an adoptive parent is as intense as physical child labor, and the moment of delivery almost more exhilarating.

"Porter," a man called out, signaling that it was our turn to come face-to-face with our baby. I was ecstatic as he placed a tiny, fragile-as-porcelain masterpiece of a child into my arms. Her familiar black eyes studied me back, and in a holy moment our hearts attached as mother and child.

I tenderly stroked her shaved head, covered with insect bites and scratches. "She is beautiful," we marveled. She silently, compliantly watched us pass her back and forth, mother to father, then brother to sister. Her ebony eyes were beckoning, as if to say, "Take me, I'm yours."

Morning light revealed a wonder that overwhelmed us all, an almost-missed miracle. The doctor announced that her palate was absolutely perfect. There would be no need for surgeries and lifelong speech therapy after all. The Great Physician had taken care of all that on His own.

Claudia Porter

Southbound Miracle

May the Lord bless you and protect you.

Numbers 6:24

I was heading south on I-5 from Seattle, joyfully singing along with the contemporary Christian tunes blaring from my car stereo. There were a few hours left on my trip home, so I settled comfortably in my seat, tap-tapping my steering wheel to the beat.

"Our God is an awesome God, He reigns from Heaven above . . . ," I sang loudly.

Suddenly a bizarre question flashed through my mind. *What would you do if someone in the lane to your left crashed right now and stuff flew into your windshield blocking your vision?*

I went silent. Where had that weird thought come from?

Yet I did ponder what I might do in such a case. I counted the lanes on the freeway: one to my left, two to my right. I decided that if such a strange thing were to happen, I'd quickly check my right rearview mirror for traffic, move across the two lanes if they were clear and stop.

I shrugged, then began listening to the music again. Yet

I was more keenly alert to my driving.

About five minutes later I heard a tremendous crash to my left. Instantaneously my windshield was covered with debris.

Oh God, oh God . . . It's happening, isn't it? Help me! I prayed. I instinctively looked in my right rearview mirror. As if on autopilot, as if I had been commanded to do so, I crossed the two lanes and pulled over onto the shoulder.

I quickly got out of my car and saw a car crushed against the concrete barrier separating the southbound and northbound lanes. Several other people parked on the shoulder near me, exited their cars, and ran to the mangled vehicle to open the passenger side. Inside a man was crumpled on the floor of his car. My fellow Samaritans pulled him from the wreckage and quickly carried him across the four lanes to where I stood. I fretted a bit as he was carried: If he had a spinal cord injury, moving him might make it worse. Yet our side of the road seemed the only safe place to lay him.

As he was placed on the ground near me, I saw him bleeding from the mouth. I feared the worst. I ran to my car and grabbed a yellow sweatsuit from my suitcase, covered the injured man with my sweatshirt, then rolled up the sweatpants to form a pillow between his head and the roadside gravel.

As I tucked the fabric under his head, he weakly muttered something strange, "No, no. Don't help me. Don't help me."

It suddenly struck me that the man might be suicidal. Could he have crashed on purpose? It seemed a stretch. But since I'd worked for three years on a psychiatric unit with suicidal patients, I didn't rule out the possibility that the accident hadn't been an accident.

A policeman appeared and asked all who had witnessed the accident to describe it. I shared my impression about the man's comments. Finally, there seemed to be little else I could do, so I got in my car and began driving home.

A few minutes later, I started to weep and shake uncontrollably and did so for the following hour. I realized that in the few seconds it had taken for the accident to happen, I could easily have been killed if I'd been surprised and lost control of my own car. But moments before the accident, a still, small voice had entered my head and prepared me, even helping me to create a plan to protect myself. Never before had I had a premonition like that. Why had that happened? Had God allowed that incident to remind me that my time on Earth might be fleeting, that at any moment I could be face-to-face with Christ?

I later realized that situation wasn't all about me.

The officer on duty phoned me at my home about a month later to tell me the injured man, desperately depressed, had indeed attempted to kill himself by driving directly into the concrete barrier. He'd since recovered from his injuries and gotten mental and emotional help. It occurred to me that rarely do officers call bystanders simply to reassure them their perceptions about an accident had been correct.

I began to see a greater picture.

God loved that desperate man and knew he was going to attempt to take his life. While allowing for his free will, God put at the ready someone who would recognize those strange few words, "Don't help me," as the opposite: a cry for help. God made certain that I would be on the freeway at that exact place and time and even be ready seconds before the accident.

I'd love to meet that man someday, but doubt I will this side of heaven. I wonder how he is treating his second chance at life? Does he see how God protected him, as I see He protected me?

Laurie Winslow Sargent

Like an Angel

Behold, I send an angel before you to keep you in the way.

Exodus 23:20

Returning to work as a nurse after an illness of six months was an ordeal in itself, but now the bitter cold and intense winds added to my stress. The employee entrance to the hospital was on the west side of the old brick building. The parking lot was on the east side across the street, so I'd have to cross the vast expanse to reach the entrance, with the unrelenting wind pushing me along.

My recent bout with pneumonia and the subsequent asthma attacks made me doubt if I could survive the walk on this subzero morning. After parking my car, I crossed the street and carefully battled the elements as I started for the entrance. Within seconds I realized it was hopeless. My weakened condition and the penetrating cold took my breath away. The icy winds blowing off of Lake Michigan pierced my lungs like shards of crystal. My chest tightened. I realized I would soon be in distress and unable to make the distance. I looked back at the warm car and contemplated whether to return to it or risk going ahead. The early morning darkness seemed to close in on me, and wafts of icy snow blew around my legs.

At that moment a shaft of light opened in the shadows on the side of the building, spilling light out of a small doorway onto the pavement ahead of me. A tall, lean figure in a long, threadbare woolen coat and knit cap stood silhouetted against the amber light from the doorway. He stood holding the door against the frigid air and waved for me to come in.

I could see the boiler room inside, an area prohibited to nursing personnel. I didn't want to be in trouble for being in a restricted area, but it was predawn, dark and cold, and I could barely breathe. My mind raced. The elderly black man raised his arm and motioned me toward him for the second time. I thanked him for getting me out of the cold and followed him past the steaming pipes of the boiler room. I had a sense of deep calm and peace as he spoke in soft tones and led me through the maze of pipes. As if he were trying to reassure me, he talked about the cold, the old pipes and cautioned me to watch my step. He opened a doorway and I was directly in front of my time clock.

I quickly punched my time card, then turned to thank him and to tell him that he had probably saved my life, but he was gone. As mysteriously as he came, he'd left.

For the weeks that followed I looked for him, but no one knew who he was. I had many questions for him: How did he know I was out there in the dark, since there were no windows on the door or on that side of the building? Why did he risk his job by giving me access to a restricted area? How did he know which was my time clock since various departments used different clocks? And why did no one know him?

The memory of that figure silhouetted against the light, motioning for me to follow, reminds me that angels come in many forms.

Naomi Follis

They Got In!

Heaven, the treasury of everlasting joy.

William Shakespeare

I was the younger of two boys and was literally a "mama's boy." Every morning that I was not on the road speaking, I had a routine. . . . I got up and went to 7-Eleven to get my mother a cup of coffee and a sausage biscuit. Mama loved a good sausage biscuit. If I was on the road, I made it a habit to call her every day no matter where I was in the world. Even in Australia and New Zealand, I got up extra early so I could talk to her awhile before she went to bed. When I got married, I bought a house a mile away from my mama so I could see her every day.

On April 11, 2003, my mother died. I was devastated. She was not only my mother, but also my advisor and my biggest supporter. We had a tremendous home-going celebration for her. It was the day before Easter, and she would have celebrated her seventy-fifth anniversary of being baptized that Easter, so it was fitting that we memorialized her that day. We brought in the best of the best singers and speakers. Les Brown (her almost-son) spoke, and I spoke and sang, and then my brother, Noble, the master musician and evangelist, spoke.

After the funeral I took the rest of the month of April off so my brother and I could get all of Mama's affairs in order. We worked closely every day and even traveled together to Virginia (where Mama was buried) a couple of times to make sure everything was perfect. We leaned on and loved each other, as always.

At the beginning of May, I felt like I was finally ready to get back to work. Then at 8:30 in the morning on May 6, I got a call from my niece saying Noble had collapsed! I rushed to his house and watched as the paramedics worked feverishly on him, and then we followed the ambulance to the hospital and waited for news. Finally a team of doctors came in and reported what we had dreaded. Noble had died of a massive heart attack.

I called my wife and told her to come pick me up because I was too shaken to drive. I got home and just sat at my desk with my head in my hands and cried, trying to fathom the fact that my big brother had died, twenty-five days after my mother. I could not believe this terrible storm was raging in my life; I did not know the storm was not over.

At 5:30 that same day, as I sat at my desk with my head still in my hands, the phone rang. My son picked it up, and I heard him gasp. He turned to me. "Dad, Aunt Rose just called to say that Granddad just died!" Eight hours after my brother and twenty-five days after my mother, my father-in-law, the Rev. Rivers S. Taylor, died. He was not just my wife's father, but my mentor, my friend, my surrogate dad. He had taken the time to talk to me over the years and taught me how to be a good father and husband. He was one of the people I respected most in the world, and now he too was gone. It was unbelievable, unfathomable, yet true.

In less than thirty days I had eulogized three of my closet allies and family members. I didn't know how I would be able to go on. I realized that no matter how positive a person is, death is always painful and always difficult. Yet, it is a road we all must walk sooner or later, so I walked the road and tried to hold on to my faith, even as my heart was breaking. I prayed for strength to somehow make it through this storm. I read the Book of Job over and over again and became acutely connected to him. I understood what it was like to be hit with one loss after another loss after another loss, without time to catch your breath, yet to fight through the pain, hold on to your faith and continue to give God the glory.

About a month after the funerals I was still struggling with the grief and the pain. One day I walked in my office and saw the message light on my phone. It was a voice from the past, the Rev. W. H. Law, an old friend of my mother's we hadn't seen in many years. I thought it was quite a coincidence that he would call now, because when Mama died, Noble and I tried to locate his number but we could not find it anywhere. So when Noble died I was doubly sad I could not reach him. Yet, here was a message, out of the blue, from Rev. Law. I was so stunned to hear his voice on the message that I could hardly dial the number.

When he answered, I was filled with emotion and said, "Rev. Law, this is Willie Jolley, I . . . I . . . am so glad to hear your voice. How are you?"

"Willie, I'm doing fine, son. Are you still doing the work of the Lord and speaking to people around the country?"

"Yes sir, I am."

"Very good, very good! You know, I tried calling your mom's house and got no answer. And then I tried to call Noble and got no answer, so I decided to give you a call and check on how everyone is doing. Tell me how your mother's doing? And how is your brother Noble?"

I was quiet for a few seconds, then managed to speak. "Well, Rev. Law, I hate to tell you this, but Mama has gone on to be with the Lord."

Rev. Law was silent for a second and then said, "What? Are you telling me that your mama got in?"

I swallowed hard. "And Noble passed away twenty-five days after Mama, and my father-in-law, Rev. Taylor, passed later the same day!"

Rev. Law exclaimed, "What? Are you telling me that your mama and your brother and your father-in-law, they all got in?"

Then I heard the phone drop. And in the background I heard this old feeble voice shouting, "Hallelujah! Hallelujah! They got in! They got in! They got in!"

He picked up the phone. "Willie Boy, I'm ninety-four years old, and I am still preaching and teaching and visiting the sick and the shut-in and those in the prisons and sending clothes and money to people all around the world. I get up early and go to bed late, working as hard as I can, doing all that I can to get in! Willie, you need to shout and celebrate, because your mama, your brother and your father-in-law—they got in!"

In those few minutes, it was like someone had lifted the burden and the grief off my shoulders and I was given a new lease on life. In only a few minutes this man had changed my whole perspective and made me realize that my mother and brother and father-in-law had gotten what we all want to get . . . they got in.

Yet, this is not the end of the story. I asked Rev. Law if he would like to get a copy of the video from Mama's funeral, where Noble gave one of the most powerful sermons I'd ever heard. He was quiet and then said softly, "Ahh . . . sure. Sure, send me the tape."

I got his address and repeated it to him, and he assured me it was correct and I told him I would get it out immediately. I hung up, addressed the package to him and sent the tape out in that day's mail.

A week or so later I was surprised when the package I sent to Rev. Law was returned to me in the mail. I looked to see why, and the message stated, "Returned to sender . . . undeliverable as addressed—no forwarding order on file." I couldn't believe it. I was confident I had the right address. I went to the computer and checked the address, and it was correct. So I picked up the phone to call Rev. Law to confirm the address one more time. When I called I heard, "The phone number is no longer in service." I dialed again: "The phone number is no longer in service."

I called the operator and asked her to check the number. She did and said that not only was it disconnected, but that number had not been working for a long time. I couldn't believe it. I had just spoken to Rev. Law at that number a week ago. How could it be?

And then it hit me. God had sent an angel in the form of Rev. W. H. Law to reach out to me and help relieve me of the overwhelming burden of grief I was bearing, and to let me know that all was well with my mother, my brother and my father-in-law. God had sent Rev. Law to let me know that "They got in! They got in! They got in!"

Willie Jolley

The Calling

But the manifestation of the Spirit is given to each one for the profit of all: for to one is given the word of wisdom through the Spirit, to another the word of knowledge through the same Spirit, to another faith by the same Spirit, to another gifts of healing by the same Spirit, to another the working of miracles. . . .

                                    1 Corinthians 12:7–10

There was nothing spoken. Words seemed unnecessary as I gazed in amazement at the most beautiful face I had ever seen in my life. I wanted to recall every detail of her divine face always. Yet now, when I try to describe it, I have no words, only the feeling of her divine presence. At the time, I didn't even question that this was happening to me. I allowed myself to feel the experience and accept the reality with peace and contentment.

I had just moved out of my parents' house when I saw this affirmation of my prayers, Mary, the Blessed Mother of God. My eyes opened, and I focused on her face. I couldn't believe she was appearing to me, of all people, and in my bedroom. It all seemed so surreal and so unbelievable. Shouldn't Mary, Mother of God, be appearing at the Vatican or some holy shrine? What possible business did she have with me?

A few months later I was returning from Italy, and as we were preparing to land in New York City a stranger approached me. The middle-aged woman said, "I just returned from a pilgrimage to Medjugorje, and I feel strongly that I need to give you this picture of Mary." You can imagine my shock as the emerald eyes of this compelling woman held me captive. Of the five hundred passengers on board the plane, she had chosen me.

Normally I would have put the picture in my room at home, but for some reason I decided to frame it and place it in my office at work. It sat on my desk for several years. One day a coworker approached me and told me he had always been drawn to the picture, but now he seemed to have a real connection. He said he was worried about his wife. She had been visiting a home in Yonkers, where oil supposedly was seeping from a statue of the Blessed Mother. The poor man thought his wife may have lost her mind.

I said softly, "It could be true." I added that I would be happy to investigate for him.

On my way that bright morning in April, I thought, *This place, Yonkers, is near the Bronx. If this miracle is indeed true, shouldn't it be happening in Rome or Jerusalem?* But as I drove up to the humble, freshly painted light blue house, I realized that, as usual, anything could happen. I would try to open my heart to the possibilities.

I arrived just before 7:00 A.M., a bit early for a Saturday, but I wanted to be sure that I had the right house, and I wanted time to sit and think about the situation. But before I could even examine the house, a tiny, wrinkled woman with silvery hair and coal-colored eyes approached my car, seemingly from out of nowhere. Her wide grin and quiet whisper assured me she was glad I came at such an early hour. In fact, it almost seemed as if she was expecting me.

As I entered her home, I was taken aback by the dizzying scent. The woman seemed to know. She grabbed my arm and whispered something in my ear. I turned to her as if in a dream and realized she had said "Rose-scented." She motioned me toward a small room off of the kitchen, and as I approached I hesitated on the threshold as the scent overwhelmed my senses. I had never experienced anything like it in my entire life—it was sweet yet pungent, light yet powerful. I can still remember how the scent seemed to surround me like a fog, lingering above my head, then flowing downward and around my body like a soft, comforting blanket.

And then I saw it. The statue of Mary was literally oozing with oil. My first instinct was to walk around trying to find the pump or electrical connection. This had to be some kind of hoax. But when I felt the oil, I knew it was real. When you come in contact with the divine, you know—you just know—and it was happening to me.

I made several visits to Muna's house after that. On one particular visit, she informed me that the oil had begun seeping from the walls and furniture as well as from the statue. She said she didn't know what to do about it, so she used cotton to catch some of the oil. She was giving away the cotton-soaked oil and offered me a bag. I accepted it, of course, brought home the precious gift, and placed it on my dresser. Little did I know that I soon would need to use it.

When I got the call several months later, I knew I had to go. I was afraid, but I knew I had to do it. The baby was only three months old when she contracted meningitis, and as I arrived at the hospital and saw all the long faces, I knew the prognosis was not a good one; she was not expected to live. If she did, the doctor said, there would be severe damage. I talked to the family, and every one of them was open to any prayers or any form of healing that might save their baby. I didn't know why or how I had come to be there or who in fact had known that I had the oil, but what I did know was that I had to use it for healing, and I had to do it now.

I walked into the immaculately white hospital room and saw the helpless child lying listlessly on the white linens, tubes coming from what seemed like every part of her tiny body. I had a very strange feeling that I knew exactly what to do. I walked over and touched her spine, gently rubbing the oil into her skin so as not to dislodge the tubes. She didn't move, but I swear I saw a twitch of a smile as I continued to rub the oil up and down her spine.

Two days later, little Eva was alert, nursing and back in her family's arms. The doctor called it a miracle. Today Eva is perfectly fine.

From the silence of that first vision, from the lack of words and the awe, from the feeling of the divine presence come the peace and the contentment in knowing that I have helped to bring joy and comfort to others. That I, an ordinary girl from New Jersey, have been given the gift of grace is still quite unbelievable to me, but I have accepted this calling. And when I am called again, I hope that I will hear and react accordingly, for if I have learned anything from this experience it is the old cliché—that it is in giving that you truly receive. And perhaps that is the true miracle.

Dawn J.
As told to Cheri Lomonte

The Red Sled

God also bearing witness both with signs and wonders, with various miracles, and gifts of the Holy Spirit, according to his will.

Hebrews 2:4

It was the day after Thanksgiving 2004, and all four of our kids were home together for the first time in a while. The house was alive with the sounds of our college-age kids teasing their little brother, Zach. The smell of holiday cooking filled the house. Outside, a fresh blanket of snow created a Norman Rockwell winter scene.

A substantial coating of snow is pretty rare by Thanksgiving, so twelve-year-old Zach pestered his two older brothers to take him sledding. Zach is a very persistent young man. In fact, after months of Zach badgering us for a cell phone, I had just recently relented and bought him one. Zach's persistent nature again paid off, and he, Jake and Mike took their sleds for an afternoon on the hills.

Marilee and I were in the midst of preparing supper and cleaning up after the tornado of the kids when the phone rang. It was Michael, our oldest, calling on Zach's cell phone. He asked if there were any Band-Aids in the car because Jake had cut himself sledding. I told him where they might be in the car and hung up. Just in case he was unable to find any, I laid a couple of Band-Aids on the table, ready to deliver if needed. Sure enough, the phone rang a few minutes later. "Dad," Mike stammered in apparent panic, "you need to get here right away. Jake is really hurt! He can't move!"

With a mother's intuition, Marilee knew before I said a word that there was something wrong.

"Where are you?" I asked Michael, trying to stay calm.

"I don't know," Mike replied. "Jake drove and I wasn't paying attention to where we were going."

I ran through a list of potential sledding spots in the area, but none sounded right to Michael. "Do you remember anything you passed on the way?" I asked.

"Groveland School," was all he could remember. I hung up and called 911. I asked dispatch to send an ambulance to the Groveland school parking lot, and Marilee and I jumped in the car.

We arrived at the school only moments before the ambulance and police. I explained our dilemma. Neither the police nor the emergency medical technicians could think of any sledding hills in the immediate area. I called Mike again and told him we were at Groveland with the ambulance and asked him if he could see a main road.

"I can't see any main road. It's all residential, but I can hear the sirens," he said.

If he could hear the sirens, we must be close, so I told him, "Try to flag us down!"

We headed east, hoping to spot them, with the police and ambulance following close behind. We drove just a few blocks when I saw something to our left.

Marilee said, "Someone is waving us down holding a red sled."

I looked left and saw no sign of the kids, but turned into a residential area, not really knowing where I was heading but knowing it was where I had to go. As we cleared the last house, I spotted the car. Then I saw them: three kids huddled by a wall at the base of the hill.

We ran to the unforgettable scene, followed by the ambulance and police. It appeared Jake had crashed the sled headfirst into the wall. The goose egg over his right eye was the size of a tennis ball and bleeding. He was conscious, but incoherent. He didn't know where he was, what day it was or what holiday we had just celebrated.

The EMTs secured his neck with a brace, gingerly lifted him onto a backboard, and rushed him to the hospital. After extensive X-rays of his head and neck, the doctor came in with the news. Jake had a bad concussion and a broken vertebra in his neck. It was hard to tell the extent of the damage until the swelling subsided, but he was able to move his legs and arms, though he had lost strength in his arms. The hospital rigged him up with a brace from his waist to his neck, and we settled in for the evening, awaiting more X-rays to determine the extent of his injuries and prognosis for recovery.

Over the next few days, family and friends lending prayers and support joined us at the hospital. We even got a surprise visit and prayers from Archbishop Flynn, who happened to be visiting someone else. The doctor finally came in and told us Jake would not need surgery but would need to continue to wear the brace.

On a follow-up visit, however, the doctor noticed Jake continuing to lose strength on his right side, so he ordered a CT scan. On Christmas Eve we got the results: The damage was more extensive than the doctors had thought; that's why Jake was losing strength in his arms. They recommended surgery soon.

I don't remember much about Christmas Eve services

that night, other than the love and support we received from the St. Therese Church choir in which we sing.

The surgery was performed a few days later. Doctors inserted a titanium plate into the front of his neck to fuse the break. It was the longest six hours of my life. The doctor met with us afterward and assured us the procedure had gone well, though the damage was much worse than originally expected. "In fact," he said, "I have never seen a break this bad before where the patient survived." It was then that I lost it. God surely has something in the future for Jake and was not ready to take him.

Our family spent New Year's Eve in the hospital while Jake recovered, and finally we had time to recollect the events on the day of the accident. We shuddered to think of what could have happened if we had not gotten there with the ambulance when we did and if Jake had tried to move with a broken neck. Marilee remarked how fortunate it was that the EMT crew had been so careful . . . and how lucky it was that Zach had brought his new cell phone to the hill.

"Who brings a cell phone sledding?" we teased.

"And how good it was that Zach flagged us down with the red sled when we were trying to find you," Marilee said.

At this, both Mike and Zach looked at us with an odd expression. "Mom, we didn't flag you down, and we didn't have a red sled. We were the only ones at that hill sledding that day."

We all sat in stunned silence for a long while, coming to the realization that they were not alone on the hill that day. Jake's recovery had been nothing short of a miracle, thanks to the fast and conscientious work of the ambulance crew, the doctors at the hospital, and to his guardian angel . . . with the red sled.

Dave Mahler

7
LOVE

And now abide faith, hope, love, these three; but the greatest of these is love.

1 Corinthians 13:13

A Knowing Friend

*F*riendship *improves happiness and abates misery, by doubling our joy and dividing our grief.*

Joseph Addison

A sigh of relief escaped me as the morning worship service ended and parents began to pick up their toddlers. Normally I enjoyed this every-other-Sunday responsibility, but today a new member was helping me. Phyllis was the mother of one of the toddlers, as was I. But our boys were opposites. My Aaron was quiet, calm and a little bigger than the other children. Her David was small, wiry and hyper.

Throughout the hour she never seemed to notice as he flew airplanes across the room, jumped on and off chairs, and zipped around with his built-in sirens going at full blast. Phyllis was pregnant too, she laughed a lot, and seemed to enjoy everybody and everything. Though I liked her, I couldn't relax in the midst of such confusion.

I left the nursery that morning with no intention of ever working with this woman again.

But being members of a small church, Phyllis and I saw each other every Sunday and Wednesday. We soon learned that we lived only blocks apart. Though I knew I should be sociable, I just couldn't imagine our boys getting along with each other. Phyllis, however, didn't give that a thought. She went right on building our new friendship and didn't seem to notice my reluctance to accept an invitation to her home for dinner—the invitation I knew I should have extended first.

Although I felt guilty, my husband and I had dinner with Phyllis and her husband, Neil, later that week. To my surprise, Aaron and David got along famously. After that we visited often in each other's homes and became best friends.

There was only one part of our friendship that made me uncomfortable. It was when Phyllis talked about Jeff, their son who had died right before David was born. I just didn't know how to respond to such a tragedy. Yet Phyllis was full of joy and love, not bitterness or anger. Though I couldn't understand it, she exhibited genuine peace.

Soon Phyllis gave birth to Jenny, and we all marveled at her beauty and newness. Several months later, our second son, Travis, was born. Everyone shared our happiness, especially Phyllis and Neil. But then, without warning, our secure, happy world fell apart. I called Phyllis from the hospital emergency room.

"It's Travis," I said, my voice and body shaking with fear. "They don't know if he'll make it."

"We'll be right there," she said quickly. And they were.

Travis died about eight hours later, due to a rare congenital heart condition doctors failed to diagnose at birth. It was sudden, shocking and the most painful thing we have ever experienced. Family and friends hovered over me, doing everything they could to help—but Phyllis *knew* how I felt. She encouraged me to talk and, on occasion, even expressed my feelings for me.

"You feel a great big hole in your heart," Phyllis said, "and there is nothing to fill it up."

Oh, how right she was. I had never felt such emptiness, such pain. On a card she wrote, "Now heaven is sweeter because Travis is there." Phyllis had traveled this road before me, and she comforted me in the following days, weeks and months with words, tears, hugs and even laughter. God had not left me alone.

A year later my husband accepted a job transfer to another city. I knew absolutely no one and deeply missed Phyllis and her sunny disposition. Since we were only an hour and a half apart, we continued to visit, celebrating the birth of her son, Mark, and the adoption of our daughter, Paula. But by the time I gave birth to our son, Jay, who had Down syndrome, Phyllis had moved to another state, ten hours away. However, cards, calls and sporadic visits continued. On any given day I might answer the phone and unexpectedly hear a familiar chuckle on the end of the line followed by, "Hi, Lou!" Time would slip away, and it was like we were young mothers again, living only blocks apart instead of being separated by several states.

Years passed, but our friendship remained strong. Then I received a late-night call from Jenny, Phyllis's grown-up daughter. Her mother had lost her battle with cancer. My heart wrenched with pain at the loss of my longtime friend, yet I had to smile as Jenny told me how her mother laughed and talked through her last night at the hospital and even heard angels singing.

And heaven is sweeter because Phyllis is there.

Louise Tucker Jones

A Mother's Love

Love is as strong as death.

Song of Solomon 8:6

It was a beautiful spring day when I arrived in Boston, where I would be one of the seminar speakers for a large inspirational event. When the director informed me that the keynote speaker wanted to meet me, I was both puzzled and pleased. I couldn't help but wonder, *Why does she want private time with me?*

After a busy morning, I was taken to the green room, where she and I hit it off immediately and had tea together. Then she told me that nearly twenty years ago she was speaking in Seattle and someone asked her to visit the hospital and pray with a young woman who was dying of liver cancer. "Cindy, I want to tell you what your husband's late wife and I talked about just before she died."

I gulped. I wasn't sure I was ready for this. I had never met Inka, Mike's wife of ten years. Of course I had gone to court and adopted her three small children after she died, but, though I hated to admit it, I had spent my seventeen years of marriage feeling alternately threatened by and grateful to her memory.

"It was hard," she continued. "Inka knew she was dying, and she told me so. And it was especially hard because she was so happy to finally have a baby girl along with her two little boys and it saddened her to realize that she wouldn't be able to raise her children. She went on to say that she knew Mike would marry again, and she wanted him to. But then she broke down and confessed that she was troubled because, while she suspected her four-year-old son and one-year-old daughter would be fine, she was so worried about the future of her six-year-old son, born with mental retardation. Inka cried, 'I just know there will never be a woman who can love him and help him with all his many special needs!'"

The speaker was holding my hands now as tears ran down my cheeks. "Cindy, I prayed with her then and there, asking God to give her peace and to provide for the husband and three precious children she would leave behind. We prayed that God would send a mother who could love and nurture the special needs of each of her children. And we prayed for that woman, whoever she might be, that God would give her all she needed for the great task at hand.

"After we prayed I looked at Inka's face, and it was full of peace as she told me, 'I know God has answered this prayer, and I can now release them all to Him.' I left the hospital room that day vowing to continue praying for the woman who would mother her children. You are the answer to that prayer—to Inka's prayer."

I sat alone in the green room, trying to sort out my feelings. I thought back to the years of raising my four children (we had another daughter five years after the adoption). The early years of our marriage had been so difficult, and I had faltered at times, wanting so desperately to be what each child needed and yet feeling so lacking. Sometimes I thought all I had going for me was the deep *desire* to be the kind of mother whose love could transform and teach and heal.

But my love could not do those things.

But God's love—and Inka's prayer—could. I thank God for His faithfulness in the lives of our children as they continue to grow as young adults who know and serve the Lord. Truly, God does answer prayers. I was merely the vessel.

Lucinda Secrest McDowell

Good Morning, I Love You!

*I love the house where you live, O Lord, the place
where your glory dwells.*

Psalm 26:8

When I speak, I tell my audiences, "As you get out of
bed each morning and stumble into the bathroom, jump-
start each day with a positive attitude. Look in the mirror
and say, 'Good morning. I love you. We're going to have a
great day!'"

Jill implemented this plan at home when their Sunday
scramble to church had become a war. It was a fight to get
her family out of bed and dressed. Yet, despite all her rav-
ing and ranting, they always arrived late, surrounded by
an angry cloud of silence.

One Sunday, she tried her new affirmation. She stood
over her husband's side of the bed and whispered in his
ear, "Good morning. I love you! We're going to have a
great day!"

Dan opened one eye and said, "What? Are you crazy?"

She just smiled and went across the hallway to their
five-year-old son's bedroom. She opened the door and

repeated the greeting. Jeff rolled over and said, "You're wrong, Mom. We're going to have a bad day!"

She smiled again and went across the hallway to check on Dan. She couldn't believe it. He was already up, dressing!

She trotted back to Jeff's room. To her surprise he too was out of bed, putting on his clothes!

That Sunday was the first in a month of Sundays they arrived at church on time and still liking one another.

So Jill turned this greeting into a morning ritual. She had been especially worried about her five-year-old's negative attitude. Each morning, she woke Jeff with her new greeting, and each morning, he gave her some sort of a cynical retort.

Her worries ended one morning when she opened his bedroom door and, before she could speak, Jeff looked up at her with his big brown eyes and said, "Good morning, Mom, I love you. We're going to have a great day!"

Margie Seyfer

My Vow

I knew I needed God, and I needed Him now. Ashamed and broken, I got down on my knees and begged Him. "Help me, Lord," I cried. "Forgive me, please forgive me, for my extramarital affair. For risking everything I loved. For pushing You out of my life."

Slowly, a peace I'd never known washed over me, proving what we all have been promised—God forgave me.

But could Allen forgive me? Could I ever forgive myself?

I knew if I trusted God, my marriage would be saved. That evening, armed with a new sense of hope, I asked my husband if we would try to work out our marriage or would we separate. With conviction he said, "I made a commitment to this marriage. I'm not going anywhere. If you want to leave, go ahead, but I'm not giving up."

I was stunned that he would want to stay, but told him I was willing to work it out as well. Then God's grace was shown through Allen when he said to me, "You are a great person. You stand up for your beliefs, and there could be no better mother for our children than you. I guess I didn't think you had any moral flaws. You made a mistake, and I forgive you."

The tears I thought I'd used up raced down my cheeks. My heart began to open up, and I wrapped my arms around my husband. I told him I would work hard to earn back his trust.

Changes began. We both agreed we needed God to be a part of our family, so we found a church and attended weekly. With the help of my newly found faith, I adjusted my attitude and began focusing on my family and all the blessings in my life. I made sure Allen knew where I was at all times and when he could expect me home. I went out of my way to prove he could trust me. His attitude changed as well. He didn't put in such long hours at work, and I could see he was really trying to get past this.

Even with all the positive changes, our relationship was still strained. The wound was still new and very deep. Life felt like a roller coaster. Everything would seem to be going along smoothly, and at any given time Allen would think about what I had done and all of the anger and hurt would surface. If the kids weren't around, he would go into a verbal rampage for a few minutes, or else he would just ignore me. I also got tired of giving a detailed itinerary every time I left the house, but knew it needed to be done. The guilt continued to weigh on my heart as I tried to maintain a positive attitude.

After a few months of emotional highs and lows, I questioned whether or not I could deal with it anymore. I wanted Allen to just forget what had happened so we could move on. It was then God showed us how to stay on the correct path. There were brochures at church giving information about an upcoming Marriage Encounter weekend. I brought it home and showed it to Allen. We decided we needed to do all we could to make our marriage work, so we signed up for the weekend.

On Friday we drove into the beautiful Rocky Mountains to a small retreat center. With our hopes high and our hearts still aching, we entered the weekend eager to heal. The days included a few large group meetings where the volunteer couples modeled good communication skills and then gave us a topic to take to our rooms to discuss. Over the course of the weekend Allen and I rehashed recent events and talked about the kids, money, forgiveness and our future. There were a lot of tears, hugs, smiles and closeness.

On Sunday afternoon, following a short, uplifting church service, all the couples were asked to stand in a circle and face their spouses. Allen and I did as we were told. We looked at each other and smiled, unsure of what was next. The minister announced, "Today you are going to relive a special moment in your lives. You are going to renew your wedding vows." My heart skipped a beat. I wanted to do this, but was Allen ready? The men went first. My insides were shaking. Allen took my hands, lovingly smiled and with tear-filled eyes, he vowed he would "take me to be his lawful wedded wife, in sickness and in health . . . till death do us part." My heart opened up, and I accepted him completely. Tears welled in my eyes. It was now my turn. I swallowed the lump in my throat and looked at this man who I had put through so much pain. It was hard to believe he still loved me, but I knew at that moment that he did. I gripped his hands tighter and vowed with all my heart to love him for the rest of my life, in good times and bad.

We sealed the vows with a kiss, and I knew at that moment our life together would last. We left behind the crumpled pieces of a troubled marriage and rebuilt a stronger foundation—this time, with God in the center.

Lyn MacKenzie

The Amazing Technicolor Dream Table

There is in all this cold and hollow world no fount of deep, strong, deathless love, save that within a mother's heart.

Felicia Hemans

Knowing that none of my four children could be home for Mother's Day, I was in a giant funk. Jeanne had called saying her teaching job prevented her from flying home. Julia and Michael, their spouses, and my five grandchildren, who all lived nearly one hundred miles away, planned to celebrate Mother's Day with me later in the week when I was in Madison giving a speech. And Andrew, my youngest, who was still in college, had just finished his finals and was busy working at a new job on campus.

So there I was, alone and lonely when I awoke on Mother's Day. After giving in to a few weepy moments before I got out of bed, I told myself that if I kept busy all day I wouldn't have time to continue my pity party. I got up, fixed my favorite French vanilla tea and enjoyed a huge mug of it out on the deck.

The day before, I'd scraped all the chipped varnish off the octagon-shaped wooden picnic table. I used my electric sander to sand the top smoother than a granite headstone, then painted it with white acrylic primer. As I drank my tea I decided to paint the second coat brown to match the deck floor when I got home from church.

Church that morning was not a very spiritual event for me as I sat there with all those grandmothers, mothers and children. Youngsters clamored to sit next to their honored mothers. I was sad and embarrassed to be sitting there alone, and glad that I'd picked a seat way in the back.

When Father Bob asked all the mothers to stand for a special blessing, my eyes filled with tears. Then I caught myself. *No! I will not give in to this self-pity stuff. I will do something to brighten my life and get out of this depressing mood.*

I looked up at the stained-glass windows and marveled at the many colors—bright red, yellow, turquoise, orange and many shades of green and blue. *That's it!* I thought excitedly, *I'll paint the picnic table in multicolored stripes!* I couldn't wait for the last song to finish.

At home I changed into my paint clothes and grabbed the box of acrylic paints. I counted the wood slats in the picnic table. Nineteen. I chose twenty small bottles of brightly colored paint, allowing one for the trim. Everything from bold primary colors of red, blue and yellow to pink, lavender, aqua, orange, purple, sage, berry and sand. I lined them all up and decided which colors would look good next to which colors and then numbered the bottles from one to twenty.

I started with purple and a small paintbrush. *Hey, this purple is the exact same color as that suit I bought for Jeanne when she lived in California!* Jeanne loved it and wore it often, and I saw her in it again some ten years later!

When I dipped my brush into the soft chocolate brown,

I thought of the brown walnut vanity I'd purchased for ten dollars at an estate sale in Denver in 1969 and refinished right in the middle of our tiny apartment living room. When my second daughter, Julia, was in sixth grade, I'd moved the vanity with the huge round mirror into her room as a special surprise. She loved it, took it with her to college and has since passed it on to her daughter.

The next color was bright Wisconsin Badger red. Boy, if that didn't remind me of Michael, my third child, who proudly wore the red University of Wisconsin Marching Band uniform for five years. Football Saturdays and post-season bowl games made wonderful adventures for Michael and me.

Next came a doublewide bright yellow center stripe, the same as Arizona State's school colors where my youngest child, Andrew, was a junior. The yellow patch also reminded me of the scorching Arizona sun the day I said good-bye to Andrew when I took him to campus his freshman year.

On that beautiful sunny Mother's Day, as I painted that picnic table, each color provided me with spectacular Technicolor memories of each of my children—memories that will live in my heart and on my deck forever.

Patricia Lorenz

Straight to the Heart

But Jesus called to them and said, "Let the little children come to me, and do not forbid them; for of such is the kingdom of God."

Luke 18:16

It was my three-year-old granddaughter, Jani, who gave me the answer to a question I'd been puzzling over.

I was visiting both of my daughters in the city that day and had taken the youngest grandchild for a walk. It was only by chance that we came upon that little park, complete with tiny hills and lovely greenery. It was like a little hideaway that not a soul knew was there. Even the sounds of traffic were blocked out.

Jani was enjoying the swing, and I sat back to watch her from a wooden bench flanked by shrubs. That was when I felt something indescribable yet so peaceful. What was that?

I knew I'd felt something like this before at our little country home, but even there I was unable to really identify it. That indescribable "feeling" was the reason we ended up buying the place.

We had been looking for an affordable home in the country and finally discovered an old farmhouse on an acre and a half thirty minutes from the city. The house had been built as a one-room schoolhouse in 1911. The basement was still a dirt cellar. Looking at this old place and thinking of giving up my beautiful home in the city with wall-to-wall carpets, a lovely fireplace and a bay window was a bit of a downer. I just didn't know if I could do it. Then we walked out across the land, and that beautiful feeling hit me. I commented to my husband, Shawn, "It feels so good here."

We looked through the old place and once again walked out in the yard, and as we traveled down a wee slope to an enclosure, that wondrous feeling again came upon me. "Shawn, I can't describe it, but it feels so good here!" I guess I told him that at least three or four times that day.

In the weeks and months that followed our purchase of the home, I received that feeling each time I walked in my enclosed "secret garden."

But I was not the only one to feel this warm energy. When we had company I encouraged each person to spend some alone time in the secret garden, and every single one reported the same warm, good feeling came over them. But what was it?

Now here I was in a park, and I had that same lovely, indescribable feeling.

I called over to my rambunctious little granddaughter. "Jani, come over here and sit with Grandma."

She climbed up on the park bench and managed to slow down her little energetic body long enough to listen.

"Jani, will you sit here with me and just close your eyes and see if you feel anything?"

Bless her, she didn't question my weird request; she merely closed her eyes and sat perfectly still. I waited to see if she would experience what I did. And then I kept waiting, as she seemed in no hurry to open her eyes. Strange inactivity for such a lively little bundle of energy!

Finally I could wait no longer. "Jani?" I touched her shoulder gently, encouraging her to open her eyes. As she did, I asked, "Jani, did you feel anything?"

Trust a child to cut through all the fuss and head straight for the heart. She broke out with a beautiful, radiant smile, and she said, "Oh Gamma, it feels like God giving me a hug!"

Ellie Braun-Haley

Don't be afraid. I'm your gardenin' angel.

Fred

I have enjoyed the happiness of the world. I have lived and loved.

Johann Christoph Friedrich von Schiller

Fred's family and friends gathered in the vestibule of the church. He'd taken care of Agnes, his wife, for their total life together except for the last year. That's when Agnes took over and nursed him—in the hospital and out. Now the ultimate caregiver, she greeted everyone with a hug and a few tears.

On a table rested memories of Fred's seventy-eight years: a college yearbook, a wedding picture, several pictures with grandsons, his military flag folded in a triangle and displayed in a wooden case, along with other sentimental memorabilia.

People milled around the table, gathered in small groups and talked softly. At last, they filed into the church.

The priest talked about how people always want to go home. Fred probably wanted to go home from the navy. He'd wanted to be with his family. Now he'd gone home; home to be with his Savior and other family members who preceded him in death. He would prepare a place to welcome Agnes and other friends and family home in the future.

After the Mass, the priest invited Fred's daughter to speak. Her words, muffled by tears, revealed the wonderful childhood she'd experienced with a loving dad. How he'd put her first by laying aside his plans so he could be involved in hers. Since her sons were too shy to speak for themselves, she read their letters, which expressed much the same sentiments. How Fred listened. How Fred shared. How Fred was always there for them. How Fred exemplified what each boy hoped to become.

Then Fred's son-in-law, Don, approached the podium. He expressed his closeness to Fred. He explained how they talked on the phone almost every day. When Don called to remind Fred of the boys' baseball games, Fred would always ask, "Want me to drive?"

Don frowned as he surveyed the congregation. "Fred was a terrible driver," he explained. "If other cars were going fifty miles an hour, Fred went eighty. If the others went eighty miles per hour, Fred went fifty. So when Fred asked if he should drive, I always answered 'No, Fred, I'll drive.'"

About that time, Don reached into his pocket and pulled out his cell phone. "Sorry," he told the congregation, "it must be really important."

People shuffled their feet, coughed, and several glanced at each other with obvious scorn on their faces.

"Hello," said Don. He paused.

"Oh, hi, Fred." Silence. "We're here at the church to celebrate your life." Don smiled. "Well, if you were here, we wouldn't be."

Fred's friends and family chuckled.

"Gee, Fred, I don't know how many people are here. Lots." Silence. "Yes, of course, Agnes has always been there for you." Silence. "Yes, they're here too. We'll all be leaving soon to go to your house for a party." Silence. "Yes, we remembered to order yellow roses." Silence. "Well, it's time for us to leave. I'm going to help host the party."

Don listened, then smiled. "No, Fred. I'll drive."

Linda L. Osmundson

Christmas Gift

It is the will, and not the gift that makes the giver.

Gotthold E. Lessing

The quiet stillness that ushers in Christmas Eve once again descends upon the Earth.

Mary finds herself alone on this most holy night, for the first time in fifty-three years. As she sits staring at the dancing flames in the fireplace, a cascade of memories engulfs her. Was it really almost fifty-five years ago that she first saw him standing there in his baseball uniform? Her heart still skips a beat as she remembers that first look of love in his eyes. The years had held many valleys and peaks for them as they raised their four children. Her mind wanders back again to a time long ago when she first noticed a limp that would continue to worsen until it stole his ability to walk. Through the tears she remembers that it never changed their love and devotion for one another, or lessened their involvement with family and friends. Alex was always there doing all that he could and more. His courage was contagious.

Alex lays awake listening to the sounds of night as it
descends on the acute care facility that is to be his home
for the next several weeks. He remembers Christmas Eves
long past—the family attending midnight Mass, the rush
to get home and the excitement of four children as they
unwrapped their gifts. Most of all he thinks of Mary, his
bride of fifty-three years. How could he ever express his
love to her and what it meant to have her stand beside
him through all the difficult days as a disease stole his
walking and working? She was always there, ready to take
on any project that needed attention and doing it so it left
his self-esteem intact. She always looked for ways to make
his life easier, purchasing a scooter for him so he could go
for walks with her and coach his beloved softball team.
Later, she made sure all his living arrangements met and
exceeded his needs. Now this year they are separated for
the first time on Christmas Eve, and it breaks his heart. For
weeks he has been thinking about what he could do to
express his love to his wife, and now with the help of his
youngest daughter his idea is about to come to life.

It's 3:00 A.M. on Christmas, and Robin checks one last
time to make sure she has everything. Snowfall in the
silence is almost sacred. As Robin heads down Interstate
74 on her way to Milwaukee, the car is enveloped in a
world of white, and the beautiful melody of familiar
Christmas carols plays softly in the background. In the
distance she sees sleeping farms, many framed in twinkling lights. As the miles slip by so do the years, and Robin
finds herself lost in the memories of Christmases past.
Those memories, however, don't begin to compare with
the anticipation she feels for the Christmas that is about to
happen.

For some years Robin had been doing the shopping for
her dad, since he can no longer shop for his wife. Several
weeks before Christmas, Robin had asked what he would

like to get Mary this year if he could give her anything he wanted. Alex shared with his daughter how much her mom meant to him and how blessed he was to have someone who cared for his every need before he even asked. He said he would give her the world if he could. Together they created the next-best idea. Robin could almost see her dad smiling through the phone as his voice held the excitement of a child who had just found the perfect gift. It was settled. Robin would purchase it and deliver it to her dad early on Christmas morning. Over the next few weeks they talked countless times about how she would get it to him and what he was going to say.

The time has now arrived. Robin sneaks into her dad's room and slips him the small box, then quietly tiptoes out as her mom arrives. Robin stays close enough to hear him try repeatedly to share what is in his heart, but each time he is overcome with emotion. Finally, Robin steps to the bed and repeats the words her dad has been rehearsing for weeks. "Mary, I love you so much, and I can never thank you for all you do for me. I want you to be my wife for all eternity."

As Robin helps him with his words, Alex slips the sparkling diamond ring onto Mary's finger. For one brief moment the years slip away, and there stand that handsome young man and his beautiful bride, pledging their love to each other. They had made it, for better or worse, in good times and bad, in sickness and in health, and because Christ was the center of their lives they would share their love for all eternity.

Laura Stephenson

"Excuse me, did I just hear somebody say
'This is the night of the deer savior's birth'?"

8

DIVINE GUIDANCE

Show me your ways, O Lord, teach me your paths, lead me in your truth and teach me, for you are the God of my salvation; on you I wait all day.

Psalm 25:4–4

Desperate Hope

Hope is the thing with feathers
That perches in the soul,
And sings the tunes without the words,
And never stops at all.

Emily Dickinson

As the train rumbled past the East Coast countryside taking my daughter and me to New York City for a mother/daughter vacation, my thoughts were as piercing as the screeching wheels of the train. *Why did he do it? Why did Greg take his own life?* He was a distant relative whom I rarely saw, yet the news that Greg had committed suicide made tears spring into my eyes and a deep sadness fill my heart. Relatives asked, "How could anyone be that hopeless and helpless?"

But I knew.

As I glanced over at my twenty-eight-year-old daughter napping next to me on the double seat, I realized with a force I hadn't felt for a long time that if I'd taken my life, I would not have the fabulous mother-daughter relationship I now enjoyed with my daughter.

Twenty-six years ago, I couldn't imagine that would ever happen. The hopelessness and helplessness had been building for months. Larry and I had celebrated our seventh anniversary, but it wasn't a happy occasion. Unwisely, I'd asked again, "Larry, why do you work so many hours? Having a two-year-old and a newborn is such hard work; I need you to help me."

He frowned. "Kathy, I've tried to help you see that I'm working all these hours to secure our financial future. That's not easy on a cop's wages." Silence surrounded us like a dense fog.

The next day, tensions escalated. *Will we get a divorce? Why can't we talk? We used to be so in love.* Just as quickly, I prayed, "Lord, what's wrong?"

That question was a prayer I prayed many times, both about my marriage and my reactions to our two-year-old daughter, Darcy. My anger toward her seemed to explode more often when I felt rejected by Larry. Her strong-willed nature, which resisted my toilet training plan and resulted in constant temper tantrums, wore me down. My reactions had deteriorated into angry spankings.

One desperate day my rage was out of control. I ran into my bedroom and slammed the door behind me. *I'm no kind of mother! I can't believe I did that!*

Then I suddenly remembered where Larry stored his off-duty service revolver.

The gun! That's the answer! The gun! A tiny, sinister voice in my head whispered, *Take your life. It's hopeless. Nothing has changed for months even though I've prayed over and over again; it's only gotten worse. God doesn't care. Otherwise He would instantaneously deliver me from my anger and heal our marriage. Larry hates me. I hate him and my life.*

With trembling hands, I opened the locked drawer and almost gasped when the gleam from the shiny barrel of the gun glinted at me so invitingly. *Darcy is better off without a mother like me. I'm ruining her for life.*

Seconds clicked off and then I reached for the cold revolver. But then a new thought suddenly popped into my mind. *What will people think of Jesus if they hear that Kathy Miller took her life?*

My hand stopped. The faces of the women in the neighborhood Bible study I led flitted before me. My family members who didn't know Christ came to mind. I thought of my neighbors I had witnessed to. *Oh, Lord, I don't care about my reputation, but I do care about Yours!*

I slammed the drawer shut and fell to my knees.

The concern about Jesus' reputation saved my life that day, and I knew it was prompted by the Holy Spirit.

I didn't have any hope at that point, but in the following months God proved Himself faithful by revealing the underlying causes of my anger, giving me patience to be a loving mom and then healing my relationship with Larry. I read in Ephesians 4:26, "Be angry, and yet do not sin. . . ." I realized that it wasn't sinful to feel angry, but it was sinful to respond in a rage or in bitterness. So I stopped trying to bury my anger and learned to express it constructively. I quit using it as a disciplinary tool and began consistently giving consequences for Darcy's misbehavior. I released Larry from holding the key to my joy and contentment and counted on God for that. As a result, Larry wanted to spend more time with me.

My reverie snapped back to the present as the train began slowing for the next stop. I looked over at my daughter, who had awakened and was gazing out the window. I smiled as I thought of her beautiful wedding we'd all enjoyed four years earlier. *I wouldn't have been there if I'd committed suicide!* The thought struck me so forcefully, like never before. Then I recalled all the happy family events I would have missed if I'd taken my life, including our son's graduation from college—despite his learning disabilities. I thought of the opportunities I'd had to speak in thirty states and five foreign countries and the forty-eight books I'd authored. I smiled thinking of Larry, my best friend, and our glorious love affair; we'd recently celebrated our thirty-second anniversary. The list went on and on. If I'd used that gun that day, I wouldn't have been at all those family events, but Larry's second wife may have been. And how my daughter and son would have grieved over a missing mother who seemed to be more absorbed in her own pain than them.

Yes, I understood how Greg could have felt so little hope—in fact, no hope at all. How I wish I could have shared with him that there is always hope, and God is faithful if we will hold on to His promises.

My daughter faced me on the train. "Mom, I'm so excited we're going to New York City together. I wouldn't have missed this for anything."

"Me neither, honey. Me neither."

Kathy Collard Miller

Doorways of Pain

The best way out is always through.

Robert Frost

If someone had told me years ago that God would use the pain of my life to help other people, I would never have believed it. I personally experienced so much emotional pain during the first years of my life that I grew weary of hurting. I was sexually, physically and emotionally abused from the time I can remember until I finally left home at age eighteen.

Though I accepted the Lord at age nine, I didn't have a life-changing relationship with Him until after Dave and I were married. It seemed my whole married life was a process of trying to get better.

I attempted to find healing, but could not understand why the process had to be so torturous. It seemed every time I made any progress, God would bring me into a new phase of recovery that always meant more pain. As I prayed about it, the Lord gave me a vision. In my heart, I saw a series of doorways, one after another. Each represented a traumatic, painful event in my life. God showed me that each one of them—such as being sexually abused at home, ridiculed at school because I was overweight or betrayed by friends at church—was a doorway of pain through which I had to pass. I saw that I'd been hiding behind many such doorways of pain, unable to free myself. To be led into freedom, I had to pass back through the same doorways of pain to get to the other side.

First, there was the pain of the abuse and then the agony from the memory of it.

My father was the main source. I was always terrified of him, even as a grown woman with four children of my own.

I was forty-seven years old before the Lord led me to confront him—face-to-face with one of my doorways of pain. I knew that I could either go back through it and come out free on the other side, or I could stay behind it, hiding and afraid of him.

Finally, I confronted my father, in obedience and by faith, but not without fear. He sat expressionless, refusing to accept responsibility for his acts or to face how devastating his behavior was to my life. He barely responded when I told him I forgave him.

Our relationship remained strained and uncomfortable, in spite of my efforts to mend it. Dave and I even obeyed the leading of the Lord and moved him and Mom to a nice home near us where we could care for their needs.

But God wasn't done with me yet. He dealt with me about His command to "honor your father and mother."

"For what?" I asked. Though I was willing to obey, I was baffled as to how to go about it. I visited them, called them and prayed for them. Then He told me to honor them from my heart for giving me life and caring for me.

Shortly thereafter, I heard some of my family members were encouraging them to watch my TV broadcast. I could not imagine what it would do to them if they tuned in and heard me tell of my abusive childhood. I did not want to hurt them, yet I knew that sharing my background really helped people. Dave, the kids and I had a family conference and decided that even though it would risk what little relationship I had with my parents, I had to follow God's will for my life.

We went to visit them and I told the truth, explaining that I was not sharing my story to hurt them, but that I had no choice if I was to help the people God had called me to help. They sat and listened calmly with no anger, no accusations, no running from the truth. My father explained that he had encountered abuse as a child also and that he was acting out of what he had learned. He claimed he had been controlled and could not have prevented himself from what he was doing. He said he was sorry and that I could share whatever I needed in my programs. Then he looked up at me and said, "I want to build a relationship with you, to try to be your father and your friend."

From that day forth, we saw some changes in him. He went to church on Easter or Christmas, but he never really said too much about it. He clearly had not given his heart to Jesus and he was still difficult to get along with. My mother told me she felt God was dealing with him, that she'd found him several times sitting on the edge of the bed crying and repeating, "I'm so ashamed of what I did to Joyce. I treated her so bad, and she's been so good to me."

Not long after that, on Thanksgiving Day, we received a call from Mother. "Dad is too sick to come to your house for dinner, but he wants you and Dave to please come over so he can talk to you about something."

The minute we walked into the room, Dad started crying. "I just need to tell you how really sorry I am for what I did to you. I have wanted to say something since you moved us near to you three years ago, but I just didn't have the guts." Then he wept with true repentance. No more excuses. No more explanations for why he did it—just sorrow that he had.

"It's all right, Daddy, I forgive you," I cried, wrapping my arms around him.

He looked up at Dave. "Can you forgive me too?" Dave wrapped his arms around us both.

I took Dad's calloused hand in mine. "Do you want to receive Christ as your Savior?"

"Yes," he sobbed.

I knelt beside him. Together we prayed the sinner's prayer . . . on Thanksgiving morning!

For days, though, Dad struggled with doubt, thinking he had been too bad to be forgiven. Finally he accepted it and asked, "Can I be baptized?"

What a privilege for me to baptize him in front of hundreds of witnesses at the Dream Center, our inner-city church in St. Louis!

Today Dad is a new man, one of the sweetest I know.

I'm thankful I found the courage to walk back through my doorway of pain. God brought healing to thousands of people—and my family—on the other side of the door.

Joyce Meyer

I Think I Can . . .

The steps of a man are established by the Lord;
And He delights in his way.
When he falls, he shall not be hurled headlong;
Because the Lord is the One who holds his hand.

Psalm 37:23-24

What appeared to be a simple sport turned into an ordeal.

It began when my husband, Jim, decided to introduce our family to the joys of snow skiing. After a couple of practice runs, our teenage son and daughter caught on quickly and zoomed off for higher ground, leaving us on the bunny slope in a cloud of powder.

Feeling like the famous red hen in my scarlet ski jacket, I sat beside Jim in the lift chair and as we ascended, I thought, *How romantic. Here we are on this beautiful snow-covered slope and the instructions sound so easy, too. The guide said, "All you have to do is lean forward and ski away."*

I glanced at my husband and he smiled, seeming confident, calm and relaxed. But I barely had time to adjust goggles, wipe my nose, and check my gloves before looking up and seeing the sign. "Jim!" I nervously gasped, "It says unload here!"

Jim leaned forward and skied off to one side. *But I'm not ready yet!* Though my pounding heart was saying, *STOP! STOP! STOP!* the monster chair kept right on moving. When I tried to stand, my backside froze to the seat. Finally, I courageously grabbed the metal arm, gave a big heave-ho and lunged forward. After a brief zip on the skis, I landed on my bottom and slid into a heap.

Two ski patrol guys promptly zigzagged out of their small cedar house. "Are you okay?" they asked while hoisting me out of the way of oncoming skiers.

"Oh, I'm fine. Thanks."

Determined, I stood up, brushed off the snow, straightened my hat, and pointed my skis downhill. At first I moved slowly. Then I began picking up speed. About halfway down I lost all semblance of control. Whizzing past other skiers, the only emergency measure I could think of was to scream, "Watch out! Here I come!"

Finally, in the midst of my panic, I remembered the instructor's warning, "To slow down, make a wedge." So I pushed my heels outward and tucked my toes inward. This creative move locked the front of my skis together, at which point I fell like a domino face first into the thick, fluffy snow.

Somehow I survived one descent, and then, in spite of my dwindling confidence, I returned to the bunny lift. I was so anxious about departing the lift that I fell off again. And again. Once, as we neared the patrol house, I heard the guides moan, "Oh no, here she comes again!" Poor fellas.

Near the end of the day, I thought *I must learn how to get off this lift or I'll never see the mountaintop.* Remembering *The Little Engine That Could,* I began telling myself, *I think I can, I think I can.*

After my last splat, another woman near my vintage advised, "Honey, if you'll scoot your bottom up to the edge of the chair before you unload, it'll be easier to stay up."

To my utter amazement and delight, it worked! The next time, I inched toward the front of the seat and at just the right time, I slid off and, while wobbling in all directions, skied away on my own! The guides shouted, "Yea, she made it!"—and everyone else joined in, including me— "Yea, I made it!"

My ecstasy was short-lived. The next morning, every muscle in my body ached. As I gingerly strained my way up the slope, I kept my eyes on the mountaintop and thought, *Somehow, I'm going to get up there.*

We began the day with another ski lesson, and our instructor, Rusty, put us to a test. He glided to the bottom of the hill and asked each one to ski down so he could evaluate our form and assign us to the appropriate class.

Most in the group were poised and controlled. Then came my turn. I began cautiously, but quickly approached Olympic speed. Instead of remembering "the wedge" that might have averted my kamikaze run, I barely missed Rusty by veering off to one side where I maneuvered 180 degrees and, in very unladylike fashion, crash-landed into the orange net fence. Rusty assigned everyone else to an intermediate class, then he held out his hand and said, "Come with me."

He helped me to my feet and flashed a good-natured grin. "I see you need a little help with your parallel turns." No kidding. I wanted to melt into the snow and disappear. But Rusty spent a few hours instructing and encouraging me. I thought, *I'm so glad I hit that fence. Look at all the individual attention I'm getting!*

On the third day, Jim and I finally took the lift to the top! What a spectacular view. The hush of fresh powder, punctuated by the aroma of evergreens, lent an awesome air to the blanketed valley below. I felt like singing "How Great Thou Art," closely followed by "The Hallelujah Chorus" to celebrate my victory.

As I stood soaking up the beauty, I pondered how life, in many ways, reminds me of skiing. We have lots of ups and downs, but if we keep our eyes on the Maker of Mountains, He'll pick us up when we fall, and sometimes He'll even carry us. Like Rusty, God knows when we need personal attention. Like Jim, He is patient and kind. And even when it feels like a sky full of snow is falling on our heads, and we feel we can't make it to the top, it's reassuring to know *He thinks I can, He thinks I can.*

Fran Caffey Sandin

Stranger in Our House

For I was hungry and you gave me food; I was thirsty and you gave me drink; I was a stranger and you took me in.

Matthew 25:35

"We need you to come get Mom earlier than planned," the e-mail read.

We made a hurried trip to bring Allen's recently widowed mother to our home to give his brother and sister-in-law a four-month break, a break they sorely needed. Allen's mother was a difficult woman.

Our conversation on the way to Arizona centered on how little we knew her. He had joined the navy at eighteen to get away from an abusive, unhappy home. In spite of letters and trips to see her, there had been no close communication between them in over forty years. "It would be easier to take in someone with no ties to the past," my husband lamented, "so bad memories wouldn't cloud our feelings now."

We knew the only way we'd be able to cope with having this stranger in our home would be for God to give us grace each day.

For over thirty years she'd lived with a husband who found jobs for her and kept her from making friends. When he died, he left her penniless with debts to pay. "Mom's scared to go home with you, because your lives are so different from what she's used to. She's afraid she won't fit in," our sister-in-law told us.

Hoping for a positive start, Allen said, "We'll take the scenic route home through the mountains, Mom, so it will be a mini-vacation."

Mom had never been off the main highways in all her eighty-three years, and was soon squealing with delight at the beauty and magnificence of the mountain scenery.

We settled her into our spare bedroom, but in spite of our efforts, her lifelong negativity prevailed. She insisted she wanted to help around the house, and that desire became difficult to deal with at times as she hovered around us in our small galley kitchen. "I could have done that," was her constant refrain. She'd sit and pout when I asked her to let me by so I could open the refrigerator door, or didn't come up with a task for her to do. My already busy life was stressed by the added job of being activity director for her.

Some moments were better. After dirtying nearly every pan as she prepared her specialties of cornbread, stuffed peppers and lasagna, she helped with the cleanup. The challenge of filling the coffee pot with exactly eight cups of water for the next morning's breakfast coffee made her giggle with delight.

She loved to hang out laundry to dry as she had years ago, but was angered because we carried the baskets of wet clothes down the steps to the lines. "How dare you!" she yelled at me as I lugged a heavy basket of wet jeans.

"How dare I what?" I replied in a tone of voice that sent her sulking to her chair. A few minutes later I apologized and explained once again why I carried it for her.

But we didn't give up. Knowing she hadn't had out-
ings of any kind for years, we took her to church, muse-
ums, art galleries and concerts to stimulate her mind. She
was amazed when our Bible study group accepted her
and called her by name. One night when everyone was
laughing uproariously, she whispered, "This is Bible
study?"

When Easter came, I made nametags for the fifteen of us
gathered around our table, hoping she would keep the
names of her great-grandchildren straight. In spite of the
nametags, she continually called our sons by the wrong
name. "Just like when we were kids, she still doesn't care,
does she?" our oldest son remarked.

Before long, it was evident her memory was going. She
would ask a question, get an answer and immediately ask
the same question. If we were going to be gone at meal-
time, she'd say, "Don't worry, I'll find something." As we
were leaving she'd ask, "What can I eat?"

It seemed that no matter what we did, we could not
please her. She had fussed about being cold, until the
ninety-degree days of summer arrived, then she complained endlessly about being too hot. Washing her hands
and showering became almost nonexistent chores.
Reminders were met with icy glares and the slamming of
her bedroom door. She began leaving her door open as she
dressed, much to the consternation of Allen. Her clothes
hamper remained empty, yet she insisted she had
changed her clothes. When she reverted back to her old
ways and off-color language, we retreated to our offices to
escape. With no happy memories to link us to her, the
days were often filled with frustrations for us.

My prayer each day was for God to give me grace to be
the person He wanted me to be. At times, I retreated to the
privacy of the basement, where I would cry out, "God,
love her through me because I don't want to!"

One night, after one of her crankiest days, I gave her the hug she'd come to expect as we said goodnight. She asked, "Why are you so good to me?" The only answer I could give was, "It is God loving you through me." I kept trying my best to involve her. One day I asked if she would like to help me can peaches. "Oh, yes! I haven't done that in nearly fifty years." As she slowly slipped the peels away and removed the pit, her mood brightened as she recalled the many jars of fruit and vegetables she used to put up when she lived on the farm.

Seeing her embroider and crochet gifts to give to the girls in her family was like watching a butterfly emerge from its cocoon. Reading our daily devotional, magazines and inspirational books led to a new outlook on life for her.

Shortly before her four months with us were over, she said, "I have just learned how to live, and it is all because of you and Allen. It took me all these years to see a better way."

I hugged her goodnight, breathed a prayer of thanksgiving and recalled God's word. "I was a stranger and you took Me in. . . . "

Anna Aughenbaugh

Caregiving

The only thing that counts is faith expressing itself through love.

Galatians 5:6

"I spend all my time trying to keep the stress off you!"

"Well, don't worry about me!" I shouted and slammed the car door. My harsh comments echoed in my mind. When I reached the elementary school where I taught second grade, I burst into tears. Ever since Emmitt's retirement, he had taken care of my relatives. He sat up during the long nights at the hospital. He checked on my relatives during the day. He even cooked meals and shared when I came home exhausted.

At school I ran to the phone and whispered, "I'm so sorry. Forgive me. I love you so! I'm just so tired."

What an excuse! He's the one who should be tired.

During the last twelve years, my husband and I have been caregivers to my mom, dad, two aunts and an uncle. Thankfully, it didn't happen all at once, but it seemed we never had time to recuperate or to have time alone with each other.

"Lord, please help us," I cried. As the only daughter of my parents, I felt a tremendous responsibility. My aunts and uncle had no children, and there was no way I could abandon any of them. We would never have done that anyway.

After a long, hard day at school that day, I came home to a clean house and a hot meal. Even though Emmitt had made "the rounds" overseeing relatives, he had time to take care of me too!

Right then and there God began to get my attention! He reminded me that He gave me this wonderful husband thirty years ago. Loving memories still linger. One Christmas, Emmitt took me in his arms and said, "Next to Jesus, you are my special gift." I remember the times he put his needs aside to buy things for our three sons and me. I could never take for granted his whispers all through the night: "I love you!"

My shame overpowered me. "Lord, show me what I can do. I never want to take Emmitt's love for granted. Thank you for helping us care for my relatives, but please show me what I can do to make the load lighter."

At bedtime that night, I asked Emmitt to pray with me. I thanked God for my husband and what he meant to me. Emmitt prayed too, and it cemented my marriage as nothing else could. It made the impatience, exhaustion and frustration of caregiving bearable. Our heartfelt prayers for guidance, wisdom and strength gave us courage and brought us closer together.

I started taping love notes on his bathroom mirror and brought him coffee in bed. I made it a point to hold his hand and say "I love you" often. I remembered those heart-throbbing times before marriage. Emmitt won me with his flirty ways. Now, I decided, it's my time to flirt!

One morning, Emmitt seemed a little grumpy from loss of sleep after sitting with my aunt all night at the hospital.

I embraced him and said, "I bet you a quarter I can't kiss you."

"Okay," he said smiling.

"You win!" I planted a big kiss on him. That did wonders!

I found out a loving glance from across the room, even while sitting up with a loved one, doesn't go unnoticed. It cushions the stress and strain.

I had let my sense of humor dwindle. I turned that around that night too. Laughter is good for the soul. "A merry heart has a continual feast" (even in caregiving, I found out).

The last time my uncle required hospital care, we both felt the stress. The doctor walked in and Uncle Steve simply exclaimed, "I guess I need a tree to fall on my head."

The doctor quickly replied, "If it did, it would hurt the tree!" Emmitt and I laughed for a long time, and that dispelled a lot of tension.

We are thankful for the Lord's guidance in reminding us not to forget all the good things, to be thankful for family, friends, doctors and nurses. They minister to hurting people daily.

God brought other things to our attention. Maintaining a positive attitude in the midst of negativity may be hard to do, but persistently emphasizing the good brings benefits to everyone.

Finally, we renewed our trust in God. In a crisis, there is confusion and threatening events all around. Worrying robs peace, which can transmit to the loved one. A calm assurance gives everyone needed rest.

As God allowed a wonderful growth in Emmitt's faith and mine, we both discovered the greatest sense of comfort. Through understanding God's love, both of us have come to know that yes, love sacrifices, but love is also the greatest thing in the world.

While other people our age talk about their recent cruises, vacations and travel excursions, I look at my husband and whisper softly, "Thank you, Lord, for this wonderful, caring man."

I'm thankful for all the relatives we cared for. It not only proved the strength of our marriage, but the depths of our love for others.

Joan Clayton

The Parable of the Coffee Filter

A soft answer turns away wrath, but a harsh word stirs up anger.

Proverbs 15:1

My brother Dan said, "I'm going home! Your bickering is making me crazy. You two fight constantly—and it wears me out."

I defended our behavior, "Hey, it's not like we disagree about *everything*. Ron and I agree on all the major issues. We hardly ever fight about 'big stuff' like where to go to church, how to raise Nick or who's a better driver (me); we just disagree about the 'little stuff.'"

He sighed and said, "Well, I'm sick of hearing you go to war over where to put the towel rack, which TV shows to watch or who did—or didn't—use a coaster. It's all dumb stuff. None of it will matter a year from now. I can tell that Ron is really mad by the way he *stomped* up the stairs. Why did you have to criticize the way he mowed the lawn? I know it wasn't perfect, but couldn't you just let it go?"

"No," I replied. "We are having company tomorrow, and

I want the yard to be perfect. So I told him to fix it, big deal! Anyway, I won, because he remowed it."

Dan shook his head, "If you keep this up, you may win the arguments, but lose your husband."

I slugged his arm. "Oh, stop being so melodramatic!"

The next evening, Ron and I went out to dinner with some friends we hadn't seen in several years. We remembered Carl as being funny and outgoing, but he seemed rather quiet and looked exhausted. His wife, Beth, did most of the talking. She told us about her fabulous accomplishments and then endlessly bragged about her brilliant, Mensa-bound children. She only mentioned Carl to criticize him.

After we ordered our dinner, she said, "Carl, I saw you flirting with that waitress!" (He wasn't.)

"Caarrrlll," she whined, "can't you do anything right? You are holding your fork like a little kid!" (He was.)

When he mispronounced an item on the dessert menu, she said, "No wonder you flunked out of college, you can't read!" She laughed so hard that she snorted, but she was the only one laughing.

Carl didn't even respond. He just looked over at us with an empty face and a blank stare. Then he shrugged his sad shoulders. The rest of the evening was oppressive as she continued to harangue and harass him about almost everything he said or did. I thought, *I wonder if this is how my brother feels when I criticize Ron.*

We said good-bye to Beth and Carl and left the restaurant in silence. When we got in the car, I spoke first. "Do I sound like her?"

"You're not *that* bad."

"How bad am I?"

"Pretty bad," he half-whispered.

The next morning, as I poured water into the coffee pot, I looked over at my "Devotions for Wives" calendar.

"The wise woman builds her house, but the foolish tears it down with her own hands." *Or with her own mouth,* I thought.

"A nagging wife annoys like a constant dripping." *How can I stop this horrible pattern?*

"Put a guard over my mouth that I may not sin with it." *Oh Lord, show me how!*

I carefully spooned the vanilla nut decaf into the pot as I remembered the day I forgot the filter. The coffee was bitter and full of undrinkable grounds. I had to throw it away.

I thought, *The coffee, without filtering, is like my coarse and bitter speech.*

I prayed, "Oh, please Lord, install a filter between my brain and my mouth. Help me to choose my words carefully and speak with smooth and mellow tones. Thank you for teaching me the 'Parable of the Coffee Filter.' I won't forget it."

An hour later, Ron timidly asked, "What do you think about moving the couch over by the window? We'll be able to see the TV better."

My first thought was to tell him why that was a dumb idea. *The couch will fade if you put it in the sunlight, and besides, you already watch too much TV.* But instead of my usual hasty reply, I let the coarse thoughts drip through my newly installed filter and calmly said, "That might be a good idea. Let's try it for a few days and see if we like it. I'll help you move it."

He lifted his end of the sofa in stunned silence. Once we had it in place, he asked with concern, "Are you okay? Do you have a headache?"

I chuckled, "I'm great honey, never better. Can I get you a cup of coffee?"

Ron and I recently celebrated our twenty-fifth wedding anniversary, and I am happy to report that my "filter" is still in place (though it occasionally springs a leak). I've also expanded the filter principle beyond my marriage and found that it's especially useful when speaking to telemarketers, traffic cops and teenagers.

Nancy C. Anderson

Knocked Off the Horse

All our acts have sacramental possibilities.

Freya Stark

I am sixty-four years old, soon to be sixty-five. My faith journey has encompassed four-plus decades and has been singularly unspectacular. My journey has been full of ups and downs, times of closeness with the Lord and times of distance, but unlike many of my friends I've never had a lot of dramatic encounters with God. And in my younger life, that worried me. I thought maybe I wasn't paying attention (well, sometimes I probably wasn't!), or God didn't have anything special to say to me. I tried many avenues: daily Mass attendance, Bible study, small faith-sharing groups, even the charismatic movement for a while. Through all of them I met wonderful people, many of whom are still in my life today. They all helped me on my faith journey, but I yearned for a "knocked from my horse" experience. It is only as I look back on my life that I see maybe I'd had them—gently—after all.

As usual, I was at an ordinary Sunday Mass in my early thirties, struggling with all the "stuff" of marriage and two

preschool children. But this particular Sunday, as I casually tossed my envelope into the basket, something had
changed. I hate to say I "heard" God speak to me, but I
really can't explain it any other way. What I heard was,
"Jan, I don't want just your money, I want all of you." It
was so real and so profound that I found myself still sitting
while the rest of the community had risen to their feet, so
overwhelming that I remember none of the rest of that
Mass. That was the beginning of years of volunteer service
that started with preschool, went on to include adult faith
development, liturgy, parish council and church committee work and even an advanced degree in theology. While
my husband worked at a job that supported our family, I
worked thirty-one years at a ministry that supported my
faith journey.

Then two years ago a very dear friend of ours died. She
and her husband lived about an eight-hour drive from us,
in the city where my husband and I had met and married
and where we still maintained a wonderful group of
friends. Since my husband was retired, I suggested we
drive up for the services and make it a mini-vacation. We
drove to the services, comforted George and spent a day or
so visiting old friends. On our return trip we investigated
some of the wonderful areas of our state we had missed on
earlier trips. It was October, there was a bit of crispness in
the air, most of the tourists were gone and we spent five
leisurely days driving home. We had a wonderful time! We
rediscovered how well we travel together, how much we
enjoy just hangin' out. One evening while enjoying dinner
from a candlelit deck overlooking a roaring river somewhere in the Sierra Madres of California, I suggested that
we take ourselves on a really long car trip, two or three
months, just roam around the Northwest. My husband
thought it was a great idea, but said, "How can we do that?
You always have commitments at church."

I guess you could say my husband's response was my "knocked off the horse" encounter. How long had I been relegating my husband and our life together to second place behind my commitments at church? He had been retired for ten years. Was it now time for me to retire?

While I was "knocked off the horse," I wasn't blinded. In fact I saw very clearly the Lord's next plan for me. My answer to my husband was, "I can give it up." It came as clearly and simply as anything that has ever been said to me. I *knew* this was right. I knew this was where God wanted me next, right beside my husband, doing all the things we had been wanting to do—things we hadn't been able to do because of my involvement. As soon as we got home I gave my pastor notice.

We made our two-and-one-half month car trip and loved every beauty-filled moment. We have refreshed ourselves and our relationships with old friends with mini-vacations and retreats. We have been to Eastern Europe to discover an unknown relative of my husband's, and we have wandered the streets of Rome. We see my daughter and grandchildren almost every week now. We have lunch together, we watch baseball together, we cook together, we laugh more, we play more. And, surprisingly enough, my church has gone on just fine without me! Other younger people with fresh ideas have stepped up and taken over the positions I once occupied—positions I thought only I could fill.

I'm happier than I have been in years. I'm less stressed. I have more time to pray.

My increased time with my husband, my family and my friends I count as increased time with my God.

Jan Kremenik

True Priorities

When I married my husband John, my life was so full, I feared I would have far more to do than time to do it. So I created a personal mission statement to define my true priorities and help me determine how to spend my time. I consulted the Bible for guidelines and selected Matthew 6:33, which spoke to me: "Seek first the kingdom of God and His righteousness, and all these things shall be added to you."

So I wrote:

> *First, the most important thing to me is my relationship with Christ. My success is first measured by how I serve the Lord with my time, talents and treasure. I make decisions based on what Jesus would want me to do, not what I feel like doing. Second, I am a faithful, encouraging, supportive wife, and I will be a loving, caring and nurturing mother, sometimes even sacrificing my own needs to ensure theirs. I work to live, not live to work. Lastly, I take care of myself physically, knowing then I will have the energy and ability to work for the Lord and my family.*

I read what I'd written and put it away, feeling good about myself. However, God soon showed me that *creating* a mission statement and actually *living* it are two different things.

I was twenty-six years old when my first child, Meagan, was born. I traveled extensively with a public seminar company, gaining success and recognition in the market-place. I was determined to be a wife and mother and career woman at the same time. Nothing would slow me down. I could change a diaper with one hand and type a proposal with another: a *good* proposal. I wanted to do it all—and succeed. So I arranged for my girlfriend, Angie, to care for Meagan when I was out of town speaking, and when Meagan was three months old, I started traveling again.

I couldn't see that my life was insane or that I wasn't following my personal mission statement. I wasn't working to live; I was living to work, striving to meet the world's definition of success, completely forgetting the one I'd written.

But then I got a wake-up call ... literally.

One late afternoon on the road, when Meagan was four-teen months old, I phoned Angie to check in, as usual. I stood at the pay phone in a hotel lobby. "Angie, hi. How's Meagan?"

"Oh Laura, we had a wonderful morning. Meagan walked today!"

Thud. I felt like I'd been punched in the stomach. *Meagan walked today. And where was I?*

My friend went on enthusiastically, "Yes, I just said, 'Come to Angie,' and she walked across the living room into my arms!"

Sobbing in the lobby of a Holiday Inn in Mansfield, Ohio, four hundred miles from home, her words echoed in my ears.

What am I doing? I shouted to myself. How could I have

missed one of the most important moments in my daughter's life? And for what? I had no one to blame but myself. I had put my career, my fame and my success ahead of my child. I had invested my time into things that weren't even part of the priorities outlined in my mission statement. I was moving so quickly in my career that I hadn't stopped to weigh the costs.

I thought of the scripture that clearly states there is no success if the family is lost. I knew I needed to align my actions with my purpose and make some changes. I vowed then to stop worrying about the quantity of work I was producing and focus instead on the quality of time I spent with Meagan. I was still committed to success—but a different kind of success.

I started saying "no" to activities that didn't support my purpose, my priorities and my mission statement. I started saying "no" to out-of-state speaking engagements and worked on building a local training business in Denver. I figured even Jesus said "no" sometimes when seemingly "good" requests for His time did not fit the overall plan for His ministry. In my Bible I found, "Now when it was day, He departed and went into a deserted place. And the crowd sought Him and came to Him, and tried to keep Him from leaving them; but He said to them, 'I must preach the kingdom of God to other cities also, because for this purpose I have been sent'" (Luke 4:42, 43).

God helped me learn to turn away from the worldly values of fame, greed and power, and discover the true meaning of success.

Six years later, I knelt in our family room. "Come to Mommy," I cooed, and our baby Johnny walked for the first time, across the room into my arms.

Laura Stack

The Band Played

For this is God. Our God forever and ever. He will be our guide.

Psalm 48:14

For years I'd dreamed about pulling up to a house and knowing, *That's the house—the house I want to build my family in.* I vowed not to be like everyone who tells house-hunting horror stories.

My newlywed husband Ward and I had spent many months praying for the perfect house to start our new life together in. We'd done all our research on the cities, neighborhoods and school districts, and the market was perfect.

But after three months of looking, I felt lost. I was becoming my worst nightmare. It was hard to find a house in Southern California that had the appeal of back east. I grew up in a very rural place with unique houses and large yards with no fences. But here they all looked alike— and I hated stucco! Was it too much to ask for a cute English-style home with wood trim, a garden and picket fence? That was my petition to God every night.

Our Realtor continued to patiently take us everywhere

and kept a positive attitude as we declined each house. But I was losing it. Emotionally exhausted and frustrated, I thought, *It's going to happen. I'm going to have to settle for a salmon-colored stucco house with the same garage door and number of windows as everyone else.*

My husband was so good. "Don't worry, Maria," he'd say. "Keep praying and have faith. God knows where we're supposed to live, and He has the perfect house for us." I was so thankful for Ward's faith and strength; he kept me going and comforted me after each stucco house we saw.

One Friday morning our Realtor called with a new listing in Costa Mesa—a three-bedroom house with a large backyard. Since I worked in the area and our church was there, I told Ward I'd go by and look at it before work. I knew exactly where the house was. It had a good neighborhood and was located near the college I attended. As I rounded the corner, I saw a For Sale sign up the street—that must be the house. As I got nearer I couldn't believe my eyes. A white picket fence surrounded a white, green-trimmed, English-style house with an old brick sidewalk entrance up to the front door. *That's the house—the house I want to build my family in.*

I was so excited, I called Ward even before I parked my car. "I found the house! Quick, you have to come! We have to put an offer on it today!"

The Realtor met us there and as Ward and I entered the house, I felt him cringe. He hated the inside. As we walked around and looked at all the old windows and stained glass, I could see beyond the seventies' rust-colored shag rug, dark blue drapes and pink walls. I could see past the old bathrooms and popcorn ceiling. Then we stepped into the backyard; it was like stepping back east. The large lawn was lined with trees, and there was even an old willow, just like at Grandma's. The big yard was out of place in Southern California. I knew then this was the house.

Still unsure, Ward suggested we needed to pray about it and sleep on it. There had been no offers on the house, and, since it had been on the market for six months, they were lowering the price. So we felt pretty comfortable about sleeping on it.

After a full day of continued house shopping, Ward found another house he wanted, so we were both stressed to the max. We lay on the bed that night, talking over both homes and praying, then finally falling asleep . . . in our clothes. We must have slept pretty hard, because when we woke, we both laughed—we still had our shoes on!

That morning we decided to make an offer on the house I loved. As we drove to look at it one more time, all the while I was praying, "God, please show me a sign." We exited the freeway, turned on the street and parked outside. Ward noticed a neighbor doing lawn work, so he strolled over to chat with him and find out his opinion of the neighborhood.

As I sat in the car praying, I heard a band practicing at the high school just across the field. It brought back memories of my high school days, when I was in the band. I sat reflecting, enjoying the community feel. Would Ward feel that too? Or would he say, "Do you hear that band? I don't think I could live with that next door!"

Ward walked back to the car and said, "Did you hear the band playing? Isn't that cool? It really makes this place feel like a community."

I knew right then this was my sign from God. We must have this house. Ward agreed. We called the Realtor and went straight to her office to sign an offer. We eagerly told her about the band playing, about how much the neighborhood felt like our community and how we'd love to live there.

She told us there were three offers pending on the

house. Just that morning, three offers had come in. The homeowners would look at them and accept the one they wanted.

My heart sank. There weren't any offers yesterday! As I began the woulda, coulda, shoulda game in my head and out loud, Ward put me in my place. "God knows the house for us. Don't worry."

But worry—and pray—I did all day long.

Early that evening we finished up dinner and talked, coming to peace with the house deal, be it ours or not. The phone rang; it was our Realtor. The house was ours! The owners accepted us above the others because of something our agent had written in a letter to them.

A letter? What letter? I asked her. She admitted writing about Ward and me, how our church and work were in that neighborhood, how we had just gotten married and how, when we heard the band practicing at the high school, we knew that was the house for us. The owners said they chose us because we liked the band playing.

My sign. God's sign. Music to my ears.

Maria Nickless

Bank on It

Next to a good soul-stirring prayer is a good laugh.

Samuel Mutchmore

I don't want to admit how debit-card dependent I am. It's getting embarrassing. One day I couldn't find my card. I looked everywhere, all afternoon. Even by the next morning there was still no trace of the card. I searched high and low, near and far—even under the sofa cushions. I found thirty-seven cents, three marbles, a T-shirt (how had we ignored that lump?), seven M&M's, a screwdriver, my favorite sunglasses and the TV remote (hey, we'd been looking for that thing!)—but no card.

I rifled through my purse for the gazillionth time. I found a ball of fuzz resembling a dead rodent, the rest of those M&M's, enough breath mints to freshen a platoon and at least four different shades of nail polish, all hidden among a ream of receipts I would never need—but still no card.

I checked our bank account online to make sure no one had used the rogue card. Nope, no extra charges (though how in the world could all those be mine?). Still, I was just this side of panic.

Why is it I wait until panic starts to set in before I remember where I really need to turn? *I'll have my quiet time with the Lord and then I can resume the hunt with more peace, less panic,* I told myself.

I opened my Bible where I had marked my place the day before—and out fell my card! I had absent-mindedly stuck it between the pages as a bookmark, a weird move spiritually *and* financially.

What a lesson my Father taught me in the pages of His Word that morning about where I should run. And believe it or not, the real treasure was not even card-related. Psalm 119:14–16 read, "I rejoice in following your statutes as one rejoices in great riches. I meditate on your precepts and consider your ways. I delight in your decrees; I will not neglect your word."

Debit cards may come and go, but our wealth is only in Him. So let's give credit where credit is due.

Or debit. Whichever.

Rhonda Rhea

9

A MATTER OF PERSPECTIVE

It is the inclination and tendency of the heart which finally determines the opinions of the mind.

Christopher Ernst Luthardt

Hot Dogs for Breakfast

Give attention to my words: incline your ear to my sayings.

Proverbs 4:20

Mom lived by herself until she was eighty, then with my sister until eighty-five. We were excited about her coming to live with us on the farm. Mom had always been my rock. As I grew into a young woman and became a mother myself, she traveled a thousand miles when each of my three children was born and stayed until they were six weeks old, taking care of my family. When we moved to the farm, she came during the busy season and helped with the cooking for a dozen extra workers, day after hot summer day. When the strawberries were ready for jam, or when the summer savory was ready for harvesting, all I had to do was call. Her hot biscuits, casseroles and cookies tasted so good after a long day of chores. And she was an expert with her needle and thread, a job I just never seem to get done. As we worked together Mom told stories of how God sustained her through the storms that touched her life.

As we prepared for her coming, her room was made ready; a welcome card and fresh bouquet of flowers awaited her arrival. I could already taste her hot biscuits and smell her spicy molasses cookies. We would go shopping together again and plan for the holidays, just as we had in the past.

The first time I asked her to make biscuits, though, she seemed confused. *That's understandable,* I thought, *she's not familiar with my kitchen.* I got out the ingredients, turned the oven on and went outside to do chores. When I came back the biscuits were sitting on the counter, but her fingers were bruised from mixing and kneading so hard. I savored every bite, knowing it would be the last time she would bake in my kitchen.

Still, I felt myself getting angry with her when I would rush in the house at the last minute to prepare supper. She'd be sitting in her chair watching the news and remark, "You poor dear, you have so much to do." I didn't want her pity; I wanted to smell one of her casseroles bubbling in the oven. I wanted to hear her laugh as we sat at the table together. But Mom didn't laugh much anymore. It took all her strength just to keep up with our farm activities and our busy family running to and fro.

Even simple things became a struggle. When we went grocery shopping, she wasn't interested in buying treats like before. She wanted to wait on a bench and I found myself rushing through the store, afraid she wouldn't be where I'd left her when I returned. When we were about to go holiday shopping, she lost her money and I searched her room for hours while she insisted an intruder stole it.

After a forty-five-minute evening drive with my husband and me, Mom forgot her home. There was confusion in her eyes as I turned down her bed and laid out her nightgown. Reading her favorite scriptures to her did nothing to ease her mind. At 10:30 she was still sitting on the side of her bed, afraid to go to sleep. As if talking to a child who has broken the rules, in a harsh and direct voice I told her she could not stay up a minute longer. She obeyed and crawled into bed. Gently, I tucked the blankets around her shoulders, kissed her cheek, left her room and burst into tears.

But as the weeks went by, we settled into a routine and I became accustomed to fitting her into my schedule. She did my dishes and I told everyone about my wonderful new "dishwasher." We laughed together again, just like we used to.

And as our roles changed, something wonderful happened. Instead of feeling sad, I felt renewed. My husband and I marveled at the way she came into the kitchen for breakfast with a smile, dressed in a pretty housecoat, and with her hairspray on. I marveled at the fact that even though she didn't read anymore, when I read from her Bible, she memorized her favorite scriptures.

Even though she was no longer telling me her stories, her minute messages held treasures. "Just look outside dear, God must be busy this morning," or at sunset, "Come see God's mansions of gold." One day she said, "I didn't think I could get up this morning, then I felt His hand in mine and I just got up and got dressed." When I heard her singing, "His Eye Is on the Sparrow," my heart soared as high as any bird in flight.

One night, I served her a hot dog for supper along with her bowl of soup. When I went to pick up her dishes, she told me to save the rest of her hot dog for breakfast. As I went past our dog's dish, I gave the leftover hot dog to Rudy, certain she would never remember. But the next morning as I was heating up the pancake griddle she came into the kitchen and said, "I'll have my hot dog, dear."

"Your hot dog?" I shot back, as if scolding a child. "I gave it to Rudy. You're having pancakes for breakfast." Her shoulders slumped as she went to her chair.

Shaking my head in disbelief, I began to pour the pancake batter, when unexpectedly another window of memory gently opened. I was a small child again standing beside my mother, a beautiful woman, in an old country church. My dress smelled like a fresh spring morning, starched and pressed lovingly by irons heated on a wood stove, fluffed out over hand-sewn crinolines. The pastor's words rang in my memory, crystal clear, as though he was talking directly to me: "Unless you become like little children you will not enter into the kingdom of heaven."

I turned off the griddle, prepared a hot dog and garnished it with her favorite toppings. Her smiling Irish eyes sparkled with a hint of mischief as I served her.

"Oh, thank you, dear. I was so looking forward to my hot dog, you know. I thought about it all night."

The pastor's words echoed again, giving me a peaceful new meaning to this phase in my mother's life.

Darlene Lawson

Good News on the Paper Route

Out of the mouths of babes and sucklings has thou ordained strength.

Psalm 8:2

Once upon a time our four sons had paper routes. Their entrepreneurial dad and I were grateful for the opportunity to help them learn about keeping commitments, working for wages and handling accounts.

We were also grateful the local paper was only a weekly.

On Wednesdays, they'd fold the papers in thirds, slide a rubber band around (on rainy days a plastic bag), and load them in their carrier bags. I'd drop the boys off one by one at their start points, then pick them up at the end of their routes. I'll never forget the dedication and determination on the face of my eight-year-old, Zach, staggering beneath the weight of his bag. His route consisted of two very long blocks of mostly retired people, who anxiously awaited their Wednesday paper. When I picked him up, no matter how exhausted he was, he glowed.

Things like this brought out the glow in me as well. Over my years of mothering, I've found no matter what I set out to teach my kids or how, God never fails to send a few lessons my way too.

Another part of delivering papers was collections. This was critical because each boy was billed for all the papers dropped on our driveway that month. To break even, each needed to collect from at least two-thirds of his customers. So collecting involved lessons in record keeping, courtesy and, most of all, perseverance.

It also took a little extra ooomph to get out the door on winter nights, when dark had fallen early and cold whipped through the hills of suburban California like a most unpopular party crasher.

On one such night, I packed the boys in the van after dinner and we headed out to do collections together. Each boy was loaded with change in his pocket, pen and clipboard in hand.

Ben's route was closest. Heater blasting, we wound our way to the first address. I stopped the car, turned off the ignition and turned to shoo my third son out the door.

The porch light was on, assuring us Ben would not stumble in the dark. But it also illuminated something special for me—a radiant smile spreading over my son's face.

"The nicest people in the world," Ben said before he stepped out into the cold. With the engine off, his brothers and I blew on our hands to keep them warm. Ben came back with dimples flashing.

We drove up four doors to Ben's next customer. As I turned off the engine, Ben beamed again. "The nicest people in the world!"

"I thought the first house was the nicest people in the world," I said.

"Yeah, but these people are too," Ben said, sincere as sunshine. Another big smile, another big tip.

We replayed this scene again and again. Soon Ben's brothers and I forgot the cold, warmed by Ben's infectious love of the people he served. Soon we were all chanting, "The nicest people in the world," in front of each customer's house.

For our family, this became a defining moment. Though our newspaper days are long gone, the lessons we learned stayed with us. Even now, "The nicest people in the world" remains part of our family's idiom—a reminder of the gladness of heart when we forget ourselves and think more highly of those we serve.

Barbara Curtis

"I liked the story about Samson.
Will there be a sequel?"

Provisions of Oil

It took every feeble ounce of strength I had to blow up the imaginary balloons and swirl the streamer. I puffed up the yellow balloon of "sorrow;" next I inflated green "regret." As a single mom of ten years, I had cried, fretted and grumbled but never before pampered myself with an all out pity-party—until now. With satisfaction, I wrapped the garish streamer of "sympathy" all around myself.

I sat slumped at the kitchen table, chin cupped in my hands, and privately enjoyed the tawdry mess in my soul.

"Good-bye, Mom!" My daughter flew past, a whirl of white ruffles and blue ribbons. "I'll phone you after the prom."

I watched her climb into the limo. The other girls in black, my daughter stood out in her Anne of Green Gables dress, left over from last year's junior prom. At that time, we had shopped to find the perfect ribbon with baby's breath for her hair and a delicate necklace to complete the look for her boyfriend. This year for her blind date, she threw on her clothes and forgot her make-up.

Left alone, my miserable soul tooted its loudest party horn. "Exhaustion." *Doesn't the work ever stop?* I moped. *The moment I get home, I take off the father's hat to earn the bread and put on the mother's hat to go bake it. I'm worn out.*

Through the tinted glass of self-pity, I looked back into the window of my single-parent experience.

Alone with my young son and daughter in our circa-1733 farmhouse, there had been no money to pay my mortgage. I felt like the widow with two children in the Book of Second Kings, who thought she had nothing at all in her house with which God could do a miracle—except a little oil.

As I had stared at my deserted barns, paddocks, cottage and pool, I wondered, *Are they my provision of oil?*

It must have been Providence that guided me, step by step, to fill my barn stalls with neighbors' horses, the split rail paddocks with a horseback riding school, my cottage with a young couple and the enclosed pool with a club of townsfolk. Relieved and grateful, I gathered up the rent checks and paid the mortgage.

But soon after, I saw flames shooting up in the woods behind the barns.

"Fire!"

Afraid for the horses' lives, I raced top speed to the house on my polio leg, only to collapse on the threshold. I crawled to the phone and made two calls, one to the fire department and another to my doctor.

The fire was extinguished, the horses were unhurt, but my heart had taken a beating—literally. More fatigue.

Not many days later, I heard the unmistakable sound of dripping. Now the roof leaked!

Thankfully, years before, I'd put the farmhouse on the National Register of Historic Places. In exchange for more paperwork, the grant money soon turned the drip, drip, drip of rain into the tap, tap, tap of hammers. Like a cape thrown over its shoulders, the rambling saltbox house became cloaked in a new wooden-shingled roof.

Now we were dry, but with no money in the budget for

heating oil, the nights grew colder. That's when the flaming autumn foliage directed me to the answer. Logs!

A state forester marked our trees, a sharecropper cut and split the wood and we carried in the logs. Wood stove heat soon filled the kitchen, drifting up to the children's bedrooms through a hole I cut in the ceiling.

For more products, gratis, I labored hard to tap maple sap, pick blackberries, pluck Concord grapes, dig carrots, hang herbs, gather apples and collect goat's milk.

As a physical therapist, I spent weekdays away from the farm, trudging in rain and snow to the front doors of the elderly. Limping on my bum leg, sometimes I thought I, not they, should be the patient. Each workday climaxed with an amusement park ride along twisting country roads in order to be home by 3:30 and greet the kids back from school.

The phone jangled me back to the present. It was my daughter.

In a depressed monotone I said, "I can't believe the prom is over already. Did you have a good time?"

"Yes, Mom, but . . . "

"If I sound a bit down, it's because I'm feeling tired."

"Sorry, but Mom!"

"Some days are just like that, you know."

"Yes, but Mom!"

"Yes, dear?"

"I was chosen prom queen tonight!"

"What?"

"It's true! I couldn't believe it when they called out my name. I'm not one of the popular girls, you know. As the master of ceremonies placed the crown on my head, I lifted my chin and thought, 'Well if this is the way it's supposed to be for me, I'll be the best queen I know how.'"

Bang, bang popped the balloons of sorrow and regret, goodbye waved the streamer of sympathy, and even the party horn of exhaustion went silent. My self-pity dissolved in the effervescence of my daughter's joy.

Through a clear window of blessing, my single-parent life looked brighter.

I realized how fun it had been to haul the Christmas tree from the woods and decorate it with red berries, silver cones and gilded nuts. How exciting it was to watch the children scamper to find chocolate Easter eggs hidden in the crevices of the Early American stone walls, the winner given the chocolate bunny in the hollow of the old apple tree. I loved the shrieks of young voices buried in heaped piles of autumn leaves and the whoosh of the horse-drawn sleigh packed with bundled kids in the falling snow.

Mustaches of cream and berries on little mouths made me laugh. Soft yellow candles aglow on young faces warmed my heart. Story time in the oak-beamed sitting room, nestled by the spacious fireplace, left me peaceful.

I saw, like the widow, a faithful God who had turned my little oil into much. I knew He, not the selection committee, had actually chosen my daughter for prom queen to help pop my pity party and inflate my faith—to go forward.

Margaret Lang

Taking Wing

It was late spring, and my young daughter, Sheridan, and I had already begun planning mother-daughter activities to share during the summer. Without my knowledge, she "adopted" a caterpillar at a local birdseed store as one way to make a memory.

Sheridan, notorious for collecting crawling critters guaranteed to make *my* skin crawl, brought home her undulating invertebrate in a covered plastic cup. Gingerly placing the striped caterpillar she'd dubbed Sunrise in a darkened corner of our kitchen, Sheridan promised to feed her, tend her and keep her at a respectable distance from me. Though never fond of things that creep, I was still fascinated by the assurance that this infinitesimal insect would soon morph into a big, beautiful butterfly. I could hardly wait to share this experience with my daughter.

Daily I watched as Sheridan emptied the cup of the mostly eaten milkweed leaves she had inserted the night before, careful not to cast away her insect gourmand in the process. I was surprised at the creature's ravenous appetite, and even more astounded by its catapulting growth. Each day Sunrise seemed to triple her girth and length. To accommodate her weight gain, on several occasions she shed her skin like a too-tight pair of panty-hose, shimmying out of it one wiggle at a time.

One momentous morning, Sunrise crawled to the lid of the cup, tenaciously attached herself and shed her skin one last time. And then, in the stillness of that magical moment, she revealed a chrysalis of shimmering green and unseen dreams . . . and . . . she waited. . . . And so did we.

Over the ensuing weeks, Sheridan and I shared our hopes for the tiny tenant residing inside the chrysalis. And in the process, Sheridan began sharing her *own* hopes and dreams with me. I realized that just like the promise of a sunrise's metamorphosis, Sheridan was shimmying out of her childhood one wobbly wiggle at a time.

One day, in the fullness of time, we beheld a brilliant butterfly, her orange-and-black stained-glass wings trembling inside the cup. We, too, trembled at her breathtaking beauty *and* at the thought of letting her go. Mustering our courage, we took Sunrise to the garden to free her, praying she'd linger among the lilacs yet awhile. She circled above the purple petals, then suddenly flew to the treetops. Alighting for just an instant, she fluttered her wings like little rays of sunshine flashing on black branches. Then she ascended higher still and finally disappeared from our sight.

Sheridan and I knew that we could never replace Sunrise, but we decided to adopt a new caterpillar every spring and raise it together. And I promised God that I would nurture my own little butterfly whose childhood was flitting away with great speed—and that one day I would love her enough to let her take wing, just as we had done for Sunrise.

Lynn D. Morrissey

Finger Play

Every child born into the world is a new thought of God, an ever-fresh and radiant possibility.

Kate Douglas Wiggin

Four-year-old Kayla nestled on Opa's lap while he read their favorite Dr. Seuss book—again. As she fought sleep, her dimpled fingers plucked idly at the roadmap veins ribbing the backs of her grandpa's hands. First one, then another, she pushed each dark blue vein into a ridge and watched it melt back down.

Suddenly she leaned forward for a closer look. Opa paused to watch as she inspected his weathered skin and compared it to her own baby-plump pink hand, touching first one, then the other. Satisfied at last, Kayla looked up.

"I think God must've practiced on you first, Opa," she said. "'Cause He did much better making me!"

Carol McAdoo Rehme

Grandma-Great

She was twelve when Teddy Meyer gave her a ring. His mistake was asking for it back. First, she took a hammer to it—slamming it flat. Then she marched across a damp field to deposit it smack in the middle of a cow paddy. "There's your ring," she said. That was seventy-eight years ago. My maternal grandmother, Barbara Cecilia Dutra LaFleur, just turned ninety. She's a full-blooded Portuguese power-house of a woman who taught me the two most important things I ever learned about God.

She's a painter, usually on large canvases, in oils, though once she painted a pine plank that hangs in my kitchen, gleaming the words of my first lesson: "Pray to God, but Row toward Shore." It sports a man in a rowboat heaving against the tide. "You can't just sit around on your fanny expecting God to fix all your problems," she'd say. "You've got to row." It seemed so refreshingly heretical to me as a child. I somehow knew she was speaking in opposition to someone or something that advocated God fixing every-thing so long as you were good enough, quiet enough, nice enough or some measure of "enough." Grandma is not always quiet, nice or good. And she never just sits on her fanny amidst a flurry of waves. She's a rower.

The second lesson came when I was much younger. It was a time of strictness and gloves every Sunday. Parents stood straight in church and children stood beside them pulling at the elastic bands of their hats or the itch of their small ties. I remember the hiss of mothers reprimanding their charges from under their breath, the building edge of threat—behave, sit up straight, the shooting stare of "stop that or else." Sunday was serious.

Grandma was babysitting all four of us kids, ages seven, six, five and four, one weekend. I don't remember the morning unfolding that Sunday when we were lost in the lollygaggle of grownups orchestrating the day. I don't remember dressing for church or driving to church. My siblings were probably little aware of it either, riding the tune of morning play and wresting into our socks, unaware of what came next, just happy and fed and twirling.

What came next was the four of us emptying out of the car and my two little brothers looking up the steps of the church in horror and then down at themselves and then up again. They began to cry and buried their faces in their hands, ashamed.

My sister and I were vaguely interested and looked them up and down. Grandma fluttered about, a sputtering of "What's wrong?" "Boys—What's happened?" My sister, the oldest, exclaimed, "Those are their pajamas!" She pointed to the neat and matching short set Grandma had dressed the boys in. That era was the heyday of matching pajamas—always purchased at Penney's or Sears. My brothers were indeed wearing their new pajamas and had been far too busy playing to notice.

So there in the parking lot where even my sister and I could commiserate with how utterly unthinkable it was to show up for church improperly dressed, there in the parking lot with two embarrassed, tearful little boys, my grandmother once again cut through all the blithering nonsense of what we so often think is paramount. "Oh, boys—God doesn't care if you go to church in your pajamas. God loves you. He doesn't care how you look. He loves you anyway."

And they stopped crying, empowered even as they marched into church heads held high and a little thrilled. They were loved and in their pajamas.

This—to me at six—was, again, blazingly heretical. I was wowed by her power to say such a thing, to proclaim it as if she knew, as if she could make the rules at a time when rules were so very important.

And of course she knew. As she said the other day when I called to ask her the cow-paddy boy's name, "I was always very definite." You sure were, and you still are. I tell her often that she is my hero. Each time she says the same thing: "No. I'm not. I'm very definite." Bingo and Amen.

Natalie Costanza-Chavez

Six Rose Hips, Two Bobby Pins and a Ball of Blue String

"Take us to the park, Mom," begged my daughter, Erin, as she reached into her pocket and pulled out the incentive. "Look at what I'll give you if you take us." Erin opened her hand, and resting on her palm for the taking were three pennies, a fishing bobber and one piece of shiny white shell.

"That's tempting, Erin," I explained, "but I have a lot of work to get done today. Let's wait and see how much I get accomplished, and we'll take it from there."

Erin turned and bounded away, content, so I thought. But within minutes she returned.

"Mom, look," she continued, "if you promise to take us to the park today, I'll give you all this." Erin again reached into her pockets, and this time laid each item delicately on our kitchen table for display.

I eagerly looked at each new incentive: six rose hips, one silver washer, a small ball of blue string, two bobby pins, one rose petal, one piece of blacktop chipped from our driveway and a chipped piece of brick.

"Wow, Erin," I exclaimed, "you mean if I promise to take

you to the park, you'd give me all this?"

"That's right, Mom. It really is a good deal."

"Well," I continued, "I think I'd feel guilty taking all of it just for taking you to the park. I'd feel like I got the better end of the deal—what do you think?"

"You're right, Mom," she answered, "that is an awful lot of stuff. Why don't you just take the six rose hips, the two bobby pins and the ball of blue string, and we'll call it even?"

"You've got a deal," I agreed. "We'll leave for the park in one hour."

Erin smiled. "Thanks, Mom—I love you!"

Tell me, how could a mom say no?

Later that evening, I began to think about Erin and her "deal." I wondered, *Do I make deals like that with God?* Do I lay before him enticing incentives if He'll promise to do something for me? Humbly, I admit I have. "Okay, God, here's the deal. If you'll heal me of my illness, I promise to teach Sunday school for a whole year." Or, "God, I'll support a hungry child every month if you'll get me that new job." Or more desperately, "God, I really need you to fix my marriage. If you'll make everything turn out all right, I promise to have a home Bible study every week without fail."

Well, I've since discovered that God doesn't always work like that. Just as I truly didn't need those six rose hips, two bobby pins and a ball of blue string, God didn't need my "incentives" to work a miracle in my life. As Erin's mother, I simply wanted to bless her with the desire of her heart—a simple trip to the park. And our heavenly father, God just wants to bless us too, though He probably gets a chuckle from what his children offer Him as a "good deal!"

Wendy Dunham

From the World of Jazz

My father was a lover of music and encouraged my brother and me to play a musical instrument in the 1920s. I played saxophone and he played trumpet in the church orchestra. Years passed and we performed for dances, parties, proms and nightclubs. I was thrilled. Jazz had me in its grip. I prayed, "God, help me lead a famous orchestra, like Duke Ellington or Count Basie."

One evening my brother and I attended an evangelistic meeting at church. The powerful sermon warned about sin and the need to get right with God. Moved emotionally, my brother, some friends and I went forward. As I knelt, I felt I should be baptized to ensure me a place in heaven.

When we rose to our feet, the pastor and people began to shake our hands and rejoice. One woman called me aside. "Howard, I am so glad you are going to be baptized. You'll be giving up the dance orchestra now, won't you?"

Her question caught me off guard. I knew that, back then, some religions didn't allow dancing, believing those actions could lead to sin. "No," I answered firmly. "There is nothing wrong with it. I've studied music hard. I'll lead a famous orchestra someday and make a lot of money."

One month later we attended the baptismal service. I

waited eagerly, and at last my brother and I were immersed. After we came up out of the water, we hurried back to the dressing room and, with our heads still wet, hustled out the back door into a waiting car. We sped away to play for a big dance. But as we drove, I ignored a surprising, strange feeling of guilt.

Time passed swiftly, and our orchestra played more and more important engagements. We reveled in our great press and our climb up the ladder of musical success.

One weekend while I was away for one of our biggest engagements, my girlfriend Wanda attended a youth crusade. Late Sunday evening I returned, eager to tell her of the good time I'd had. But she would talk only of her new-found joy and peace in Christ Jesus.

"Howard," she said, "the Lord has completely forgiven my sins and transformed my life. I'm saved!"

Although I didn't understand it completely, I was glad for Wanda. After all, I told myself, a little religion never hurt anyone. I had mine, so I thought, and now she had hers.

I was shocked, though, when she refused to go dancing or even to the movies. "Those are things of the world," she warned. "I must give them up to follow Christ."

We'd talked often of getting married, and when I proposed, I couldn't believe my ears.

"I love you," she said, "but I love Christ more. Therefore, unless you accept Jesus Christ as your personal Savior, I must leave you because we have nothing more in common with each other."

Wanda's words cut deep. I knew I wasn't willing to change my ways, though losing her was the last thing on earth I wanted to happen. But her terms were too high. Too stubborn and proud, I told myself I could live without Wanda or her Savior. I tried to lose myself in my music and the pleasures of the world.

But the more I tried, the more I realized I was only

fooling myself. I was miserable in mind and soul. I became restless, wretched and dissatisfied with everything the world had to offer. My unhappiness began to affect my music. I couldn't play as I used to. The men in the band were puzzled. Actually, I couldn't understand myself. The music of the band didn't grip me anymore. The spine-tingling feeling that once thrilled me as we poured out the big band sounds was gone. Without Wanda and peace of heart, my music was nothing at all.

One Sunday night in my misery, as I sat in Wanda's church again, her pastor preached a powerful sermon. I was so convicted by the Holy Spirit that I went to the altar where the pastor and church members knelt in prayer for me. On my knees, I poured out my heart to God in tears.

That night God answered my prayer—and Wanda's prayer. For the first time in my life I knew that somewhere, somehow, God had something for me to do for Him.

From that night on, things began to happen. I threw away my cigarettes and gave up smoking and drinking. Still, I hoped secretly that I could have Christ, Wanda *and* the dance orchestra.

Then came the biggest dance event of the season. All my old gang and my orchestra went to a popular night-club to see one of the most famous orchestras in the United States.

I entered the big hall, drawn as if by a big magnet to the bright lights and the jazz music. When I got inside, I did not experience the secret thrill I had hoped for. The music of the band didn't excite me. Beads of perspiration stood out on my forehead. I trembled all over. Some of our own band members noticed. "Howard, are you sick?"

Turning quickly from the bar, I walked as fast as I could to the nearest exit. The clean, cool night air swept over me.

"Oh, God!" I cried out, "I know I prayed to lead a band, but now I'll give up everything to serve You the rest of my life!"

At that moment, He flooded my soul with peace and joy I'd never known before.

The band couldn't believe my announcement.

"Howard, you're going to leave the band?" they exclaimed.

"Yes," I replied. "I feel God wants me to leave it. At times I even feel as though He wants me to preach the gospel."

Then began the opposition of my friends. "You're crazy to leave the orchestra!" "What's wrong with you?" "Your religion won't last. Just wait and see." "Jazz is your life. You will be back in the orchestra in two weeks."

On and on it went, but confidence in my Lord brought me through all the opposition. And through it all I was determined that someday I would enter Bible school and prepare myself as a preacher.

A few years later, Wanda and I entered college to prepare for Christian service. This time when I proposed, she gave a resounding, "Yes!" We graduated and were married in June 1944.

My pastoral ministry continued for fourteen years, when I resigned to accept an invitation from Dr. Billy Graham to become the first black associate evangelist on his crusade team. Little did I realize when I gave my life to Jesus Christ that He would use me in the way He has. Traveling the world in this ministry, I also conducted Bible conferences and the weekly Hour of Freedom radio broadcasts, plus produced countless articles and tapes, touching millions of lives.

Today, times have changed—most churches allow dancing. Sometimes people ask, "Howard, now that the rules have changed, are you sorry you gave up your big band?"

I answer with all my heart, "Not at all! See, while I thought He wanted me to lead an orchestra, He wanted me to lead His people . . . to Him."

Howard O. Jones

The Wreath

Faith, like light, should always be simple and unbending; while love, like warmth, should beam forth on every side and bend to every necessity of our brethren.

Martin Luther

"Oh, for the things I might have said, the things I might have done." My eyes were riveted to the inscription beneath the oil painting. Unlike the light and airy Impressionist paintings my mom and I had seen that day at the Art Institute of Chicago, this masterpiece depicted a somber funeral wreath on a glossy black door. The Monets receded from my memory, but this poignant inscription seared its way into my consciousness: "Oh, for the things I might have said, the things I might have done." What finality!

On the subway ride home I thought about Mom. She sat close beside me, yet she was so distant. *There are many things I could have said to Mom or done for her—but I didn't. Now that I'm in college, I wonder if it's too late?*

Storybook vignettes of the past flashed before my mind.

As a young daddy's girl, every night after dinner I sat on his lap and proudly slipped the paper ring from his Roy Tan cigar onto my finger. Instead of helping Mom with the dishes, Dad and I worked a picture puzzle. When my girlfriend slept over, Dad played a prank by putting Jell-O in the foot of my bed. After he got the surprised reaction he wanted from me, he tried to clean up the strawberry delight with a towel. But it was my servant mom who wiped my toes, changed the linens and laid out fresh towels. Funny, I don't recall thanking her for her services.

As I grew older, Dad and I, each with a long stride, walked quickly down the street, while Mom, with her shorter legs, lagged farther and farther behind. Occasionally we paused to wait for her, but never long enough for her to catch up.

At a recent big gathering, I tucked my arm in Dad's and stayed close by his side, while Mom was the furthest thing from my mind.

The subway jolted to a stop. *From now on, it's going to be different. I want Mom to see how much she means to me.* I stole a glance at her seated beside me, prim in her suit and hat, her mind somewhere else.

"What are you thinking, Mom?"

"Oh, just about the troubled girls at my school."

Mom was a devoted teacher, and I knew she helped disadvantaged children in a number of ways. But I hadn't realized before now how deeply she felt for these children. *I wonder if I really know her; I guess I only know about her.*

That night, I gave Mom the hug usually reserved for Dad. She stood somewhat awkwardly, almost like a child who didn't know how to respond.

Lying in bed I asked God, *What can I do to reach her with my l love?* Then it occurred to me that perhaps her British heritage was the key. *After all, she likes everything English. Maybe I can even try to change my tomboy persona, which often conflicts with her ladylike preferences.*

I asked the next day, "Mom, could we have a cup of English tea together this afternoon?"

Startled, she replied, "Why, yes . . . of course, dear."

I noticed how carefully she laid out her best china, with silver teapot, pitcher of cream and bowl of sugar, even adding a plate of Scottish shortbread, my favorite. She set the tea service on the low table and poured the tea she had brought back from England. As we held our cups and saucers somewhat stiffly, we talked about her recent trip to Cornwall to search out her relatives.

From that day forward, our tea party was repeated, each afternoon at three, just like clockwork. Soon formal talk became relaxed chatter. She gave our chat time a name, "girlie gab," and giggled like a schoolgirl when Dad came around to see what we were up to. She even unlocked the longings and secrets of her heart. Each day our lives were woven together more tightly.

Throughout the summer, we took an oil painting class, planted geraniums in big pots, shared our favorite historic novels and excitedly discussed the book she was writing. But no matter how full our days, every afternoon we took time out for our cup of English tea.

In later years, and for too many of them, my marriage took me miles away from her, that is, until the autumn of her life. Dad had passed on, she suffered a mild stroke and I longed once again to intertwine our hearts like the branches of a vine. So I brought her back east with me. This was the summer to delight her with the laughter of children and the playfulness of puppies. It became the autumn to shuffle through leaves, feed the ducks, picnic by the brook. It turned into the winter to snuggle by the fire, carol at the piano and peruse family photos. It broke into the spring to sniff country lilacs, hear the mockingbird's song and, most importantly, to sip a cup of English tea—together.

Then it was over. My brother wanted her with him, and I steeled myself for the looming finality of her departure for the Midwest. The book of the things I might have said and the things I might have done was closing. There was nothing more I could do.

"Good-bye, precious Mom," I said at the airport, through tears. Her soft and radiant smile of thanks was all I needed.

Another summer came and went before I laid a wreath at her gravesite—a personal wreath interlaced with bright memories. How transformed it was from the cold wreath in the Art Institute painting, because I'd heard the plea of the artist to love before the hour has passed.

Margaret Lang

10

MAKING A
DIFFERENCE

*Each person has inside a basic decency
and goodness. If he listens to it and acts on
it, he is giving a great deal of what it is the
world needs most. It is not complicated but it
takes courage. It takes courage for a person
to listen to his own goodness and act on it.*

Pablo Casals

Smiley

*Do not lay up for yourselves treasures on earth,
where moth and rust destroy and where thieves
break in and steal; but lay up for yourselves
treasures in heaven.*

Matthew 6:19-20

I was in the prima donna, self-centered phase of seventeen, and my motives were simple—to enhance my final health assistant grade. To accomplish my goal before high school graduation, I volunteered at the nearby convalescent center.

For weeks I grumbled to my boyfriend. "I can't believe I'm stuck with tending to old people for free." He agreed. I soon realized that the bright yellow uniforms my classmates and I were required to wear made matters even worse. On our first day at the center, the nurses took one look at our sunshiny apparel and nicknamed us "The Yellow Birds."

During my scheduled days, I complained to the other "yellow birds" about emptying bedpans, changing soiled linens and spoonfeeding pureed foods to mumbling mouths.

A tedious month passed; then I met Lily. I carried a tray of food to her room, and her bright blue eyes appraised me as I entered. Soon I became very aware of the kindness behind them. After talking with her for a few minutes, I realized why I hadn't noticed Lily before, even though I had been past her room numerous times. Lily, unlike so many of the other residents, was soft-spoken and undemanding. From my first day at the geriatric center, I had learned that the staff had their favorite patients, usually those who stuck out in some characteristic way. From joke-tellers to singers, the louder and more rambunctious the patients, the more attention they received.

Something inside of me immediately liked quiet, unassuming Lily. Strangely, I even began to enjoy our talks, which proved Lily's genuine kindness stemmed from her relationship with God.

"Come here," she smiled to me one rainy afternoon. "Sit down. I have something to show you." She lifted a small photo album and began to turn the pages. "This was my Albert. See him there? Such a handsome man." Her voice softened even more as she pointed to a pretty little girl sitting on top of a fence. "And that was our darling Emmy when she was eight years old."

A drop of wetness splattered on the plastic cover, and I quickly turned to Lily. Her eyes spilled tears. "What is it?" I whispered, covering her hand with my own.

She didn't answer right away, but as she turned the pages I noticed that Emmy was not in any other photographs. "She died from cancer that year," Lily told me. "She'd been in and out of hospitals most of her life, but that year Jesus took her home."

"I'm so sorry," I said, disturbed that God would take away this beautiful woman's daughter. "I don't understand why He let her die. You're such a true follower of His."

"It's okay," she smiled slightly, meeting my eyes. "God has a plan for every life, Karen. We need to open our hearts to Him regardless if we understand His ways or not. Only then can we find true peace." She turned to the last page. Inside the worn album was one more picture of a middle-aged Lily standing on tiptoes and kissing a clown's cheek.

"That's my Albert," she laughed, recalling happier memories. "After Emmy died, we decided to do something to help the children at the hospitals. We'd been so disturbed by the dismal surroundings while Emmy was hospitalized." Lily went on to explain how Albert decided to become "Smiley the Clown."

"Emmy was always smiling, even in the worst of times. So I scraped together what fabric I could find and sewed this costume for Albert." She clasped her hands in joy. "The children loved it! Every weekend, we'd volunteer at the hospitals to bring smiles and gifts to the children."

"But you told me you were poor; how'd you manage that?" I asked in amazement.

"Well," she grinned, "smiles are *free* and the gifts weren't anything fancy." She closed the album and leaned back against her pillows. "Sometimes the local bakers donated goodies, or when we were really hurting for money, we'd take a litter of pups from our farm. The children loved petting them. After Albert died, I noticed how faded and worn the costume was, so I rented one and dressed as Smiley myself; that is, until my first heart attack, about ten years ago."

I left Lily's room that day consumed with thoughts about how generous she and Albert had been to children who weren't even their own.

Graduation day neared, and on my last day of volunteer services at the ward, I hurried to Lily's room. She was asleep, curled into a fetal position from stomach discomfort. I stroked her brow, worrying about who would care for her the way I did. She didn't have any surviving family members, and most of the busy staff simply met her basic needs, giving her no extra attention. At times, I wanted to proclaim Lily's virtues to them, but she'd stop me, reminding me that the good things she'd done in life were done without thoughts of self.

"Besides," she would say, "doesn't the good Lord tell us to store our treasures in heaven and not on this earth?"

Lily must've sensed my inner torment above her bed that day as she opened her eyes and touched my hand. "What is it, dear?" she asked, her voice concerned and laced with pain.

"I'll be back in two weeks," I told her, explaining about my high school graduation. "And then I'll visit you every day. I promise."

She sighed and squeezed my fingers. "I can't wait for you to tell me all about it."

Two weeks later to the day, I rushed back to the center, bubbly with excitement and anxious to share with Lily the news of my graduation events. With a bouquet of lilies in my hand, I stepped into her clean, neat, unoccupied room. The bed was made, and as I searched for an answer to Lily's whereabouts, my heart already knew the answer.

I threw the flowers on the bed and wept.

A nurse gently touched my shoulder. "Were you one of the yellow birds?" she asked. "Is your name Karen?" I nodded, and she handed me a gift-wrapped box. "Lily wanted you to have this. We've had it since she died because we didn't know how to get in touch with you."

It was her photo album. Written on the inside cover was the scripture Jeremiah 29:11: "'For I know the plans I have for you,' declared the Lord, 'plans to prosper you and not to harm you, plans to give you hope and a future.'" I clutched it to my chest and departed.

Three weeks later, my horrified boyfriend stood before

me. "You can't be serious," he said, pacing back and forth. "You look ridiculous."

We were in my bedroom and as I tried to view myself in the mirror, he blocked my reflection. "You can't be serious," he repeated. "How in the world did you pay for that thing anyway?"

"With my graduation money," I answered.

"Your what?" he exclaimed, shaking his head. "You spent the money that we saved for New York on *that*?"

"Yep," I replied, stringing on my rubber nose. "Life is more about giving than receiving."

"This is just great," he muttered, helping me tie the back of the costume. "And what am I supposed to tell someone when they ask me my girlfriend's name? That it's Bozo?"

I looked at my watch. I had better hurry if I wanted to make it to the children's hospital on time. "Nope," I answered, kissing him quickly on the cheek. "Tell them it's Smiley . . . Smiley the Clown."

Karen Majoris-Garrison

On the Other Side of the Door

Remember me, O Lord, with the favor You have toward Your people; Oh, visit me with Your salvation.

Psalm 106:4

I tap lightly on the door to the hospital room, never knowing what awaits me on the other side. As a minister to the sick for the Catholic Church, I regularly visit patients in hospitals and nursing homes, as well as those homebound.

Today the response is a gruff "Come in." Impatient, even a little angry. Nevertheless, I approach the bedside. "How's it going today?"

A snort. "Not good."

"Oh, I'm sorry. Not a good day, huh?"

"Not a good month," Joe snaps back.

I wait, sensing Joe has more to say. He is a big, burly man, a construction worker I'd guess. His beefy hands display calluses. My list says his age is forty-six, and the gray that flecks his full beard confirms it.

"They found cancer in my lungs," he volunteers, pointing to his chest. "Now, it's here." He waves his hand toward his head derisively. "In my brain. I start radiation today."

"Oh Joe, I'd be so frightened if that happened to me."

"I am afraid," Joe replies, his tough veneer cracking. "So afraid."

When I ask if he wants to pray, Joe nods slightly. We ask for healing and for courage. We thank God for His presence in Joe's life, especially now, and invite Him to go with Joe into radiation treatments.

Next when I knock I hear a timid "Yes," on the other side of the door. Maria is an attractive woman with short, curly black hair and sad brown eyes. She's crying softly when I enter the room. She hesitantly raises her eyes to me and sees my badge announcing me as a Eucharistic minister.

"I think God's mad at me," she whispers in a lilting Spanish accent.

"Oh, my," I murmur and sink into the visitor's chair.

"I tried to kill myself." Out pours a story of estranged relationships, a mentally challenged son and a single daughter twice pregnant whose children she cares for. "Why me?" she pleads.

"I don't know. But I do know God loves you and will see you through." Words are inadequate. Mostly, I listen and cry and pray with her.

Next, Fred regales me with jokes from the moment I walk up to his bed. "Did you hear what the scientist said to a stubborn, argumentative clone?"

"Tell me," I smile.

"'Why can't you be a reasonable facsimile?'" Fred's belly laugh rocks the bed. He later reveals to me that he has blood clots in his legs. "If one of those puppies breaks loose, well, I'm either going up," his forefinger and eyes point knowingly toward the ceiling, "or down." Dramatically, the finger and the eyes drop to the floor.

"I'm betting it will be up," I say. "God needs laughter in heaven."

"Yeah, but not yet!" His twinkling eyes tell me he would add a smile here or in the hereafter.

Next, more joy awaits me. Mom is in the shower, and Dad is gently rocking the firstborn child, telling him how wonderful his future is going to be. Dad answers my questions about name and weight, never taking his eyes off the angelic face of his son. When Mom joins us, we all trace the sign of the cross on the baby's forehead and pray that God will walk with him all the days of his life.

Sometimes the joy is in the form of a face lined with age. John, behind the next door, has that face. He is a farmer, and days in the sun have toughened his skin and given him a permanent squint. These days he can only move about with the aid of a walker. Today he receives the news. "I'm going home!" he fairly shouts at me. Then, more softly, with tears glistening, "I'm going home."

There is no response to my next knock, so I tiptoe in. Mary is ninety, frail and small. There is only one light on, and it seems to focus on her hands, busy praying the rosary. When I tell her I'm a Eucharistic minister, she reaches out and takes my hand, entwining the rosary around both of our hands. As we talk, she quietly says, "I hope they don't cut my legs off." We pray God will preserve her legs.

There is no door to knock on in ICU; only curtains separate the beds. I stand at the foot of one, praying for a slight, elderly man who is comatose. I turn and literally bump into a young man who, unknown to me, had been praying with me.

"Are you his son?" I ask gently.

"No, I was visiting a friend, but he needs prayers."

I nod in agreement. "Don't we all?"

"I do," he states firmly. "Will you pray for me?"

"I will. What's your name and how do you want me to pray?"

Sam tells me he is fearful of losing his job and that he is grieving his father's death. I plan to write his request on the list of prayer intentions in the chapel, but somehow I sense we should pray together now. So, amid the hustle and bustle and all the noise and confusion of ICU, we bow our heads and pray about Sam's concerns.

I am occasionally asked why I continue to be a volunteer caregiver. "Don't you find it sad? Don't you ever wonder what you will say?" Sure I do. But being able to share with those who are most vulnerable because of illness or age, and knowing that I bring them some measure of comfort is a reward in itself. The incredible faith and courage I encounter during these visits awes me.

No, I never know what awaits me on the other side of the door, but whatever it is I know I will come away enriched and humbled.

Nancy Baker

A Christmas Visit

Remember the prisoners as if chained with them, and those who are mistreated, since you yourselves are in the body also.

Hebrews 13:3

Following a three-year military assignment to Germany, my husband was transferred to Fort Polk, Louisiana, in 1984. Our European tour had been filled with opportunities to help others, and at no time did our outreach seem more meaningful than at Christmas.

Each year we opened our house to the men and women from my husband's unit who were unable to go home for the holidays. To my three small children, the meaning of Christmas wasn't merely Santa Claus or the toys under the tree, but the opening of heart and home to others.

As the muggy days of summer shortened into fall, I wondered about the direction of our holiday outreach. My husband's office was staffed with married personnel; everyone had a home to go to on Christmas. But the stockade (prison) on post held thirty men who would have no visitors.

A family meeting sealed our commitment, and a call through channels authorized our visit. Eagerly we began our preparation. We purchased gifts: paper tablets, pens, envelopes and stamps to encourage the recipients to write notes to loved ones far away. Toilet articles, socks, jigsaw puzzles and decks of playing cards were carefully wrapped by little fingers before being tucked into larger gift boxes.

Their slippery hands greased in butter, the giggling children formed gooey cereal into festive red and green treats. With glee they wrapped each one in colorful plastic secured with festive bows. Pumpkin bread, baked in individual loaf pans, filled the house with a pungent aroma. Thick chocolate fudge, poured hot into baking pans, cooled into mouthwatering treats.

Pocket-sized New Testaments and scripture verse cards recounting the birth of the baby Jesus were included, along with our own personal holiday greetings. Then we sprinkled candy around the gifts before the outer boxes were covered with brightly colored paper and shiny ribbon.

On Christmas Eve, we packed the gifts into our car and left the warmth of our quarters. Riding in silence, we passed row after row of houses outlined with glowing bulbs. The children, usually bouncing with energy and anticipation, were noticeably subdued.

The final path leading to the stockade stretched dark and desolate. The dreary compound, surrounded by a tall fence topped with barbed wire, stood in stark contrast to our cozy, cheerful home.

My husband showed his identification at the guardhouse, and we were given permission to proceed. Without a sound we gathered up the boxes and entered the stockade. The men stood in formation to welcome us.

As we presented our gifts, my husband and I shook each man's hand, wishing them well, hoping they could feel our compassion and concern. While we filtered through the ranks, the children babbled their Christmas greetings, bringing smiles to discouraged faces.

That simple outreach started a family tradition. The following Christmas other families joined us, and the next year even more people became involved. I don't know if we took Jesus into the prison with us on those cold December nights, but I know we found Him there.

Debby Giusti

Sprinkled with Prayer

I know no blessing so small as to be reasonably expected without prayer, nor any so great but may be attained by it.

Robert South

Our son, a personal chef who lives sixteen hundred miles away, calls us once a week. It's wonderful to hear Dan's news about how the family is doing, especially our grandson. But it's especially gratifying to share our son's contagious exhilaration for his true passion in life—preparing delicious food for people.

In addition to creating scrumptious, home-cooked meals for his hardworking clients, he also gives them the blessed gift of time, freeing them to do more important things besides shopping for groceries and preparing dinner—like breaking bread together with their families.

Several weeks ago, Dan called with the latest updates on his thriving business, mouthwatering new recipes and a client's unusual request. "Today Sarah asked me to bake cookies for her nephew who is serving in the military in Iraq. She wants to send him a taste of his Texas hometown."

"Super idea, Dan. Mind if I make a suggestion?"

"Sure. I'm listening."

"Why don't you add an extra special ingredient to that recipe of yours?"

"Now I'm curious, Dad. What are you talking about?"

"While you're mixing the batter and baking those treats, pray over them. When you deliver them to Sarah, mention exactly what you did. Then tell her to be sure and sprinkle those cookies with lots of prayers while she's wrapping them."

"That's different. Where'd you hear that?"

I could sense Dan's interest as I explained, "A group called Kairos conducts Christian retreats in prisons. As they prepare for the retreat they bake special 'prayed over' cookies for the inmates who will be attending. Neat, isn't it?"

Dan didn't have much to say after that except, "Interesting. Thanks for the suggestion, Dad."

The following week, Dan's call began with an exuberant, "Guess what?"

I had no clue. "Something good happened?"

"Remember that extra ingredient you mentioned? Well, I not only prayed over the cookies headed for Iraq, I also prayed over all my clients' meals this week."

His words warmed my heart. "That's my boy."

"There's more! I sold a record sixteen hundred dollars in gift certificates this week!"

"Congratulations, Dan. When did you say you started praying?"

I could almost feel his smile, all the way from Texas.

Tom Lagana

If God Had an Eraser

If God had an eraser,
What would He erase away?
Would He erase the clouds,
And make the sun shine every day?
Would He erase oppression?
Would He choose to make us free?
Would He rid the world of wars,
Of pain and poverty?
Would ugliness and ignorance,
Be among the first to go?
Would we all be beautiful,
And know all there was to know?
Would He eliminate our anger,
Our pettiness and greed?
Would He grant us all our wishes,
And fulfill our every need?
Would He choose to rub out sadness,
So we'd never need to cry?
Would He eradicate all illness,
So we'd never need to die?

Would He erase anxiety,
Our fears and worries too?
Would He rid the world of suffering,
Or leave that for us to do?

Ellen Javernick

Willie

You save an old man and you save a unit; but you save a boy, and you save a multiplication table.

"Gipsy" Smith

As a teacher of learning-disabled children, I felt I had an extra portion of patience. That changed the moment seven-year-old Willie entered my classroom. The brown-headed boy seemed to be the poster child for distractibility. Every sound, either in my room or out in the hallway, was a resounding alarm to Willie, pulling his attention from the important learning matters at hand. The movement of a pencil across a page mesmerized him. If an adult walked past our door, he focused there. A flicking light became his fireworks. His attention went everywhere but to me and to the words inside his book. His reading was laborious and slow. He laughed, he hopped, he hollered, and learning took a back seat. Whenever Willie went anywhere or did anything, it was at breakneck speed. He once caught his foot in the chair he sat in and twisted it, badly injuring it. I had never seen before nor since anyone sprain an ankle while sitting down.

At the parent-teacher conference, his mother helplessly confessed he acted the same at home. In the classroom I set limits and gave him structure, which he always tested like a young colt against a new fence. This approach was the direct opposite from his home life, where chaos and no discipline were the order of the day. I began to resent his mother for this. I decided she was at fault for some of the trouble I experienced at school. I thought mean thoughts about her and gritted my teeth at her son. I counted the days to the end of the school year. Summer looked better and better—no Willie.

Two weeks before the end of school, Willie's mom burst into my classroom in a Willie-style speed, wearing a Willie-style smile on her face. "I hear you are doing some summer tutoring."

I saw my summer melting away with visions of this small hurricane tearing around my beloved small house. Quickly recovering, I explained my times, fees and rules. I kept my fingers crossed she wouldn't like my terms. To my utter dismay, she agreed to everything. Cringing, I thought about Willie and my china cabinet meeting in an untimely fashion.

Getting up to leave, she turned and said, "Do you remember your reading teacher?"

I thought about Mrs. Rounds sitting in her rocking chair in front of our classroom. She had the sweetness of candy and the calmness of a rock. She taught me the importance of words, and I loved her for it.

"Yes, I do," I replied.

"I remember mine too," Willie's mom said to me, straightening her rumpled skirt. "She taught me how to read, and I still pray for her. Don't even know if she is alive or dead, but I pray for her to this day. Each time I read a story, or the *TV Guide*, or a letter, or e-mail, I think about that woman. I loved her. You remind me of her." With that she left the room.

I stood a humbled woman, my irritations washed away.

As Willie bounced to class the next day, I gave him a big hug and told him what a wonderful, smart young man he was. Caught off guard for a minute, he stood perfectly still, then quickly recovered and whirled about my room touching everything. I smiled. I found myself thinking happy thoughts about Willie as he went about his usual way in the class. I began to notice positive actions and his endearing mannerisms. I was finally ready for the task of Willie.

That summer we sat on my living room floor as I continued to teach letters and sounds to this remarkable child. I saw good progress in his reading and in my attitude. Before Willie left each day, I took something small and fragile out of my china cabinet for him to look at and hold, oh so carefully. Then we put it gently back in its place. In this unexpected way he began to learn how to be still, if just for a moment. I learned how to stretch my patience.

I waved good-bye to Willie at the end of the summer. He and his mother were moving. I imagine him praying for me one day when he is a grown man and looks at all the words he can read. I hope he reads a lot.

Robin Lee Shope

Boundaries

Therefore humble yourselves under the mighty hand of God, that He may exalt you in due time, casting all your care upon Him, for He cares for you.

1 Peter 5:6

"I don't have a drinking problem, okay? And you are not my mother! I can go to bars if I want. I can have a few beers. You don't know anything about it!"

"Clint, we're not talking about a few beers here. I saw your trash can outside. It's overflowing with liquor bottles."

"What are you, the FBI? You got surveillance cameras or something?"

"Clint, I'm not spying on you—it's just that you have a problem."

"I don't have any problem! I go to school. I get the job done. If I have such a problem, how come my college teachers think I'm great? Maybe you're the one with the problem!"

"Clint, you can't get through the day without a drink— you're an alcoholic."

He said nothing. The silence and tension grew by the second. Finally he spoke, so quietly it frightened me. "I'd like you to leave. You're not welcome here anymore."

In a way, Clint was right. I was the one with the problem. His addiction to alcohol had created just as serious an addiction in me: codependent caretaking. This twenty-one-year-old son of my best friend had been sent to live near us and attend our local college. Now he was consuming my life, and he wasn't even my kid. I was driven to try to rescue him, fix him and prove to his mom that I could be the one to "save" him.

I didn't realize how deeply I had fallen into this self-destructive behavior until one night when sirens woke me. I sat straight up in bed and grabbed the phone. My husband looked over at me groggily. "Honey, it's two o'clock in the morning. Who in the world are you calling?"

"Didn't you hear those sirens? I have to make sure Clint wasn't in an accident."

"Honey, this is ridiculous, just go back to sleep."

"No! I know he's been driving drunk. We need to go drive around and look for him. His mother would never forgive me if—"

He stared at me in disbelief. "Why are you so obsessed by all of this? I'm tired of losing sleep over his problems. He's not losing any sleep, why should we?"

The next morning I made a phone call to Mike, a member of my church and a substance abuse counselor. He was himself a recovering alcoholic. He listened kindly as I unloaded the whole story of Clint's drinking problem. I waited for him to tell me exactly what should be done to "save" Clint from himself, but instead, he said, "We could probably sit here and talk about Clint for hours, but what about you?"

"What about me?"

"Don't you have goals you're working on? I seem to

remember you were a pretty good songwriter. Have you written any lately?"

I was dumbfounded. I hadn't thought about my music since Clint came to us. In fact, I hadn't thought about myself at all.

"I guess I've been pretty busy with Clint," I said sheepishly.

"That won't work, Carla. You'll end up betraying yourself and getting lost in the process. Then you won't be any good to anyone."

I protested, "But you're a substance abuse counselor. You know how much someone like this needs help."

"He does need help. But he needs it from one person: God. Do you want to try and fill those shoes?"

I fell silent. His words stung because they were absolutely true. I was trying to be somebody's messiah again. "Well, what am I supposed to do?"

"You're supposed to live your life. You're supposed to take care of you and let Clint take care of Clint. Carla, your concern for him is wonderful, but you have to set boundaries, and you have to quit encroaching on his. You can't force him to stop drinking. The more you steamroll over his boundaries, the more he'll get angry. The more you put your own life and plans on hold, the more you'll get angry. After awhile, everyone's just angry."

"I want to help him. I don't want him to get hurt anymore."

"That's good. You *should* want to help him. But you have to let him help himself. If you don't, he'll probably feel so guilty he'll drink more. You have to detach; care about him but let him go. And someday, when he figures things out for himself, he might even come back and thank you."

And then Mike did the most amazing thing. "I'd love to talk to you more, Carla, but I won't," he said. "My little boy is outside waiting for me to play baseball with him. That was my plan for the afternoon, and I'm going to stick to my plan. Maybe we could talk another time."

He didn't say he couldn't talk anymore. He said he wouldn't. He had a plan. He had boundaries, and no one's imagined emergency or daily crisis was going to get him off track and ruin his day. No wonder he had so much peace in his life.

I thought about all the caregivers I knew—paramedics, pastors and counselors, the most caring people in the most caring professions—who quit after only three or four years. I was ready to crack after only three or four *months*. I had to stop trying to do everything for Clint. It was painful, but I had to leave him to his own choices.

A month later Clint moved away. Our parting was less than friendly. Then I heard he was in prison.

Nine years later I saw him again, his baby daughter sleeping soundly on his lap while his wife heated a bottle in the kitchen. He worked as a supervisor and was the most peaceful looking man I had ever seen.

I grinned. "Clint, I'm so proud of you. I'm so amazed at your transformation. What happened?"

"I got sober," he said plainly. "You do drugs and drink, you lose your life."

"How did you get clean?"

"People stopped giving me chances. I hit bottom and realized that I only had one chance left, and I better help myself for a change. It took awhile, but I had the help of a good woman."

"You sure have a beautiful wife," I said.

"Actually," he added, "I had the help of *two* good women," and he looked right at me and smiled.

Mike was right. Nearly a decade later, in his own way, Clint had thanked me. He was over his drinking problem, but I was the one who had really recovered. I had implemented my plan to set boundaries. Over the years, whenever I fell into those old "messiah" patterns, I went back to the simple words of a man who faced people's crises every day, but never lost himself in the process: "I have a plan for this afternoon; I'm going to play catch with my son."

And like Mike, while helping others, I too am going to stick to my plan.

Carla Riehl

The Friday Christmas Tree

The interests of childhood and youth are the interests of mankind.

                                        Edmund Storer Janes

"Mommy," six-year-old Brian* cried, as he pulled on his pajamas, "the other kids said we're going to have a Christmas tree for the house! What's a Christmas tree?"

Snug in their small bedroom at this Christian shelter for women and children, Jenny Henderson held him and four-year-old Daniel close. "It's a beautiful tree that helps people be glad for Jesus," she said. "People decorate them at Christmas time. They buy each other presents and put them under the trees."

Daniel wrinkled his nose. "What's 'decorate' mean? What's Christmas?"

Their mother sighed. All the years she had lived with the boys' father, he refused to let them celebrate anything, no matter how much she pleaded. No birthdays. No holidays. And certainly no Christmas.

---

*Names have been changed.

So the boys had never blown out birthday candles, watched TV, decorated a Christmas tree, hung up stockings, eaten a big Christmas dinner or opened any gifts.

When the Henderson home became so sad with all the arguing, controlling and bossing, Jenny and the boys moved to the shelter home. Now they were free to celebrate everything, including Christmas, with the other mothers and children there.

Jenny gave Daniel a hug. "I'll tuck you both under the covers and tell you a wonderful story about Jesus and Christmas."

She recounted the detailed story of the first Christmas night, then told them about decorating a Christmas tree, giving Christmas presents to each other, and telling God thank you for baby Jesus.

"Wow!" Brian cried. "I want to love baby Jesus, too. And I want to decorate a Christmas tree, too!"

"Me, too!" Daniel echoed. "Please, Mommy, please!"

Jenny laughed. "Mrs. Naples, the house manager, says we're going to have a big Christmas tree decorating party this Saturday. All the kids who live here will be able to help, including you two."

Brian and Daniel were so excited, they could hardly get to sleep. And the very first thing Daniel asked when he woke up the next morning was, "Is it Saturday yet? Can we decorate the tree yet?"

Finally, that Friday, they heard a great shout. "The tree's here!" All the children scrambled down the stairs. There at the front door were three men carrying the biggest, most beautiful, fragrant evergreen, so big it almost stuck in the doorway. The men set it up on a stand, and everyone gathered around. It almost reached the ceiling!

"Can we decorate it right now?" Daniel asked.

Mrs. Naples laughed. "No, remember it's still Friday, Daniel. We'll have our decorating party tomorrow."

Just then she got a phone call in the office. It was the boys' father. Since Mr. Henderson had never hurt the boys, he was allowed to come to the shelter and take them out on visits. He was coming the next day to take them out for a while—right at decorating time.

The boys loved their father, of course. But they did so want to decorate their very first Christmas tree. "Please, Mrs. Naples," Brian begged, "could we put just one pretty thing on the tree tonight? Just one small decoration?"

The house manager looked at the beautiful tree. She looked at the two boys and she looked at the other children. "Well, what do you think, children?" she asked. "Would that be fair? Let's take a vote."

"Yes!" they all shouted.

A short time later, all the children helped carry not just one little decoration, but whole boxes of them into the living room. They set them around the waiting tree.

"All right, boys," Mrs. Naples said to Brian and Daniel. "You have an hour. During that time you may decorate to your hearts' content. We won't plug anything in, but you take out anything in any of the boxes. Tomorrow while you're gone we'll take the decorations off so the other children can have their chance putting them on. But tonight is your night."

Then she shooed the other children away and left the two boys alone.

Brian and Daniel had never been so happy in their entire lives. They picked up each shiny ball, each shimmering garland, each handful of icicles, as carefully as if they had been made of diamonds, then placed them lovingly on the tree.

A little later, Mrs. Naples stopped by to see how they were doing. All around the bottom branches—as high as little boys' arms could reach—glittered joyful ornaments of blue, red, green, gold and silver, plus loop upon loop of garlands, and handfuls upon handfuls of icicles.

But instead of standing there admiring their work, the two boys were on their knees with their eyes closed tightly, praying.

"Thank you, dear Jesus," Brian began, "for getting bornded at Christmas time. And thank you for letting us decorate your Christmas tree. That's the bestest Christmas present I could ever get."

"Oh, and, Jesus," his little brother added, "when Daddy comes here tomorrow and sees our beautiful tree, please let him like it and not be mad. And help him want to love you, too."

Brian thought a moment. "You're right," he agreed. "*That* would be the bestest Christmas present of all."

Bonnie Compton Hanson

Theosis

On January 1, I walked with a dear friend, Bonnie, a nurse on the cardiac unit of one of our Valley hospitals. I had just chosen my theme for the year—as always, something that I wanted to grow toward, journal on and find scriptures to support. Eagerly I told her about this year's theme word, Theosis.

"Theo is a word for God and *osis* is 'the process of.' So," I explained enthusiastically, *"theosis* is 'the process of His life lived out through us in community with others.'"

Bonnie paused. "You won't believe this," she said. "I had a lesson on your theme just yesterday."

She explained how, at work, she was assigned a newly admitted elderly woman in a semi-coma from a heart attack. The woman's vital signs were not good, and Bonnie was quite sure she would die within the hour. She rushed to the chart to see if the family had been notified, and learned the woman had no family in Arizona and was here visiting a friend. The friend had been notified, but had not yet arrived.

Bonnie explained, "I went back into the patient's room, stood by her bed and, even though she was unresponsive, I felt a really strong spiritual sense in the room. I knew she should not die alone, so I sat down by the bed, rubbed her arms gently and prayed out loud, releasing her to Jesus' care. Within moments, the woman breathed her last breath calmly and died in my arms."

As we walked and talked I didn't know if Bonnie was short of breath from our brisk pace or from reliving the moment. She continued to tell how she had headed back to the desk, feeling so grateful that she'd been with this dear woman when she died, when suddenly the elevator door opened and a woman frantically rushed off saying, "Is she still alive, is she still alive?"

Bonnie told the patient's friend that she was sorry, she had just passed away a few minutes ago. The woman asked, "Did a priest arrive in time to be with her?"

"No, but I was with her, and prayed with her in her final moments."

"Oh, thank you, thank you! For much of her professional lifetime she was the head administrator of a large Catholic hospital out east. In fact, many people called her 'The Mother Teresa of the East,' she was so beloved. Her one desire as she approached the end of her life was that she would not die alone."

Bonnie continued to walk and talk faster. "As we stood in silence, contemplating all that had just occurred, all of a sudden I recognized her and said, 'Do you know who I am? I was one of your nursing students. You were one of my favorite instructors when I was in school!' Then we began to cry together. I told her, 'You taught me well.'"

"Theosis." Bonnie and I giggled as we said the word at the same time.

His life lived out through us in community with others.

Naomi Rhode

The Stranger at Our Door

Every time a man unburdens his heart to a stranger he reaffirms the love that unites humanity.

Germaine Greer

"I forgot to stop for gas in Salt Lake City," my husband Bob said.

Hearing the urgency in his voice I scanned the horizon, seeing only the rugged Utah terrain as we headed west toward the Great Salt Flats. "I was supposed to remind you. I'm sorry." I glanced at the fuel gauge. "We'll find something."

"I didn't want to worry you, but I haven't seen a station at any of the exits."

"None at all?"

He shook his head. "We missed the ones right outside Salt Lake City."

I tried not to panic and watched for signs indicating gas at the off ramps. "Come on, God, find us a gas station," I said, sending up a lighthearted prayer.

The next ramp showed a no-service sign. Discouraged, I

began to pray in earnest. What would we do? We had many miles behind us, and nothing in front of us but an endless stretch of the white salt flats.

I scoured the map. "We have one more hope. The village of Knolls is up ahead."

"We've been driving with the low-fuel light on for miles. We'd better find a station there." His voice echoed concern.

My heart began to pound as doubt won out over my confidence. When the exit appeared, the city marker sign was free from a no-service sign. "Thank you, Lord," I whispered as we rolled up the ramp.

But at the top, my heart sank. The sign loomed at us as we reached the overpass above I-80. Before us stretched the endless white salt plains—empty, desolate and hopeless. We sat in silence, wondering what we could do.

To my surprise a lone car and driver sat across the road. "He must be out of gas, too," I said.

"I'll find out," Bob said as he stepped outside and walked to the stranger's automobile.

When Bob returned, he climbed inside and shrugged. "He said he's resting."

"Resting?" I glanced at his license plates. "He's from Utah. He couldn't have driven far enough to need to rest in this desolate area." My mind spun with fear, conjuring up a thief or a murderer waiting for his prey.

"He offered us gas if we have a siphon. He said he has a full tank."

"That's great," I said, relieved.

But Bob wasn't smiling. "We don't have anything to use as a siphon."

My relief catapulted to the ground. "So what then?"

"He offered to follow us until we run out of gas and then drive me to the nearest gas station and bring me back. What do you think?"

"And I'd have to stay behind alone with the car?" My

fear roared in my head. "How do we know either of us will be safe?" Stories filled my thoughts of people robbed or murdered.

"Do we have another choice?"

"No," I said, ashamed. The man had offered to help us.

Still, concern filled Bob's face. "Why would anyone be willing to drive a stranger forty or more miles up and back for gasoline?" I pondered his question. But what choice did we have?

He hurried back to the stranger's car, returned, then climbed inside and placed his hand on my arm. "We'll be okay. Where's our faith?"

Where's our faith? The words rang in my head as we descended the ramp and returned to the barren salt flats. I glanced over my shoulder and observed the young man following us, still praying he didn't have harmful intentions.

My prayers continued, asking for safety and reassurance.

Time passed as I stared at the mileage meter and the gas gauge that now sat on empty. In desperation, I studied the map again, this time with greater hope. "Bob, if we can make it to the Bonneville Speedway, the map shows a gasoline station. It's not far ahead."

"We've been driving over sixty miles already and we're past empty. We'll never make it." Bob used cruise control, turned off the air-conditioning, everything to help us conserve fuel.

My chest tightened with every mile as my prayers grew more fervent. Finally in the distance, I saw a small speck taking shape, closer and closer—Bonneville Speedway.

"Thank you, God," I whispered while tears beaded in my eyes.

We exited and rolled to a gasoline pump. The stranger pulled in beside us, then waved before heading toward the highway.

Bob gestured to him to stop and hurried to the sedan. When I opened the door, I saw Bob offering the young man a gift of money for his kindness, but the stranger shook his head no.

I approached them. "Please take the money," I said. "It was such a relief to have you behind us."

As I spoke, I winced at my earlier distrust of the stranger. "We'll feel better if you let us show our thanks. I've never prayed so much in my life."

His face twisted with emotion as he accepted the bills. "Faith and prayer is what we need."

I looked into the man's gentle eyes, a man whom I had feared might be a criminal, and said, "You helped God answer my prayers."

"And you answered mine," he said.

My brow wrinkled in question.

"My sister is very ill, and I'm going to see her empty-handed. I've spent all my cash on gas for my car." He lifted the bills we'd given him. "Thank you."

We paused, looking at each other in silence before we said good-bye. I watched him, filled with awe, as he pulled away from the gas station and return to the highway.

In the guise of strangers, God had answered both our prayers.

Gail Gaymer Martin

Music for the Soul

*M*usic is the child of prayer, the companion of
religion.

Francois Auguste-René de Chateaubriand

I really hate hospitals. They always strike me as cold,
indifferent institutions. Perhaps that's why I was running
late that morning. I grabbed the video camera, whispered
a prayer and ran out the door in a frantic rush. I had made
it a priority to videotape my daughter Becky's show choir
concerts during her senior year in high school. With the
many performances this December, I was running ragged
trying to keep up. I questioned if this program would even
be appreciated by the patients at Spaulding Rehabilitation
Center in Denver, a hospital for severely injured patients
requiring long-term care and therapy.

When I walked in, I noticed an attempt at warmness. A
Christmas tree with lights stood in one corner on the pol-
ished, white linoleum floor. The nurses were polite,
although somewhat distant and perhaps a bit annoyed.
They worked busily with a quiet, professional efficiency.

The sixteen-member choir arrived. The young men

looked handsome in their black tuxedos with red cummerbunds and bow ties. The girls were equally attractive in long black formal gowns with red flower corsages. They began singing in the lobby to patients brought from their rooms. I was touched as I watched many of the patients wipe tears from their eyes as they heard traditional holiday songs. One wheelchair-bound man, a victim of a serious automobile accident I learned, smiled as he tried to put his hands together to clap in gratitude. I filmed the faces of the young people in the choir as they realized how their music had moved this small but significant audience. Becky's eyes brimmed with tears.

When this performance was over, a prim nurse in a white starched uniform approached the group to say many of their patients couldn't leave their rooms to attend the concert. She asked if they would mind going into some of the rooms and singing to those patients. The kids didn't hesitate a second. The choir director pulled out the pitch pipe, gave them the pitch and off they went into the first room, caroling.

As they entered, the nurse told me this patient had been at Spaulding longer than anyone else. This paraplegic patient, now in her seventies, was so excited about the kids coming to sing, she put on her Christmas sweatshirt for the occasion. I walked in behind the choir, still trying to get some video shots for the family memoirs. Sure enough, she had on her sparkling holiday sweatshirt and the brightest smile I'd ever seen.

We strolled from one room to the other. These bright, cheerful young people, with warm cheeks and smiling faces, moved through an ocean of broken bodies. As we approached the last room, the nurse escorted us to the doorway and warned that we would not get much response. These two patients were more critical.

I followed the choir in, the camera rolling. The first

patient was in a coma and unaware of our presence. The other, an elderly man with a full head of gray hair, smiled at us. There were numerous machines hooked up to him, all making their life-tracking sounds. I noticed a hole in his throat where a trach tube was inserted.

The choir was singing a folk carol titled "Tiny Little Baby." It had a rather striking rhythm and repetitive verse. As they sang over and over the words, "tiny little baby, tiny little baby, tiny little baby born in Bethlehem," the elderly man began singing with them, his face animated and joyful. The sound of his voice came from his trach tube instead of his mouth but, nonetheless, it was enthusiastic and heartfelt.

I was the last one out of the room. He turned his head to me and from his trach tube I heard, "Thank you."

The prim nurse, who had issued the warning prior to us entering, was waiting as we left. She smiled at me and quietly thanked us all. I smiled back and said, "He was singing with us."

She laughed and in a rather sarcastic tone said, "Yeah, right."

I could tell she didn't believe me, so I persisted. "Yes, he was! He was singing with us!"

The nurse put her arm around me. "Honey, he hasn't said a word in the two years since his accident. He doesn't speak, let alone sing."

"Really? Well, he did today. Would you like to see it?" I asked, pointing to the camera.

At first she seemed reluctant, then nodded. I rewound the tape, pushed replay and handed her the camera. She watched silently for a moment, then her expression began to glow with a newfound radiance. She excitedly motioned to her fellow nurses across the room to come see. They left their stations and crowded around my camera. One by one they seemed to be trapped by the exuberance of the moment, hugging one another, and jumping up and down. Watching tears run down their faces, I could see through their professional façade. *How they must struggle every day*, I thought, *dealing with defeat, fighting the great enemy—the suffering of the soul and of the human spirit.* I had to ask myself, *Who would volunteer to work with people so broken?* I suddenly realized the prim, starched nurse had shed many tears for her patients. All my preconceptions evaporated; I was humbled.

I smiled at Becky as she filed out the door of the center with her fellow choir mates. The look in her eyes told me I was not the only one changed by our experience there that morning.

I walked back to the car slowly, reflecting upon what I had seen and felt. Somehow the air seemed cleaner and crisper now, gravity diminished, and the sunshine felt warmer. I had witnessed pure joy, unselfish love and, for an instant, felt the touch of the Divine.

Suzanne Vaughan

The Agnes Story

I wandered up and down the streets of Honolulu at 3:30 in the morning. Since I live on the East Coast, it felt like 9:00 A.M. to me. I was wide awake and hungry for breakfast, but found nothing open before dawn.

Up a side street I found a little place. I went in, took a seat on one of the stools at the counter, and waited to be served. This was one of those sleazy places that deserved the name "greasy spoon." I mean, I did not even touch the menu. I was afraid that if I opened the thing something gruesome would crawl out. But it was the only place I could find.

The fat guy behind the counter came over and asked me, "What d'ya want?"

I told him, "A cup of coffee and a donut."

He poured a cup of coffee, wiped his grimy hand on his smudged apron, then grabbed a donut off the shelf behind him. As I sat there munching on my donut and sipping my coffee at 3:35, the door of the diner suddenly swung open and, to my discomfort, in marched eight or nine provocative-looking and boisterous prostitutes.

It was a small place, and they sat on either side of me. Their talk was loud and crude. I felt completely out of place and was just about to make my getaway when I overheard the woman sitting beside me say, "Tomorrow's my birthday. I'm going to be thirty-nine."

Her "friend" responded in a nasty tone, "So what do you want from me? A birthday party? What do you want? Ya want me to get you a cake and sing 'Happy Birthday'?"

"Come on!" said the woman next to me. "Why do you have to be so mean? I was just telling you, that's all. Why do you have to put me down? I don't want anything from you. I mean, why should you give me a birthday party? I've never had a birthday party in my whole life. Why should I have one now?"

When I heard that, I made a decision. I sat and waited until the women had left. Then I called over the fat guy behind the counter and I asked him, "Do they come in here every night?"

"Yeah," he answered.

"The one right next to me, does she come here every night?"

"Yeah," he said. "That's Agnes. Yeah, she comes in here every night. Why d'ya want to know?"

"Because I heard her say that tomorrow is her birthday. What do you think about us throwing a birthday party for her—right here, tomorrow night?"

A smile slowly crossed his chubby face and he answered with measured delight, "That's great! I like it!" Calling to his wife, who did the cooking in the back room, he shouted, "Hey! Come out here! This guy's got a great idea. Tomorrow's Agnes's birthday. This guy wants us to go in with him and throw a birthday party for her—right here—tomorrow night!"

His wife came out of the back room all bright and smiley. She said, "That's wonderful! You know, Agnes is one of those people who is really nice and kind, and nobody ever does anything nice and kind for her."

"Look," I told them. "If it's okay with you, I'll get back here tomorrow morning about 2:30 and decorate the place. I'll even get a birthday cake."

"No way," said Harry (that was his name). "The birthday cake's my thing. I'll make the cake."

At 2:30 the next morning I was back at the diner. I had picked up some crepe paper decorations at the store and made a sign out of big pieces of cardboard that read, "Happy Birthday, Agnes!" I decorated the diner from one end to the other. I had that diner looking good.

The woman who did the cooking must have gotten the word out to people on the street, because by 3:15 every prostitute in Honolulu was in the place. It was wall-to-wall prostitutes . . . and me!

At 3:30 on the dot, the door of the diner swung open and in came Agnes and her friends. I had everybody ready and when they came in we all screamed, "Happy Birthday!"

Never had I seen a person so flabbergasted . . . so stunned . . . so shaken. Her mouth fell open. Her legs seemed to buckle a bit. Her friend grabbed her arm to steady her. As she was led to one of the stools along the counter we all sang "Happy Birthday" to her. As we came to the end, "Happy birthday, dear Agnes, happy birthday to you," her eyes moistened. Then, when the birthday cake with all the candles on it was carried out, she lost it and openly cried.

Harry gruffly mumbled, "Blow out the candles, Agnes! Come on! If you don't blow out the candles, I'm gonna!" And, after an endless few seconds, he did. Then he handed her the knife and told her, "Cut the cake, Agnes. Yo, Agnes, we all want some cake."

Agnes looked down at the cake. Then without taking her eyes off it, slowly and softly said, "Look, Harry, is it all right with you if I . . . what I want to ask you is . . . I mean is it all right if we don't eat it right away?"

Harry shrugged and answered, "Sure! It's okay. If you want to keep the cake, keep the cake. Take it home if you want to."

"Can I?" she asked. Then looking at me she said, "I live just down the street a couple of doors. I want to take the cake home and show it to my mother, okay? I'll be right back, honest."

She got off the stool, picked up the cake and, carrying it like it was the Holy Grail, walked slowly toward the door. As we all stood there motionless, she left.

When the door closed there was a stunned silence in the place. Not knowing what else to do, I broke the quiet by saying, "What do you say we pray?"

Looking back on it now it seems more than strange for a sociologist to be leading a prayer meeting with a bunch of prostitutes in a diner in Honolulu at three-thirty in the morning. But it just felt like the right thing to do. I prayed for Agnes. I prayed for her salvation. I prayed that her life would be changed and that God would be good to her.

When I finished, Harry leaned over the counter and said, "Hey, you never told me you were a preacher. What kind of church do you belong to?"

In one of those moments when just the right words came, I answered, "I belong to a church that throws parties for whores at three-thirty in the morning."

Harry waited for a moment, then he answered, "No, you don't. There's no church like that. If there was, I'd join a church like that!"

"There is a church like that, Harry—started by a man who did *just* that. Let me tell you about Jesus. . . ."

Tony Campolo

"Today I learned that Moses partied on the Red Sea."

More Chicken Soup?

Many of the stories and poems you have read in this book were submitted by readers like you who had read earlier *Chicken Soup for the Soul* books. We publish at least five or six *Chicken Soup for the Soul* books every year. We invite you to contribute a story to one of these future volumes.

Stories may be up to twelve hundred words and must uplift or inspire. You may submit an original piece, something you have read or your favorite quotation on your refrigerator door.

To obtain a copy of our submission guidelines and a listing of upcoming *Chicken Soup* books, please write, fax or check our Web site.

Please send your submissions to:

Web site: *www.chickensoup.com*
Chicken Soup for the Soul
P.O. Box 30880, Santa Barbara, CA 93130
fax: 805-563-2945

We will be sure that both you and the author are credited for your submission.

For information about speaking engagements, other books, audiotapes, workshops and training programs, please contact any of our authors directly.

In the Christian Spirit of Giving

Since 1995, Health Communications, Inc., authors Jack Canfield, Mark Victor Hansen and their coauthors have helped the less fortunate by donating part of the proceeds of each book to related charities.

Hundreds of inmates wrote to share their miraculous personal and spiritual transformations after reading *Chicken Soup for the Soul* stories. In August 2000, Jack, Mark and prison volunteer Tom Lagana co-authored *Chicken Soup for the Prisoner's Soul*. Since then we have distributed more than 150,000 books to men, women and youth in correctional facilities through the generosity of *Chicken Soup for the Christian Family Soul*, *Chicken Soup for the Christian Woman's Soul*, churches, prison volunteers and groups such as Kairos, Prison Fellowship Ministries and many other organizations.

Now a portion of the proceeds from *Chicken Soup for the Christian Soul 2* will help fund the distribution of additional copies of *Chicken Soup for the Prisoner's Soul* and *Chicken Soup for the Christian Soul 2* for inmates.

It is our hope and dream that we can use these God-given tools to help change the lives of those who desperately need our care, love and support—one story at a time—one inmate at a time.

For more details on how to obtain books for those behind bars, prison staff, chaplains and volunteers may contact:

Tom Lagana
P.O. Box 7816
Wilmington, DE 19803
phone: 302-475-4825
e-mail: *Tom@TomLagana.com*
Web site: *www.TomLagana.com*

Who Is Jack Canfield?

Jack Canfield is one of America's leading experts in the development of human potential and personal effectiveness. He is both a dynamic, entertaining speaker and a highly sought-after trainer. Jack has a wonderful ability to inform and inspire audiences toward increased levels of self-esteem and peak performance.

He is the author and narrator of several bestselling audio- and videocassette programs, including *Self-Esteem and Peak Performance, How to Build High Self-Esteem, Self-Esteem in the Classroom* and *Chicken Soup for the Soul—Live*. He is regularly seen on television shows such as *Good Morning America, 20/20* and *NBC Nightly News*. Jack has co-authored numerous books, including the *Chicken Soup for the Soul* series, *Dare to Win* and *The Aladdin Factor* (all with Mark Victor Hansen), *100 Ways to Build Self-Concept in the Classroom* (with Harold C. Wells), *Heart at Work* (with Jacqueline Miller) and *The Power of Focus* (with Les Hewitt and Mark Victor Hansen).

Jack is a regularly featured speaker for professional associations, school districts, government agencies, churches, hospitals, sales organizations and corporations. His clients have included the American Dental Association, the American Management Association, AT&T, Campbell's Soup, Clairol, Domino's Pizza, GE, ITT, Hartford Insurance, Johnson & Johnson, the Million Dollar Roundtable, NCR, New England Telephone, Re/Max, Scott Paper, TRW and Virgin Records. Jack has taught on the faculty of Income Builders International, a school for entrepreneurs.

Jack conducts an annual seven-day Training of Trainers program in the areas of self-esteem and peak performance. It attracts entrepreneurs, educators, counselors, parenting trainers, corporate trainers, professional speakers, ministers and others interested in developing their speaking and seminar-leading skills.

For further information about Jack's books, tapes and training programs, or to schedule him for a presentation, please contact:

Self-Esteem Seminars
P.O. Box 30880
Santa Barbara, CA 93130
phone: 805-563-2935 • fax: 805-563-2945
Web site: *www.jackcanfield.com*

Who Is Mark Victor Hansen?

In the area of human potential, no one is more respected than Mark Victor Hansen. For more than thirty years, Mark has focused solely on helping people from all walks of life reshape their personal vision of what's possible. His powerful messages of possibility, opportunity and action have created powerful change in thousands of organizations and millions of individuals worldwide.

He is a sought-after keynote speaker, bestselling author and marketing maven. Mark's credentials include a lifetime of entrepreneurial success and an extensive academic background. He is a prolific writer with many bestselling books, such as *The One Minute Millionaire, The Power of Focus, The Aladdin Factor* and *Dare to Win,* in addition to the *Chicken Soup for the Soul* series. Mark has made a profound influence through his library of audios, videos and articles in the areas of big thinking, sales achievement, wealth building, publishing success, and personal and professional development.

Mark is the founder of the MEGA Seminar Series. MEGA Book Marketing University and Building Your MEGA Speaking Empire are annual conferences where Mark coaches and teaches new and aspiring authors, speakers and experts on building lucrative publishing and speaking careers. Other MEGA events include MEGA Marketing Magic and My MEGA Life.

He has appeared on television (*Oprah,* CNN and *The Today Show*), in print (*Time, U.S. News & World Report, USA Today, New York Times* and *Entrepreneur*) and on countless radio interviews, assuring our planet's people that "You can easily create the life you deserve."

As a philanthropist and humanitarian, Mark works tirelessly for organizations such as Habitat for Humanity, American Red Cross, March of Dimes, Childhelp USA and many others. He is the recipient of numerous awards that honor his entrepreneurial spirit, philanthropic heart and business acumen. He is a lifetime member of the Horatio Alger Association of Distinguished Americans, an organization that honored Mark with the prestigious Horatio Alger Award for his extraordinary life achievements.

Mark Victor Hansen is an enthusiastic crusader of what's possible and is driven to make the world a better place.

Mark Victor Hansen & Associates, Inc.
P.O. Box 7665
Newport Beach, CA 92658
phone: 949-764-2640
fax: 949-722-6912
Web site: *www.markvictorhansen.com*

Who Is LeAnn Thieman?

LeAnn Thieman is a nationally acclaimed professional speaker, author, and nurse who was "accidentally" caught up in the Vietnam Orphan Airlift in 1975. Her book, *This Must Be My Brother*, details her daring adventure helping to rescue three hundred babies as Saigon was falling to the Communists. An ordinary person, she struggled through extraordinary circumstances and found the courage to succeed. LeAnn and her incredible story have been featured in *Newsweek* magazine's "Voices of the Century" issue, FOX News, CNN, PBS, BBC, PAX-TV's *It's a Miracle*, and countless radio and TV programs.

Today, as a renowned motivational speaker, she shares life-changing lessons learned from her airlift experience. Believing we all have individual "war zones," LeAnn inspires audiences to balance their lives, truly live their priorities and make a difference in the world.

After her story was featured in *Chicken Soup for the Mother's Soul*, LeAnn became one of *Chicken Soup's* most prolific writers, with stories in eleven more *Chicken Soup* books. That, and her devotion to thirty years of nursing, made her the ideal co-author of *Chicken Soup for the Nurse's Soul*. She went on to co-author *Chicken Soup for the Caregiver's Soul*, *Chicken Soup for the Father and Daughter Soul*, and *Chicken Soup for the Grandma's Soul*. Her lifelong practice of her Christian faith led her to co-author *Chicken Soup for the Christian Woman's Soul* and now *Chicken Soup for the Christian Soul 2*.

LeAnn is one of about 10 percent of speakers worldwide to have earned the Certified Speaking Professional Designation awarded by the National Speakers Association and the International Federation for Professional Speakers.

She and Mark, her husband of thirty-five years, reside in Colorado, where they enjoy their "empty nest." Their two daughters, Angela and Christie, and son, Mitch, have "flown the coop" but are still drawn under their mother's wing when she needs them!

For more information about LeAnn's books and tapes or to schedule her for a presentation, please contact her at:

LeAnn Thieman, CSP
6600 Thompson Drive
Fort Collins, CO 80526
1-970-223-1574
www.LeAnnThieman.com
e-mail *LeAnn@LeAnnThieman.com*

Contributors

Several of the stories in this book were taken from previously published sources such as books, magazines and newspapers. These sources are acknowledged in the permissions section. If you would like to contact any of the contributors for information about their writing or would like to invite them to speak in your community, look for their contact information included in their biographies.

The remainder of the stories were submitted by readers of our previous *Chicken Soup for the Soul* books who responded to our requests for stories. We have also included information about them.

Janice Alonso is a wife, mother, teacher and "professional" volunteer. In the last five years she has lived her lifelong dream of becoming a published writer. She thanks Bruce, Andrew, Joseph, Alisa and her mother for their support. Please visit her Web site, *www.janicealonso.com*, and leave her a message.

Nancy C. Anderson (*www.NancyCAnderson.com*) is the award-winning author of *Avoiding the "Greener Grass" Syndrome: How to Grow Affair-Proof Hedges Around Your Marriage*. She is also a popular speaker at women's and couples' events. Nancy lives in California with her husband of twenty-six years and their teenage son.

Anna Aughenbaugh and her husband chose to have God as head of their home. They have three children and thirteen grandchildren. Anna draws on the trials and blessings in her multifaceted life for her freelance articles. Time spent with family, hiking, cooking and working as a deaconess bring her joy.

Nancy Baker resides in College Station, Texas, with her husband and golden retriever. She enjoys traveling, reading and walking. After retirement she pursued her lifelong love of writing and has been published in anthologies, national magazines and devotionals. She is a hospital and a hospice volunteer.

Margaret Berg received her B.S./B.M. from Case Western Reserve University and Cleveland Institute of Music, M.Ed. from University of Cincinnati and Ph.D. from Northwestern University. She is an associate professor of music education at University of Colorado. She enjoys playing violin, hiking and being a mom. Please e-mail her at *berg@buffmail.colorado.edu*.

Pegge Bernecker lives in Fort Collins, Colorado, and delights in her family, dogs, nature and companioning people on their spiritual journey. She teaches in a formation program for spiritual directors. The author of *God Anytime, Any Place*, her new book, *Becoming a Spiritual Gardener*, will be published in 2006. See her Web site: *www.PeggeBernecker.com*.

Ellie Braun-Haley is a former newspaper correspondent and began a more personal writing career by publishing two books for teachers of small children. She has since published a book of stories on heavenly intervention, has written short stories for a number of books and is coauthor of *War on the Homefront,* a look at spousal abuse.

Irene Budzynski, R.N., lives in New England with her husband of thirty-six years. Her writing has appeared in *Heartwarmers, Heart Touchers, Chicken Soup for the Teenage Soul IV* and *Chicken Soup for the Caregiver's Soul.* E-mail Irene at *budd@yahoo.com.*

Dianne E. Butts writes for Christian magazines and compilation books and is writing her own books. Her work has appeared in Great Britain, Bulgaria, Poland, Canada and Korea. Besides writing, she enjoys riding her motorcycle with her husband, Hal, and gardening with her cat, P.C. They live in Colorado. Visit her Web site: *www.DianneEButts.com.*

Dr. Tony Campolo, an ordained minister and speaker, has worked to create, nurture and support programs for at-risk children in cities across North America and has helped establish schools and universities in several developing countries. He is a media commentator on religious, social and political matters and author of thirty-two books. Visit his Web site: *www.tonycampolo.org.*

Arlene Centerwall is a retired registered nurse with many years experience in all fields of nursing, including teaching and management. She won second place in the American Christian Writer's Association contest and second place in the Cameron Press contest. Arlene has been published numerous times in several anthologies and magazines. She is a poet and presently involved in a book for teenagers. She volunteers by visiting the elderly and pet-sitting.

Virginia Cheeney is an educator, author and poet dedicated to redemptive teaching and writing for the glory of God. Virginia resides in the Great Smoky Mountains of Tennessee with Dave and their adopted daughter, Karen. You may contact Virginia at: *dvcheeney@vallnet.com.*

LindaCarol Cherken is a lifelong Philadelphian. Her writing has taken her from an interview with the Beatles for her school paper to weekly food and health columns for the *Philadelphia Daily News* to a syndicated advice column. Today, she writes features for newspapers and magazines, including essays for several of the *Chicken Soup* books.

Joan Clayton has been published in three other *Chicken Soup* books. She is a retired teacher and now writes full-time. She has been published in many anthologies and magazines. She is the religion columnist for her local newspaper. Visit her Web site at *www.joanclayton.com.*

David Cooney's cartoons and illustrations have appeared in numerous *Chicken Soup for the Soul* books as well as Christian magazines, including *The Lutheran, Presbyterians Today, Charisma, The Door* and *Devo 'Zine.* He lives with his wife,

Marcia, and their two children, Sarah and Andrew, in Miffling, Pennsylvania. He can be reached at *david@davidcooney.com*.

Natalie Costanza-Chavez is a poet and writer. She writes a spirituality column called Grace Notes for the *Fort Collins Coloradoan* and lives with her husband and two boys in Colorado. She can be reached at *grace-notes@comcast.net*.

Dean Crowe is a certified Personality Trainer, published author and inspirational speaker at churches, businesses and schools. Visit her Web site at *www.deancrowe.org*.

Barbara Curtis, award-winning author of *The Mommy Manual* and *Lord, Please Meet Me in the Laundry Room* as well as over seven hundred articles, finds tons of material as mother to twelve children, grandmother to nine (so far!). Visit her at *www.barbaracurtis.com* or *www.mommylife.net*.

Kathy B. Dempsey is the president of KeepShedding! Inc., a company that helps individuals and organizations grow by "shedding their skin." Kathy speaks at conferences and workshops and is the author of *Shed or You're Dead™: 31 unConventional Strategies for Growth and Change*. She has a nonprofit organization called *SpiritualShedding.org*. Please visit *www.KeepShedding.com* or e-mail her at *Kathy@KeepShedding.com*.

Pat Dodson is Garrett's mother. She is married to Dave Dodson, and they also have a daughter, Amanda. Pat enjoys traveling, boating and fishing. She continues to support ataxia-telangiectasia research, providing public awareness and hoping to help find a cure for this disease. Please e-mail her at *pdodson@yucca.net*.

Richard Duello is a pilgrim, husband, father, ironworker. He didn't used to write because he couldn't spell. He reads very little fiction because he finds real life more intriguing. He worked in the oil fields of Texas, survived a hurricane in Mississippi and hung steel in Georgia. People fascinate him, children teach him.

Wendy Dunham is a mother of two fantastic children, a registered therapist for differently-abled students, and an inspirational writer. She can be reached at (585) 637-7305.

Jan Dwyer received an M.B.A. from the University of Chicago in 1991. Owner of Boundless Potential, she helps clients make courageous leaps in customer service, communication and career development. She is a speaker, trainer and consultant and enjoys swimming and studying the Bible. Please e-mail her at *Jan@JanDwyer.com*.

Edna Ellison, Ph.D., international humorist and author of eight books, will have three more published in 2006–2007. Known as the "guru of Christian mentoring," she's been published by Focus on the Family, where her life story has also been featured. For booking information, see *www.newhopepubl.com* or e-mail her at *ednae9@aol.com*.

Kerrie Flanagan is a freelance writer who lives in Colorado with her wonderful family. She enjoys curling up on her big green chair to read a good book, spotting moose at Tunnel Campground and searching for people to beat at Scrabble. She can be reached via e-mail at *Kerrief@frii.com*.

Naomi Follis is a graduate of Purdue University School of Nursing Calumet Campus and has a diploma from Long Ridge Writers Group. She currently resides in Oklahoma City, Oklahoma, where she continues to write and enjoys painting and the study of Native American history and Bible prophecy.

Nancy B. Gibbs is a weekly religion columnist, author and motivational speaker. Nancy has had twenty stories published in various *Chicken Soup for the Soul* books. Her writings have appeared in numerous magazines, anthologies and devotional guides. Visit her Web site at *www.nancybgibbs.com*. You can contact her via e-mail at *Daiseydood@aol.com*.

Audrey Gilger currently works as a freelance writer for various publications and newsletters. She also works as a pediatric nurse and owns an online consignment shop. Audrey lives with her husband, four children and two in-laws in beautiful Amish country, Pennsylvania. Please e-mail her at *gilger5@msn.com*.

Debby Giusti is a freelance writer living in the Atlanta area. Her work has been published in numerous magazines, including *Woman's World, Southern Lady, Family, Army Magazine* and *Our Sunday Visitor*. Currently, she is writing full-length inspirational romantic suspense and can be reached by e-mail at *willoworks@mindspring.com*.

Frances Griffin founded Le Voyage, her childcare center, in 1983. She received her B.S.Ed. in special education and M.Ed. in counseling from Georgia State University. Now retired, Frances continues to work informally with parents and children, and teaches a Bible study class. She can be reached at *fbg413@comcast.net*.

Speaker-artist **Bonnie Compton Hanson** is author of several books for adults and children, including the popular Ponytail Girls series, plus hundreds of published articles and poems. She also mentors new writers and leads writing seminars. Write to her at 3330 S. Lowell St., Santa Ana, CA 92707; call 714-751-7824 or e-mail *bonnieh1@worldnet.att.net*.

Jean Palmer Heck is an international speaker specializing in communication and leadership. A former TV news anchor and corporate spokesperson, she works with executives who want to deliver messages that have Real-Impact. She has trained people from thirty-two countries. Contact her at *jean@real-impact.com* or 317-873-3772. Please visit *www.real-impact.com*.

Allan Hirsh, M.A. is a psychotherapist, trainer and cartoonist. His latest book, *Relax for the Fun of It: A Cartoon and Audio Guide to Releasing Stress*, is available at *www.caramal.com*. Contact Allan at *relax@allanhirsh.com* or visit his Web site, *www.allanhirsh.com*.

Since 1976, **Judy Howard** has owned Buckboard Antique Quilts. Visit *www.buckboardquilts.com* to view her 250 quality quilts at affordable prices. *Heavenly Patchwork—Quilt Stories Stitched with Love* by Judy is available on *www.heavenlypatchwork.com*. All book profits go to charity.

Mark Ippolito received his master's of physician assistance from the University of Nebraska and his bachelor's of science as a PA from Rutger University in 1980. He has been a certified Physician Assistant who worked in a wide variety of clinical settings from rural areas to urban areas, as well as helicopter medevac, back country rescue and federal prison clinics.

Stephani Marlow James is a freelance writer. Her writings appear in various anthologies, including *Chicken Soup for the Father and Daughter Soul*. She resides in Kansas City, Missouri, with her husband and daughter, who are prime sources of her inspiration.

Ellen Javernick is a first-grade teacher in Loveland, Colorado. She's the author of sixteen books for children and numerous articles for readers of all ages. She enjoys being Grams to her three grandaughters. Tennis is her favorite sport. You can reach her at *javernicke@aol.com*.

Willie Jolley is an award-winning speaker, singer and author. He is the author of *It Only Takes a Minute to Change Your Life* and *A Setback Is a Setup for a Comeback*. He can be heard daily across America on his syndicated radio program. His Web site is *www.williejolley.com*.

Dr. Howard Jones served as a visiting professor for evangelism at Crown College in St. Bonifacius, Minnesota and there established the Dr. Howard Jones Chair of Evangelism. Each youth college gives a scholarship to a student who feels called as a pastor evangelist and missionary in this country and abroad. He authored numerous books, including his autobiography, *Gospel Trailblazer*.

Louise Tucker Jones is the author of *Dance from the Heart* and coauthor of the award-winning book *Extraordinary Kids*. A popular speaker, Louise shares God's grace in difficult times. She has published articles in numerous magazines, including *Guideposts*, and contributed to other *Chicken Soup* titles. Louise resides in Oklahoma. Her e-mail is *LouiseTJ@cox.net*.

Jan Kremenik received a B.S. in nursing and her master's in practical theology from the University of San Diego. She lives in Southern California, where she enjoys traveling with her husband and their grandchildren and singing in her church choir. She is working on an inspirational book and a novel. Her e-mail is *sjkrem@aol.com*.

Tom Lagana is a professional speaker, author and engineer. He is coauthor of *Chicken Soup for the Volunteer's Soul, Chicken Soup for the Prisoner's Soul* and *Serving Time, Serving Others*. He can be reached via e-mail at *Tom@TomLagana.com*, or through his Web site: *www.TomLagana.com*. Or you can write to him at P.O. Box 7816, Wilmington, DE 19803; or call 302-475-4825.

Margaret Lang received her bachelor of arts from Brown University in 1963. She teaches women and children's groups in California. Margaret has eight stories being published in *Chicken Soup* books and one in *Christian Miracles*. Her daughter is a physician/missionary, her son is a youth pastor, and she has two granddaughters.

Darlene Lawson lives on a farm with her husband in eastern New Brunswick, Canada. They have three grown children and one princess granddaughter. Her writing continues to expand and move her into new areas of ministry. She can be reached at *antenna@nb.sympatico.ca*.

Sylvia Boaz Leighton credits her German/Puerto Rican heritage for her love of baking and dancing. Her family's mission is to be ambassadors to the world and to share God's love with everyone. She has worked at the University of California, San Diego, for over thirty years. Her passions are grandparenting, family and serving others. E-mail her at *Sylvia@library.ucsd.edu*.

Cheri Lomonte is a photojournalist who began her career by photographing pictures of the Madonna. After hearing heartstopping personal accounts associated with Mary, she recorded the stories to share with others in her book, *The Healing Touch of Mary*. She lives in the Hill Country of Texas.

Patricia Lorenz is a member of St. Jerome's Church in Largo, Florida, and thanks the Lord every day for her many blessings. She's an art-of-living speaker, author of five books and a top contributor to the *Chicken Soup for the Soul* books with stories in twenty-five of them. To hire her as a speaker, e-mail *patricialorenz@juno.com* or visit *www.patricialorenz.com*.

David Mahler received his bachelor's degree in accounting from the University of Notre Dame in 1978. **Marilee Mahler** received her bachelor of arts degree from Notre Dame in 1978 and a master's in directing from Roosevelt College. The Mahlers have raised four children, and all are all active in theatre and music.

Karen Majoris-Garrison is an award-winning author whose stories appear in *Woman's World, Chicken Soup for the Soul, God's Way Books* and *God Allows U-Turns*. A homeschooling mother of two children, Abigail and Simeon, Karen credits God and "family life" as the sources of her inspiration. Please e-mail her at *InnHeaven@aol.com*.

Award-winning novelist **Gail Gaymer Martin** writes for Steeple Hill and Barbour Publishing with thirty-five contracted novels. She has also authored over twenty worship resource books. Gail is a keynote speaker and teaches writing in the United States and abroad. Visit her web site at *www.gailmartin.com* or e-mail her at *gailgmartin@aol.com*.

Lucinda Secrest McDowell, a graduate of Gordon-Conwell Theological Seminary, is an international conference speaker and author of six books, including *Spa for the Soul, What We've Learned So Far, Quilts from Heaven* and *Amazed by Grace*. She enjoys giving innovative presentations through her ministry, "Encouraging Words That Transform!" Contact her through the Web site *www.EncouragingWords.net*.

Joyce Meyer is a best-selling author and one of the world's leading practical Bible teachers. Through her ministry, Joyce has taught numerous subjects, authored over seventy books and conducts nearly twenty conferences each year. Joyce's television program is broadcast to two-thirds of the globe and her radio program is on hundreds of stations worldwide. Her life is a remarkable testimony to the dynamic, saving work of Jesus Christ. Call her at 1-800-727-9673 or visit *www.joycemeyer.org*.

Sarah Michel is an international speaker, trainer and author who lives in Colorado Springs with her husband and two daughters. Her book, *Perfecting Connecting*, was published in 2004, and her weekly career advice columns appear in newspapers nationwide. Please visit her Web site at *www.PerfectingConnecting.com*.

Kathy Collard Miller is a popular women's conference speaker both nationally and internationally, having spoken in thirty states and five foreign countries. She is also the author of forty-eight books, including *Princess to Princess* and *Partly Cloudy with Scattered Worries*. Visit her at *www.KathyCollardMiller.com*.

Janet Lynn Mitchell is a wife, mother, author and inspirational speaker. Her book, *A Special Kind of Love*, published by Broadman and Holman and Focus on the Family, and the first two books in her Hands-On Faith series by Carson-Dellosa, are now available.

Stacie L. Morgan has Ph.D. in strategic management. She is an international speaker, strategy consultant and author. Her published works include *Spiritual Strategy in a New York Minute*, *Professional Strategy in a New York Minute*, and *Balancing Tomorrow, Today—AT HOME*. She may be contacted through the Web site *www.balancedmanagement.com*.

Lynn D. Morrissey wrote *Love Letters to God: Deeper Intimacy Through Written Prayer*, other books, and devotionals for numerous bestsellers. An AWSA and CLASS speaker/staffer, and soloist, she specializes in prayer-journaling and women's topics. She and her husband Michael and daughter Sheridan live in St. Louis, Missouri. Contact her through e-mail at *words@brick.net*.

Jean C. Myers volunteers with the Disaster Child Care program sponsored by the Church of the Brethren. Wearing many hats—Regional Coordinator, Disaster Project Manager, Trainer and Coordinator with the Critical Response Team—Myers has traveled extensively to provide care for traumatized children and to train volunteers. She is an active member of the Little Swatara Church of the Brethren in Rehrersburg, Pennsylvania and is a wife, mother and grandmother.

James A. Nelson holds a B.A. in economics from Eastern Washington University. Divorced with seven grandchildren and four children, he has self-published a book entitled *The Way It Was and The Way It Is—Forty-Nine Nostalgic*

Short Stories. He has been published over sixty times locally, nationally and internationally.

Maria Nickless is the *New York Times* best-selling coauthor of *Chicken Soup for the Bride's Soul* and *Chicken Soup for the Mother of the Preschooler's Soul.* She is a member of the Crossing Church in Costa Mesa, California, with her husband and two young children. She can be reached at *www.bridesoul.com.*

Linda L. Osmundson lives in Fort Collins, Colorado, with her husband of forty years. Her articles have appeared in children, parent, travel, teacher and religious magazines, *Chicken Soup* books and *Family Circle.* She enjoys art, Dixieland music, crafts, golf, reading and grandparenting. You can reach her at *LLO1413@msn.com.*

Mark Parisi's "Off the Mark" comic panel has been syndicated since 1987 and is distributed by United Media. Mark's humor also graces greeting cards, T-shirts, calendars, magazines, newsletters and books. Please visit his Web site at *www.offthemark.com.* Lynn is his wife/business partner and their daughter, Jenny, contributes with inspiration (as do three cats).

Donna Partow is one of America's most popular Christian authors and motivational speakers. Donna toured with Women of Virtue for three years, and her books have sold more than three million copies. Her Web site, *www. donnapartow.com,* is packed with free resources to strengthen believers in spirit, soul and body.

Bruce Porter received his doctor of divinity degree from Promise Christian University. Reaching out to hurting people at Columbine High School; after 9/11; in Erfurt, Germany; Israel; Sri Lanka; Beslan, Russia; and Red Lake, Minnesota; are but a few of his response efforts. He is the author of three books. E-mail Bruce at *bruce@torchgrab.org.*

Claudia Porter is an experienced speaker, author, teacher, Christian ministry leader, musician, wife, mother and friend. She received a B.A. in literature and creative writing from the University of Arizona and a K-12 teaching certificate from the University of Missouri. Claudia is a master encourager. E-mail her at *claudia@torchgrab.org.*

Frances Pace Putman, B.A., M.A.Ed., is a wife, homeschooling mom and freelance writer/editor from Birmingham, Alabama. An active member of her church, Frances enjoys spending time with her family, including her husband, Ted, and children Caroline and Will. E-mail her at *fpputman@aol.com.*

Carol McAdoo Rehme, a frequent editor and contributor to the *Chicken Soup* series, finds her inspiration in stories and shares it as both author and speaker. With a passion for the aged, Carol directs a nonprofit, Vintage Voices, Inc., which takes interactive arts programs to the frail elderly. Contact her at *carol@rehme.com* or see *www.rehme.com.*

Kayleen Reusser has written hundreds of articles for publications including *Today's Christian Woman, Grit* and the *Fort Wayne News-Sentinel* newspaper, where she specializes in travel and features. She is also the editor of a jail chaplaincy newsletter. Please e-mail her at *Kjreusser@onlyinternet.net*.

Rhonda Rhea is the author of *Who Put the Cat in the Fridge?* and other fun books, and has a new Christmas book coming in 2006. She is a radio personality and humor columnist and speaks nationwide. Rhonda lives in the St. Louis area with her pastor/husband and five children. See her Web site: *www. RhondaRhea.net*.

Naomi Rhode, C.S.P., C.P.A.E., Speaker Hall of Fame, Cavett Award winner, is past president of the National Speakers Association and 2006 president of the International Federation for Professional Speakers. Naomi is a cofounder of SmartPractice, a Phoenix-based company servicing health-care professionals. Naomi finds her joy in following Jesus and sharing his love with family, friends and audiences both corporate and Christian.

Carla Riehl is a national speaker and author. Her motivational seminars on peak performing and assertiveness skills are favorites among Fortune 500 companies and women's groups. Carla won an Emmy and Clio for singing national TV commercials. She inspires her audiences to soar with their strengths! Please contact her at her Web site: *www.carlariehl.com*.

Dan Rosandich is a cartoonist based in Michigan. Thousands of his cartoons and illustrations have been published worldwide. Dan's popular Web site, *www.danscartoons.com*, now licenses his images from presentations, books, newsletters, magazines, etc. Dan can also create "custom" cartoons. Contact him at *dan@cartoons.com*.

Fran Caffey Sandin is a nurse, writer and speaker, physician's wife, mother and grandmother living in Greenville, Texas. She has authored *Touching the Clouds: Encouraging Stories to Make Your Faith Soar* (NavPress) and *See You Later, Jeffrey* (Tyndale) and contributed to sixteen other books. Visit Fran's Web site at *www.fransandin.com*.

Laurie Winslow Sargent is the author of *Delight in Your Child's Design* (2005, Tyndale) and *The Power of Parent-Child Play* (2003, Tyndale, WinePress), and contributor to additional titles. At *www.ParentChildPlay.com*, Laurie offers articles/excerpts, helpful parenting and writing links, and events information regarding her parent education workshops and radio broadcasts.

Michael Jordan Segal is a social worker, author and inspirational speaker. His "miraculous" comeback story was first published in *Chicken Soup for the Christian Family Soul*. Since then he's had many stories published in anthologies, magazines and newspapers. To contact Mike, please visit *www.InspirationByMike.com* or call Sterling International Speakers Bureau at 1-877-226-1003.

Margie Seyfer, Impact Presentations, is a snap, crackle and pop speaker and customer service trainer. This story is in her keynote "Attitude Is Infectious!"

She enjoys Jazzercise, gardening and church. She is the author of *From Attitude to Zeal—26 Insights for Energizing your Life.* Web site: *www.margieseyfer.com.*

Robin Lee Shope recieved her bachelor of science, with honors, from UW Whitewater in 1975. WIth over twenty years teaching experience, she is presently a Study Skills teacher. Robin has authored over two hundred articles and short stories. Her novel, *The Chase,* by Revell Publishers is out in bookstores now. A trilogy will soon be added, so be sure to keep watching.

Christine Smith is the mother of three, grandmother of twelve, and is also a foster parent. She enjoys writing anecdotes about her family and friends. She believes there is no greater joy than to share her faith in God and to see it reflected in those she loves.

Laura Stack, M.B.A., C.S.P. (Certified Speaking Professional) is "The Productivity Pro®." She is the president of an international consulting firm specializing in productivity improvement in high-stress industries and the author of the bestselling book *Leave the Office Earlier* (Broadway Books, 2004). Increase your personal productivity at *www.TheProductivityPro.com.*

Gloria Cassity Stargel writes for *Guideposts, Decision* and others. Like a fine antique, her award-winning book, *The Healing*—a cancer-survivor's story of thirty-two years—gains value with age. Read portions at *www.bright morning.com.* Order online or phone 1-800-888-9529 or write to Applied Images, 312 Bradford St., NW, Gainesville, GA 30501.

Laura Stephenson serves as manager of Berean Christian Stores in Cincinnati. She pursues interests of reading, writing and teaching. She is the mother of three adopted children and seven beautiful grandchildren. Alex and Mary Ann are the parents of her roommate, Robin.

Dick and **Melodie Tunney** have been involved in contemporary Christian music for more than two decades. They are the recipients of ten Dove Awards, one Grammy award and have received many other accolades. Dick and Mel are parents of two daughters, Whitney, a student at Baylor University, and Kelsey, a student at Wheaton College. They reside in Brentwood, Tennessee. They can be reached at *tunney4@comcast.net.*

Suzanne Vaughan, author of the book *Potholes and Parachutes,* is a motivational speaker and seminar leader who has delivered programs to corporations and associations for over twenty-five years. She is past president of the Colorado Speakers Association. You can reach her at 720-886-9236 or through her Web site: *www.suzannevaughan.com.*

Bobbie Hamlet Wilkinson is a freelance writer and artist whose creativity inspires everything from painting tractors to uniquely renovating the barn she and her husband live in. Her greatest passions are her family and appreciating the beauty that surrounds her. Contact Bobbie at *bobbiewilkinson@earthlink.net* or visit her at *www.artbybobbie.com.*

Lori Williams often writes about international adoption and the special-needs child. She and her daughter, Aurelia, enjoy biking, scrapbooking and gardening. Lori would love to hear from other adoptive mothers; she may be reached at *dewlaw@cox.net.*

Veronica Wintermote received her bachelor of science with honors from Oral Roberts University in 1992. She is currently a part-time stay-at-home mom living in Aberdeen, Washington, with her husband and their two sons. Veronica enjoys singing, swimming and camping. She hopes to do more inspirational writing in the future. Please e-mail her at *mamamote@aol.com.*

Thousands of **Bob Zahn's** cartoons have been published in all the leading publications. He has over one thousand greeting cards to his credit as well as several humor books. His e-mail address is *zahntoons@aol.com.*

Jeanne Zornes, M.A., Communications (Wheaton Graduate School), is a widely published Christian author and conference speaker. Her books include *When I Prayed for Patience, God Let Me Have It!* (Kregel). She and her husband have two young adult children, who pursued music interests. Learn more about Jeanne at *www.allaboutquotes.com/awsa.*

Also Available

Chicken Soup African American Soul
Chicken Soup Body and Soul
Chicken Soup Bride's Soul
Chicken Soup Caregiver's Soul
Chicken Soup Cat and Dog Lover's Soul
Chicken Soup Christian Family Soul
Chicken Soup Christian Soul
Chicken Soup College Soul
Chicken Soup Country Soul
Chicken Soup Couple's Soul
Chicken Soup Expectant Mother's Soul
Chicken Soup Father's Soul
Chicken Soup Fisherman's Soul
Chicken Soup Girlfriend's Soul
Chicken Soup Golden Soul
Chicken Soup Golfer's Soul, Vol. I, II
Chicken Soup Horse Lover's Soul
Chicken Soup Inspire a Woman's Soul
Chicken Soup Kid's Soul
Chicken Soup Mother's Soul, Vol. I, II
Chicken Soup Nature Lover's Soul
Chicken Soup Parent's Soul
Chicken Soup Pet Lover's Soul
Chicken Soup Preteen Soul, Vol. I, II
Chicken Soup Single's Soul
Chicken Soup Soul, Vol. I-VI
Chicken Soup at Work
Chicken Soup Sports Fan's Soul
Chicken Soup Teenage Soul, Vol. I-IV
Chicken Soup Woman's Soul, Vol. I, II

Available wherever books are sold • For a complete listing or to order direct:
Telephone (800) 441-5569 • Online www.hcibooks.com
Prices do not include shipping and handling. Your response code is CCS.